Prostitution

Prostitution
Sex Work, Policy and Politics

**Teela Sanders, Maggie O'Neill
and Jane Pitcher**

Los Angeles | London | New Delhi
Singapore | Washington DC

SAGE Publications Ltd
1 Oliver's Yard
55 City Road
London EC1Y 1SP

SAGE Publications Inc.
2455 Teller Road
Thousand Oaks, California 91320

SAGE Publications India Pvt Ltd
B1/I 1 Mohan Cooperative Industrial Area
Mathura Road, New Delhi 110 044
India

SAGE Publications Asia-Pacific Pte Ltd
33 Pekin Street #02-01
Far East Square
Singapore 048763

Library of Congress Control Number: 2008934311

British Library Cataloguing in Publication data

A catalogue record for this book is available
from the British Library

ISBN 978-1-84787-065-0
ISBN 978-1-84787-066-7

Typeset by C&M Digitals (P) Ltd, Chennai, India
Printed in the UK by the MPG Books Group
Printed on paper from sustainable resources

CONTENTS

LIST OF FIGURES

LIST OF TABLES

ACKNOWLEDGEMENTS

Many thanks to Kate Green for permission to reprint the image on the cover. Images are contributed from the 'Working Together to Create Change' participatory action research project, funded by Walsall South Health Action Zone led by Maggie O'Neill and Rosie Campbell in partnership with Walsall Community Arts, Walsall Youth Arts, local support agencies, local residents and local sex workers (www.safetysoapbox.co.uk). Images reprinted (Figures 3.1, 4.1, 4.2, 4.3, 10.1) with kind permission of artist Kate Green. The images are a product of the expression and sharing of sex workers and residents, and we thank everyone for their commitment to this art project.

Maggie and Teela would both like to thank our students, past, and present, who have taken such a keen and critical interest in the sex industry and our own work. We have been privileged to teach our own research and hopefully inspire others. We would particularly like to thank Susan Lopez-Embury for her knowledge and the time and expertise she dedicated to writing parts of Chapter 6. Her continued efforts to work for sex worker rights are an inspiration.

Finally, but most importantly, the authors would like to thank the sex workers and staff in support projects who have contributed their time, knowledge and views to inform our research over many years.

1

THE SOCIOLOGY OF SEX WORK

This first chapter will describe and debate the different theoretical and sociological/criminological perspectives on prostitution and the sex industry as well as the 'rights' and 'wrongs' of prostitution or sex work. Introducing students to the complexities of language and the implications of the different sociological and feminist debates, this chapter moves beyond the polarized perspectives of prostitution as either 'violence against women' or 'sex as work', to explore theories of women's involvement in sex work and how theories are grounded in data evidence.

The chapter begins with a brief look at the place of 'the prostitute' in historical texts that includes contemporary analysis of the construction of 'the prostitute' in official discourses (medical, legal and political).[1] Next, we outline the key theoretical positions on prostitution and sex work and offer some examples of empirical work undertaken on this issue. Feminist debates on the 'prostitute body' demonstrate divided views that focus upon victimhood and exploitation in contrast with agency and choice. The rise of the 'sex as work' perspective is described in relation to the advent of activism among sex workers and campaigns for rights. Analysing these debates, we look beyond the binary of either 'exploitation' or 'choice' to the nuances of theoretical analyses that attempt to understand the lives of women, men and young people who are involved in selling sexual services. Finally, drawing on the differing perspectives, this chapter argues that this body of literature, including philosophical, criminological and sociological debates, results in a 'sociology of sex work' which has developed over recent years and combines the global and local politics of the sex industry.

--------------------------------- **Historical Constructions of the 'Prostitute'** ---------------------------------

Prostitution was not always seen as deviant behaviour. The earliest records of prostitution show that it took place in temples: to visit a prostitute was to make paeans to the goddess. In fact, one of the earliest known deities was Inanna – a female prostitute (Bassermann, 1993). Later forms took place in religions that were referred to as 'cults' of Venus, and all through ancient history there is evidence of temple prostitution across

Mesopotamia and the Near East. Though goddess worship persisted, resistance to prostitution began in around 1200 BC when ancient Israel disapproved of erotic religions in surrounding societies (Eisler, 1995). In 350 AD, Christians succeeded in prohibiting temple prostitution in Rome and, as time went on, the systematic denigration of sexuality, particularly female sexuality, engendered increasingly intolerant attitudes towards prostitutes. Since then, as we document in Chapter 6, sex workers have been organizing for their rights and staging resistance to oppression sporadically throughout history. Prostitution came under harsher regulations during the Victorian era and even more so in times of war, as prostitutes were blamed for the venereal diseases prevalent among soldiers. As we see in Chapter 7, the current discourses and laws regulating sex work are framed by these puritanical campaigns that sought to regulate the morality and hygiene of prostitutes and led to the making of an outcast group.[2]

Historical constructions of 'the prostitute' in literature, media, political and official discourses have been fascinated with the 'whore' image which has dominated the cultural imagination. Pheterson (1989: 231) neatly summarizes: 'The prostitute is the prototype of the stigmatized woman' defined by unchastity which casts her status as impure. The 'prostitute', or the 'whore', is contrasted to the female mirror image of the 'Madonna' which portrays the image of pure femininity: that is, sacred and holy. The 'Madonna/whore' binary projects the status of the prostitute woman as a failed example of womanhood, defined by her immoral sexual behaviours, and someone to be avoided (Pheterson, 1993).

O'Neill (2001: 124–53) argues that the status and representation of the prostitute in the public imagination are maintained through and by a set of self-sustaining discourses which are part of the representation of women more generally from tradition to modernity and postmodernity. Moreover, it is important to look at the cultural texts that symbolically represent the prostitute through time. On the one hand, the prostitute is made morally reprehensible, a victim, impure, depraved and suffering marginalization and 'whore stigma' (Pheterson, 1989) and, on the other, she is a body-object of fascination and desire. We can find many examples of the aestheticization of female sex workers that include fantasies and desires associated with the 'whore' and the purchase of sex (Corbin, 1990; Stallybrass and White, 1986). In current times, prostitution is seen as part of a postmodern leisure phenomenon, yet 'One response to the diseased/adored, menace/remedy dichotomy of the "prostitute" is the formal and informal regulation of prostitution' (O'Neill, 2001: 130).

Currently women working as prostitutes are perceived as 'bad girls', contravening norms of acceptable femininity, and increasingly criminalized by state, policing practices and the lack of effective action taken by policy-makers to address the complexities of women's and men's lives in the broader context of poverty, globalization and capitalism and an understanding that, in consumer capitalism, 'sex sells'. Some aspects of sex workers' experiences are not so different from the experiences of prostitutes in earlier centuries. Social stigma, social exclusion and reduced personal safety are central to the lived experience of sex workers as they have been throughout the documented history of prostitution. Yet, with the opening up of sex markets and a growth in the commercial sex industry, especially in relation to the 'adult entertainment' industry, one would expect a loosening of regulation and control – however, this is not so, as we see in Chapter 7. How then might we theorize prostitution and what do sociology and criminology offer?

Theorizing Prostitution

Prostitution is an inherently social activity (Matthews and O'Neill, 2003). Davis (1937: 744) asks, 'Why is it that a practice so thoroughly disapproved, so widely outlawed in western civilisation, can yet flourish so universally?' In his article in the *American Sociological Review,* he presents a functionalist approach: that the complexity of buying and selling sex boils down to the fact that as an institution, prostitution serves a useful function – it is a 'necessary evil'. Alongside the 'functional' approach is the pathological approach developed by Lombroso and Ferrero. *Criminal Woman, the Prostitute and the Normal Woman,* originally published in Italian in 1893 offers a pathological approach to why some women sell sex. Lombroso is considered a founding father of criminology, bringing scientific methods to the study of crime. Lombroso's theory of the atavistic offender, is that a criminal is born, not made, a throwback to earlier, more primitive times, bearing the evidence on their bodies of small heads, heavy jaws and more body hair than their 'normal' counterparts. *Criminal Woman* ... was a key text, and still inspires some scholars of biological positivism. Female prostitutes had the smallest cranial capacity of all female offenders – even lower than 'lunatics'. 'Almost all anomalies occur in prostitutes than in female criminals, and both categories have more degenerative characteristics than do normal women' (Lombroso and Ferrero, 2004: 8). The argument goes that the propensity for evil in criminal women far surpasses that of criminal men.

Mary McIntosh (1978), arguing against functional and pathological models, provides a more rigorous sociological analysis, asking why should it be that men demand sexual services and women supply them especially in so-called 'liberated times'. For McIntosh, the answer resides, in part, in the ideology of male sexual needs. Taking an ethnographic approach, Hoigard and Finstad (1992) argue that it is involvement in criminal sub-cultural milieus that leads some people into sex work. Eileen McLeod's (1982) feminist socialist research develops the sub-cultural theory by arguing that it is economic conditions that shape involvement in sex work. 'Women's generally disadvantaged position in the context of capitalist society is central to their experience as prostitutes ... Women's entry into prostitution is characterised by an act of resistance to the experience of relative poverty or the threat of it' (1982: 26). McLeod's research highlights the experiences of sex workers who explain the economic reasons for their sexual labour:

I do it purely for the money. I did work for six years as an office junior and in factories and then I became unemployed. When I was out of work I was at a friend's house when one of her clients called and he said 'I like your friend!' I was really desperate and that is how I got into it. (1982: 26)

Feminist analysis has developed since McLeod's early work and incorporates and develops sub-cultural as well as economic/poverty analyses with theories of patriarchy, as well as sex worker rights and more complex understandings of the multiple subject positions of women who sell sex (O'Neill, 2001, 2007a).

In the initial stages of feminist analysis of prostitution in contemporary society, prostitution was treated in a reductionist way as a deviant activity, and as sexual slavery (see Barry, 1979; Dworkin, 1981; Hoigard and Finstad, 1992; Jarvinen, 1993). More recently it has been treated as an understandable (and reasonable) response to socio-economic need within the context of consumer culture, and within a social framework which privileges male sexuality (Green et al., 1997; Hoigard and Finstad, 1992; McClintock, 1992; McIntosh, 1978; McLeod, 1982; O'Connell Davidson, 1998; O'Neill, 2001; Pheterson, 1986; Phoenix, 1999). Feminist work in this latter area has mostly focused upon violence against women, sexuality and/or the pornography debate (see Hanmer and Maynard, 1987; Hanmer et al., 1989; Hanmer and Saunders, 1984; Segal and McIntosh, 1992). Jo Brewis and Stephen Linstead have produced an interesting exploration of the temporal organization of sex work in relation to the labour process (1998); and Jackie West has explored the politics of regulating sex work focusing upon comparative analysis between Australia, New Zealand, the Netherlands and the UK (2000).

West's analysis explores the complex intersections between local politics, sex worker collectives and regulatory contexts marked by increasing differentiation within prostitution and a blurring of the boundaries between legalization and decriminalization. There are complex implications for sex workers, including sex worker discourse having substantial impact (but not radical transformative change) under certain conditions. For example, these include opening up debates on labour law reform; the significance of sex worker discourse upon local initiatives such as zoning in Utrecht; a combination of industry growth and legalization encouraging investment; and the links between mainstream leisure industries and prostitution becoming more extensive. West's analysis focuses upon the impact of sex worker discourse, and the influence sex worker collectives have on the changing regulation of prostitution. The impact of sex worker discourse is an important and under-theorized aspect of the sociology of prostitution, as we see in Chapter 6.

Phoenix (1999: 3) argues that involvement in prostitution is made possible for some women by the social and material conditions in which they live. In her ethnographic work she explored the structural influences operating on individual women and the subjective symbolic landscape within which their involvement in prostitution was made meaningful. Similarly, O'Neill (2001, 2007b, 2008) problematizes feminist theorizing and feminist research, specifically the epistemological and methodological issues involved in knowledge production and recommends that we develop more participatory, constellational and hybrid ways of doing and re-presenting research with women and young people working as prostitutes. This may include working through participatory action research and using creative methodologies with performance artists and/or photographers. She also problematizes the categories 'prostitute' and 'prostitution' by drawing upon self-reflexive ethnographic accounts of women's lived experiences, the available literature and fictive or cultural texts to explore neglected gender issues, especially around subjectivities and difference.

Sanders (2005a, 2008a) has developed a feminist analysis of the contemporary sex industry focusing upon violence, off-street working, exiting and clients. Sanders is one of a number of sex worker theorists who combine activist work with sociological and criminological analysis. Moving away from framing prostitution as 'deviant' and drawing heavily on individuals' experiences and narratives about their involvement in sexual labour, Sanders notes the similarities between sex work as a profession with other forms of body and emotion work.

Yet, despite the richness of the feminist literature, two polarized feminist perspectives emerge as the most salient and are subsequently represented in public discourses. The arguments are reduced to a small number of basic assertions which avoid the complexities of prostitution. First, women working as prostitutes are exploited by those who manage and organize the sex industry (mostly men). Moreover, prostitution and the wider sex industry serve to underpin and reinforce prostitution as a patriarchal institution that affects all women and gendered relations. Second, in contemporary society, prostitution for many women is freely chosen as a form of work, and women working in the sex industry deserve the same rights and liberties as other workers including freedom from fear, exploitation and violence in the course of their work. Additionally, sex work or erotic labour can actually be a 'liberatory terrain for women' (Chapkis, 1997: 1). Both perspectives are overly simplistic and ignore the relevance of economic circumstances and inequalities between men and women, as well as the diversity of workers in the industry.

Prostitution has been the subject of ongoing feminist debate between radical, socialist, liberal, neo-liberal and postmodern feminists for many years. How did these binaries emerge? One point of commonality across the binary positions is that modes of regulation have been exercised on the bodies of women selling sex both in the UK and Europe as well as across the globe (Bullough and Bullough, 1987; Corbin, 1987, 1990; Finnegan, 1979; Lim, 1998; Meil Hobson, 1990; O'Connell Davidson, 1998; Roberts, 1992; Truong, 1990; Walkowitz, 1980). So, it is across the bodies of sex workers that feminist debates play out. It must be pointed out that the theory as well as the policy has consistently concentrated on the 'female' body in relation to prostitution: male sex workers and transgendered sex workers have not been problematized through these theoretical binaries in the same way that gender and power relations have been central to theoretical frameworks that attempt to understand prostitution. It is the female body, and the use of a woman's sexuality and sexual body, that become the focus for theory and consequentially, policy.

Feminist Debates on 'The Prostitute Body'

Prostitution became an ideological and political target of early wave feminists who sought to address the inequalities of a patriarchal culture which disadvantaged women in all areas of public and private life. Early Western feminist theorizing on prostitution looked upon the place of the female body as 'a female object'.

The 1970s saw a further turn as the social construction of gender became the latest lens through which women's position in society and culture could be understood. A critique of the differences between sex and gender was strengthened by 'feminisms of difference' (such as women of colour, lesbians, and women in the sex industry). This critique of the essentialist position of the reproductive female role promoted a view that minimizes difference between the sexes. This allows a new perspective on how bodies can be viewed and disassociated from biology. It is within these wider feminist discussions that theorizing about prostitution also shifted.

Bell (1994: 2) examined how the 'othering' of the 'prostitute body' was evident in the discursive construction of 'the prostitute' across a spectrum of historical periods and information sources from Plato, to feminism, and media portraits. Bell documents how there has been a continual construction of 'the prostitute' body through a process of 'othering'. This has been done by contrasting the failed prostitute body with some primary image of female perfection: good/bad; healthy/diseased; agent/victim.

Bell (1994: 12) notes that 'the prostitute body was produced as an identity and prostitution as a deviant sexuality'. This is very evident in the medical and legal discourses amongst popular texts in the 1900s (such as Freud, Havelock Ellis, William Acton). From analysing these texts, Bell concludes: 'The prostitute body was produced as a negative identity by the bourgeois subject, an empty symbol filled from the outside with the debris of the modern body/body politic, a sign to women to sublimate their libidinal body in their reproductive body' (1994: 72). In short, Bell states that the enduring image of the failed prostitute body is a symbol and signal to all other women in society to act up to the reproductive sex role of 'the female' and to suppress other forms of desire. There was a continuation of the 'othering' of the prostitute body beyond male writers, commentators and decision makers in the second wave of feminism in the 1980s.

Second wave feminists looked at prostitution in relation to wider gender relations in society, in particular, the oppressive institutions that existed which ultimately gave men control over women. Pateman (1988) wrote in *The Sexual Contract* that the marriage contract was fundamental to patriarchy as it was a socially acceptable way that men could get access to women's bodies. Pateman saw that prostitution was an extension of this form of oppression, and that the institution of prostitution gave men privileged access to purchase the sexual acts of women. Pateman states: 'Prostitution is an integral part of patriarchal capitalism ... men can buy sexual access to women's bodies in the capitalist market' (1988: 189). Pateman goes further by stating what she terms 'the contractarian' perspective on prostitution: that the prostitution contract is a free exchange between a prostitute and a customer and that it can be considered a trade. Pateman then goes on to contest this argument by relying on a traditional Marxist perspective that condemns capitalism for the status and position of wage labourers. Pateman compares the prostitution sexual contract to that of the ordinary employment contract between a wage labourer and an employer. She states that the prostitution contract comes to symbolize everything that is wrong in the employment contract. The image of the prostitute mirrors the status of the wage labourer and 'patriarchal capitalism is pictured as a system of universal prostitution' (1988: 201). Other writers supported this view that prostitution was ultimately the oppression of women, whether these accounts were arrived at via an economic argument (Pateman), or were simply stated from a gender and power perspective. For example, MacKinnon (1987, 1989) argued that prostitution was the extreme example of how society constructs female sexuality as only an object of male desire.

There have been criticisms of these feminist perspectives. Pateman (1988) accepts the separation of women into (bad) prostitutes and (good) wives, continuing the 'othering' of women. Scoular (2004a: 345) concludes how this 'domination theory' over-determines gendered power dynamics and reduces prostitution and women just to their sex acts. Scoular goes on to note that this essentializes women and 'fails to move outside the phallocentric imaginary' (2004a: 345). Further, the radical feminist theories reduce women's identity to a single trait, regardless of the structural effects of money, culture and race.

The radical feminist arguments have been developed since the 1980s and appear in more recent feminist arguments that connect prostitution to sexual slavery and the overall oppression of women on a local and global level. Barry (1995) defines prostitution as sexual exploitation: 'when the human being is reduced to a body, objectified to sexually service another, whether or not there is consent, violation of the human being has taken place'. Barry describes a four-stage process in which prostitution becomes sexual exploitation: (1) distancing; (2) disengagement; (3) dissonance; and (4) disembodiment. It is these stages, Barry argues, that objectify the female body and separate sex from the human being. Similar arguments about the theoretical contradiction that women can consent to prostitution when it is fundamentally sexual exploitation have been made by Raymond (1999), Farley (2004) and Jeffreys (1997). Further, Farley (2005) puts forward theoretical arguments that state that prostitution is always harmful to both the women who 'prostitute' themselves and women's position in society in general. More recently, Jeffreys (2008) argues that states which have legalized prostitution, or made provisions for regulation, are acting as pimps and are continuing the male domination of women.

This argument has come to be known as the abolitionist or prohibitionist perspective because the solutions focus only on the eradication of prostitution, concentrate on the suffering and victimization of women and argue that because the nature of prostitution commodifies the body for the use of men, there can be no consent. This reading of victimization states that a woman can never be a 'sex worker' because she is turned into a 'sex object' by structural and power inequalities between men and women (Barry, 1979; Dworkin, 1996).

Theoretical perspectives that locate oppression and violence in the intrinsic nature of prostitution are somewhat supported by the evidence of the difficulties and distress associated with some types of sex work. Few scholars would argue about the connections between some forms of sex work – particularly street level – with violence, murder (Kinnell, 2008), drug use (May and Hunter, 2006; Surratt et al, 2004), homelessness (McNaughton and Sanders, 2007), poor health (Jeal and Salisbury, 2004), and other indicators of social deprivation. However, despite these realities, motivations and consequences of abuse and addiction being part of the story for some people, there have been long-standing criticisms of making simplistic links between the survival strategies of sex work with a lack of choice, consent or voluntarism (Phoenix, 2007/8). The negative elements of prostitution are only one side of the story, as those involved in sex work express a diverse range of experiences, many far removed from stories of abuse, coercion and control.

Critiques of the victimhood perspective

Bell (1994) analyses the narratives of Pateman and MacKinnon and concludes that these writings and perspectives which became dominant in the 1980s, actually reproduce 'the prostitute body'. Bell argues that this line of thinking which locates the prostitute as a powerless victim within a masculine discourse actually silences the voices of women, refuses to acknowledge women's agency and results in the reproduction of 'the prostitute body'. Equally, as Maher (2000: 1) notes, taking the position that woman who sell sex are only victims, powerless and not in control of their circumstances leaves women 'devoid of choice, responsibility, or accountability'. In addition, in terms of thinking about workable solutions and approaches to managing prostitution from a policy perspective, the pursuit of eradication does not provide a viable solution to address wider social inequalities. Consequently, the 'victimhood' perspective has been greeted with challenges from other branches of feminist thought and women's rights groups.

There are strong arguments against the idea that women cannot consent to prostitution. Empirical evidence from studies which examine the relationships that sex workers have with their clients identifies how the transfer of power from the sex worker to the client is not always done in such a way that the client has complete control over the worker (see Hart and Barnard, 2003). Bodily exclusion zones (Sanders, 2005b), and strategies to separate out selling sexual services exist, preventing 'selling the self' (Brewis and Linstead, 2000b) as others would imply.

There are indeed other important dynamics to consider in the prostitution relationship. Factors of class, power relations and wealth all interplay with gender and race relations to influence the client–sex worker relationship. In the case of prostitution, O'Connell Davidson (2002) criticizes the social and political inequalities that form the basis of market relations that underpin prostitution. Questioning whether sexual capacities constitute property that can be legitimately offered as a commercial transaction, O'Connell Davidson (2002: 85) highlights the complexities of labour, and in particular sexual labour, as a 'transfer of powers of command over the person'. Arguing from a Marxist perspective, O'Connell Davidson (1998) describes how labour is not separate from the person but through the process of buying labour, the purchaser has direct power over the person. This argument leads O'Connell Davidson to argue that prostitution is

> an institution which allows certain powers of command over one person's body to be exercised by another ... he pays in order that he may command the prostitute to make body orifices available to him, to smile, dance or dress up for him, to whip, spank, massage him or masturbate him. (1998: 10)

O'Connell Davidson offers a more sophisticated examination of the relationships of power that exist in the prostitution relationship. Her concerns are more about the conditions under which women can make choices and the fact that there is often an imbalance of power in the transaction between sellers and buyers of sex. This raises some more interesting questions about how power plays out in transactions between women and men.

Shifting Ideas: Agency, Choice and Difference

The feminist rift that began between the radical feminists and the radical/cultural feminists in the late 1960s and early 1970s found a new battlefield in prostitution discourse. The emergence of second wave feminism signalled the development of the sex worker rights discourse to counteract other arguments promoted by radical feminism which some 'sex positive' feminists would argue have been damaging to the position of women and even dangerous for the experiences, livelihoods and political power of women in the sex industry. Emerging arguments from the 1970s spoke out against the 'victimization' of sex workers' perspectives but instead put forward a perspective that was based on human rights, sexual freedom and diversity amongst women's experiences.

This ideological shift was symbolized by a change in language, as the use of the word 'prostitute' was considered problematic because it separated out this category of women from all women, and explained her existence only through her identity as a 'prostitute'. The word 'prostitute' was also a legal term which signalled crime, deviance, and the need for 'reformation'. This term also was a significant way in which stigma continues to be directed at this group of women. The term 'sex worker' was coined as a way of identifying that sexual labour could be considered work and that the woman's identity was not only tied up with the performance of her body. Carol Leigh, a COY-OTE (Call Off Your Old Tired Ethics) member and prostitute also known as Scarlot Harlot (see her testimonies in Delacoste and Alexander, 1987), coined the term 'sex work' in the 1980s to avoid the 'connotations of shame, unworthiness or wrongdoing' of the word *prostitute* and assert 'an alternative framing that is ironically both a radical sexual identity ... and a normalization of prostitutes as "service workers" and "care-giving professionals"' (Bernstein, 1999: 91). The new terminology solidified the movement's demand for recognition as workers entitled to labour rights (see Chapter 6 for further details). This debate about language has continued as the Criminal Justice and Immigration Act 2008 proposed to remove the word 'common prostitute' from law as the government recognized the stigmatizing effects of this label.

The backlash against radical feminist ideas centres on the notion that by constructing women involved in prostitution as only 'victims', the objects of male oppression and passive in their own lives, the 'agency' of women is denied. This argument about 'agency' essentially refers to women's free will and their ability to make decisions about their circumstances and how they use their bodies. What has come to be known as the 'choice' argument strongly acknowledges that women can recognize the constraints they face by the structures around them (for instance, economic structures such as job opportunities and oppressive conditions caused by poverty or living on welfare benefits). This perspective does not wholeheartedly or simplistically assert that women choose to work in the sex industry in the way that they may decide on a career as a beautician or nurse. The routes to which women enter into prostitution are varied (see Chapter 3), but recognizing elements of consent and choice are key to this 'sex work' argument. Phoenix (2000: 38) states that there are certain conditions through which women are sustained in prostitution, therefore, for some women, prostitution 'makes sense' within their limited economic, social and material conditions. Findings from observations of Chicago's ghettos suggest that sex work is a rational 'resource exchange' for men and women who are part of an overall low-wage economy, where life is structured by persistent poverty, risks and destitution (Rosen and Venkatesh, 2008). These authors argue that 'sex work offers *just enough* money, stability, autonomy, and professional satisfaction' rendering the decision as rational within the context of their lives (2008: 418). Within the recognitions of structure (e.g. wanting to change the poor conditions they experience, or wanting to provide a better life for their families), and by recognizing opportunities to use sexual and body labour in the sex industry, women make choices about entering and working in the sex industry.

The nuances of this argument are important as scholars define this theoretical position beyond the simple concept of 'free will'. Chapkis (1997: 67), for instance, explains how some women make an informed 'rational choice' to work in prostitution, rather than a 'free choice', available to few individuals in a society that is structured hierarchically by race, sex and class. Kesler (2002: 223) summarizes that women may not be presented with a free choice, absent from constraints of opportunity, but ultimately all non-prostitute women who make decisions about entering into marriage or employment do so within a particular set of constraints under the present patriarchal capitalist system. It is within these wider contexts of women making decisions about their circumstances, survival and future that some theorists move away from the radical feminist perspective that reduces prostitution to sexual exploitation and force.

The debates about agency and choice are intensified when discussing the situation of women in developing countries who make stark choices between extreme poverty, starvation and the likely infection of HIV; and using their sexual bodies to survive (Evans and Lambert, 1997; Wojcicki and Malala, 2001). Campbell (2000: 479) conducted research with sex workers in a South African gold mining community and concluded that to speak only of sex workers' powerlessness is 'unduly simplistic'. Law (2000: 98) describes how women in South-East Asia migrate around the province to work in sex tourism destinations. Yet these women are constructed by many official agencies as passive victims who are being coerced and trafficked across borders into prostitution rather than considering that women are actively responding to their poor economic situation and the wider economic infrastructure of a neo-colonial country.

Many protagonists of the 'sex as work' and 'choice' perspectives have come from the sex work community and the testimonies of sex workers play an important part in these perspectives. Nagel (1997: 2) and other feminists who work as porn actresses, peep show workers, and sex providers recognize that their certain 'economic and racial privilege' means their participation in the sex trade is by choice, yet there are many women for whom this is not the case. It is in the testimonies of sex workers that the diversity of experience is real. Testimonies range from exploitation, coercion, survival strategies, to women who place themselves somewhere along the 'choice' spectrum (see, for example, the collections by Delacoste and Alexander, 1987, and Nagel, 1997).

The shifts in theoretical thinking relating to women involved in the sex industry are evident through the political positions and grassroots activities of non-governmental organizations (NGOs) and advocacy groups. Law (2000) who researched sex workers and assistance agencies in South-East Asia (Bali, the Philippines and Thailand) saw how the discursive practices, attitudes and activities of NGOs that carry out HIV/AIDS programmes are in the process of shifting away from the dominant idea that the 'prostitute' is always the victim. These changes stem from practical priorities to 'empower' women to protect themselves from HIV and keep themselves safe. Such priorities have been attacked by those against the harm reduction perspective as taking a more 'agency-centred' approach to participatory education that has been viewed as encouraging prostitution by some who believe in the 'victimhood perspective'.

The limitations of 'sex as work'

The 'sex as work' discourse (see Brewis and Linstead, 2000a) that prioritizes attention to the skills, labour, emotional work and physical presentations that the sex worker performs, has been the theoretical underpinning of legal and social changes that have made provisions for legitimate sex work. There has been some progress made by the sex workers' rights movement and in some countries (Germany and New Zealand, for example) working conditions and employment rights have been achieved (see Chapter 6). Yet in countries such as the UK, where sex workers face criminalization rather than the recognition of rights, the notion of 'sex as work' becomes further problematized at a theoretical and practical level.

There are striking differences between prostitution and mainstream employment such as the significant likelihood for sex workers of being robbed, attacked, raped or even killed (Kinnell, 2008). It is on the issue of violence that O'Connell Davidson (1998: 64) draws out the reasons why sex work is not like other occupations. She points out there are other professionals, such as plumbers, sales personnel, and estate agents who enter houses alone to meet strangers, and occasionally we hear of violence or even fatalities. Only in sex work is it prevalent that if a customer is unhappy, he will beat, rape or murder the service provider because 'there is no popular moral doctrine which tolerates hostility towards "dirty plumbers" only "dirty whores"' (O'Connell Davidson, 1998: 64). The lack of social acceptance of 'sex workers', in both cultural, social and political terms, means that women who work in all areas of the sex industry are still affected by the social stigma that is connected to the 'whore stigma'. Thompson and Harred (1992) and Thompson et al. (2003) uses comparative research with women who work as strippers a decade apart to demonstrate the continued negative attitudes, stigma and destabilizing effects of working in what is still considered a 'deviant' occupation. It is this evidence, despite whether consent and choice have been exercised, that makes working in the sex industry different from working in mainstream occupations which have legitimacy and acceptance even if they mirror the activities that happen in the sex industry.

Beyond Binaries

Models of 'victim' or 'worker' have also been criticized because they tend to 'dichotomize agency' (Maher, 2000: 1) and ignore the complexity of power and resistance that defines the sex worker's experience. Empirical findings from a study of homeless women in an English city, half of whom had engaged in street-level sex work, argue that women's motivations were in part related to systemic familial abuse and coercive, abusive partners (Harding and Hamilton, 2008). However, the interpretation of these life circumstances argues that locating the consequences of 'abuse' and 'coercion' should not necessarily mean victimhood, as this framework misunderstands the women's positions and therefore any practical assistance (such as social work) intervenes from the wrong starting point. Instead, the authors argue that 'respecting a woman's decision to sex work, however diminished her ability to choose for herself might be, is crucial in demonstrating a non-judgemental attitude towards vulnerable women' (Harding and Hamilton, 2008: 15).

There are alternative ways of understanding the place of vulnerable people in the sex industry without adopting either the 'exploitation' or 'choice' argument. Phoenix and Oerton (2005: 97) criticize the uni-dimensional simplification that reduces involvement in prostitution to victimhood. These authors argue that while it may appear that defining women in the sex industry as 'victims' may suggest they will be provided with more assistance and welfare interventions, on the contrary, the recent (regurgitated) official discourse of 'victimhood' justifies government regulation, criminalization and exclusion of women and children involved in prostitution. They argue that this happens for two reasons: (1) the rhetoric of victimhood is used to blame individuals for their own situation (for instance, they are involved and stay in prostitution because they are victims); and (2) in order to blame individuals, the concepts of 'consent', 'voluntarism' and 'coercion' are simplified. This means that official agencies who adopt the 'victimhood' approach can use the argument that women are 'choosing' to stay in prostitution, and therefore can mobilize sanctions, disposal orders, compulsory drug treatment and other 'orders' to change behaviour through the criminal justice system (see Chapter 7).

The further problem of the 'victimhood' philosophy is that the approach makes individual women responsible for the existence of prostitution (and in local areas this is reduced to names and lists of 'prolific street prostitutes' who are to be removed). The wider social implications and reasons for the existence of the sex industry are not addressed as part of any solutions, but instead the 'social problems' of prostitution become individualized to 'problem women' (see Scoular and O'Neill, 2007). Scoular and O'Neill challenge the ideological effects of policy, practice and representations that mark prostitutes out as stigmatized Others and argue for a politics of inclusion that brings sex workers into research, debates and dialogue as subjects (not objects).

The wider context of work

West and Austrin (2002) note that gender relations, sexuality and work, which are central dynamics of the sex industry, become overlooked in theoretical debates as the preoccupation tends to be bifurcation of exploitation or choice. Instead they call for a more nuanced approach to understanding the sex industry through the lens of work, occupations and networks. Drawing on the work of Adkins (1995) and McDowell (1997) amongst other scholars, West and Austrin (2002: 486) argue that gender relations in the context of the sex industry need to be understood in terms of the production of identities and the wider networks in which the markets operate. Taking on this criticism of the way in which the sex industry is studied, Sanders (2008c) examines how there are ancillary industries that support the sex industry, providing a robust and ever-expanding informal economy around the sex industry. Six ancillary industries that facilitate and support the sex markets are sketched: premises, advertising, security, transport, presentation, recreation and hospitality. These supporting industries provide work for both men and women who are not sex workers but provide services and facilitate the operation of the sex industry.

A Sociology of Sex Work

Scoular (2004a) reviews how different feminist theorists who assume a range of positions offer a spectrum of interpretations on the subject of prostitution. By reviewing different theoretical lenses, Scoular (2004a: 343) concludes that prostitution cannot be viewed in just one way but is contingent on a 'diversity of structures under which it materializes'. An example of the localized climates and conditions under which people who work in the sex industry understand their experiences is explored in the collection of works by Kempadoo and Doezema (1998). This collection debates and recognizes the complex conditions under which sexual labour is exchanged. Their concentration on non-Western perspectives of sex work highlights how the transnational, socio-cultural and economic structures that operate at a global level are influenced by the local context of lifestyles, familiar patterns, sexual norms and values, experiences of racism, colonial histories and sexism. Other forms of power beyond those of gendered inequalities need to be central to any theorizing about the rights and wrongs of prostitution. With these differences at the forefront, Scoular calls for a 'discursive space for a transformative feminist theory which seeks to utilize the disruptive potential of the counter-hegemonic and "resisting" subject to challenge hierarchical relations' (2004a: 352).

Weitzer (2000: 3) calls the differences in the feminist arguments the 'sex war' between 'sex objects vs. sex workers'. The differences in perspectives somewhat reflect the diversity of the sex industry and the complexities of situational experiences which are influenced by the local and global context. This statement by a peep show worker sums up how there cannot be any generalizations made and how rigid standpoints that refuse to recognize diversity fall short of any complete explanation of the nature of the sex industry, exploitation, consent and choice:

> There is no standard sex worker. Each woman has her own reasons for working, her own responses of boredom, pleasure, power and/or trauma, her own ideas about the work and her place in it. This work can be oppression or freedom; just another assembly-line job; an artistic act that also pays well; comic relief from street realities; healing social work for an alienated culture. What is at work within each woman that lets her accommodate this situation? Intense denial, infallible sense of humor, co-dependency, incredible strength, a liquid sense of self? The only safe thing to say is that we're all in it for the money. (Funari, 1997: 28)

Perhaps the future of building theoretical frameworks through which the sex industry can be understood is in the fertile, international social movements that exist around the sex industry. It is in identity politics which speaks from the hearts and experiences of those involved in working, managing, and living within the sex industry, that the complexity of the issues are most evident. Whilst macro structural forces affect all our opportunities for work, economic survival and lifestyle choices, there are variables such as geography, gender, class, and ethnicity that are equally as powerful in determining our choices. In addition, the state, with its both oppressive and transformative mechanisms, is a crucial dynamic that affects the status of sex workers, especially their exposure to vulnerability, violence and stigma.

Notes

1 These discourses are taken up in more detail in Chapter 7 with reference to prostitution as a crime against morality and the subsequent regulatory discourses and practices enshrined in law.
2 This paragraph was written by Susan Lopez-Embury.

Suggested Reading

Doezema, J. (2001) 'Ouch! Western feminists' "wounded attachment" to the "third world prostitute"', *Feminist Review*, 67(Spring): 16–38.
Kesler, K. (2002) 'Is a feminist stance in support of prostitution possible? An exploration of current trends', *Sexualities*, 5(2): 219–35.
O'Connell Davidson, J. (2002) 'The rights and wrongs of prostitution', *Hypatia*, 17(2): 84–98.
Raymond, J.G. (1999) 'Prostitution as violence against women', *Women's International Forum*, 21(1): 1–9.
Scoular, J. (2004) 'The "subject" of prostitution: interpreting the discursive, symbolic and material position of sex/work in feminist theory', *Feminist Theory*, 5(3): 343–55.

Study Questions

Level one

- What are the historical constructions of 'the prostitute' body and how can these be criticized?

Level two

- What are the differences between first and second wave feminist perspectives on prostitution?

Level three

- Why is the dichotomy between 'choice and exploitation' not always a useful theoretical framework through which to understand the complexities of sex workers' lives?

2

THE CULTURAL CONTEXT OF
COMMERCE AND SEX

This chapter will explore the cultural context within which the sex industries exist and the complexities of the different types of sex markets. The first section explores why the cultural context of the sex industry is a necessary lens through which commercial sex should be analysed. Second, an outline of the different types of markets is given, including the definitions of 'direct' and 'indirect' sex work. Third, the different types of actors that perform roles in the sex industry are described. Fourth, the occupational cultures of different sex markets are sketched out in order to demonstrate the ways in which venues and markets are organized. Fifth, we provide an overview of the modes of advertising that are prolific. Sixth, the role of the Internet and technology is explored more critically as a significant dynamic of change. Finally, questions are explored about whether the sex industries are expanding.

Sex, Commerce and Culture

The context in which the sex industry exists has a major influence on the nature, shape, organizational features and general characteristics of commercial sex in any given setting. O'Neill (2001: 1) calls for 'a feminist socio-cultural analysis of prostitution in changing times' that uses 'renewed methodologies' to represent the social sphere and the lived experiences of women. The cultural context of the sex industry can alter within regions and localities as well as across countries. Without acknowledging the different contexts and the influential local and national dynamics that can affect an informal economy like the sex industry, information and knowledge about what takes place can become biased and distorted. For instance, Agustin (2005: 618) criticizes the overall production of knowledge about the sex industry by academics, researchers and policy-makers, stating that what we know is a result of an unbalanced obsession with certain features of sex and commerce: 'A paradoxical combination of moral revulsion and resigned tolerance has permitted the sex industry's uncontrolled development in the underground economy and also impeded research on the phenomena involved.' The concentration of knowledge about the sex industry often rests with a very narrow type of commercial sex: 'prostitution' and in particular 'street prostitution'. This is only one aspect of sex work as it refers to a formalized commercial exchange between two people (usually a heterosexual man as the buyer and woman as the seller) rather than studying the broader relationship dynamics between commerce and sex.

To make this knowledge imbalance clearer, the point is that by concentrating on 'prostitution', the focus becomes only the actual selling of sex for money. What are not examined are the micro-relationships between the seller and buyer, or the wider economic and social setting within which the sex industry exists. For instance, what sex acts are sold and how are these decided upon? What sexual acts are requested and how are they performed and experienced? In addition, all parties – not just female or male sex workers – involved in the organization of commercial sex need to be contextualized. Each market has its own peculiarities and nuances that reflect its geographical space, whether it is located in the private or public sphere, and whether it is illegal, legal or occupies a 'grey' area of the law where some aspects are outlawed whilst other activities are not.

Narrowing the sex industries to prostitution and, in particular, street prostitution, can only perpetuate stereotypes and feed the concerns from health and criminal justice agencies about 'risky' women, rather than examining the broader sex industries that operate in many different parts of society. Not studying the sex industry in its entirety has the effect of producing a false dichotomy between types of sex industries. To move away from this narrow approach, Agustin (2005: 619) calls for a cultural studies approach to the sex industries that examines 'commercial sex in its widest sense, examining its intersection with art, ethics, consumption, family life, entertainment, sport, economics, urban space, sexuality, tourism and criminality, not omitting issues of race, class, gender, identity and citizenship'.

By referring to the cultural context of the sex industry it is inferred that the whole of the sex industry needs to be examined in relation to the everyday lives of individuals, businesses and relationships. The socio-cultural context of the sex industry determines what selling and buying sex means, resulting in many different values and interpretations based on a localized context. Another reason the cultural context is important is because there are significant cross-cultural differences in the social meanings of the consumption of sex. For instance, O'Connell Davidson (2003), in an article that uses empirical research from six countries across the globe to argue against criminalizing men who buy sex as a viable solution to stop sexual exploitation, highlights that buying sex has different cultural meanings for groups of men depending on their age, life-stage and the values that are attributed to buying sex in that culture. There are complex differences across the globe in the pressure to perform masculinity by either engaging in commercial sex or abstaining from it, at various life-stages and ages, meaning that 'normal' masculinity is closely linked with the sex industry.

These social meanings are also influenced by political climates and are usually in a process of change and flux. For instance, with the rise of lap dancing bars in Western cities and the mainstreaming of this type of activity as part of the everyday night-time economy, more people have been exposed to this form of entertainment

(Collins, 2004). Other cultural changes can be identified in the rise of 'adult only' stores, online access to pornography, and online stores for women, as well as the genre of Ann Summers parties (Storr, 2003) and sex toys (Comella, 2008) and male strippers for women (Montemurro, 2001). Another example of change in attitudes can be seen with the symbolic legislation of Sweden that has criminalized men who buy sex since 1999 (Scoular, 2004b). This is an example of how a government can intervene to try to shape cultural meanings of commercial sex.

The social context must be defined in its broadest sense as it is this context that determines how the sex markets operate, are organized and the experiences of the people who work in them. From a meta-analysis of 681 'prostitution' articles published from 1996–2004, Harcourt and Donovan identify several core influences that impact on sex markets:

> Typically social and legal sanctions against sex workers merely succeed in displacing the activity into other localities or into a different kind of working arrangement. Every country, and every region with those countries, has a different composition to its sex industry – shaped by history, social and economic factors, legal framework, and policing practices.
>
> (2005b: 201)

What is often missing from an analysis of the sex industry is the location of people as individuals who have lives, relationships and experiences outside the sex industry. The need for this deeper, more complex analysis is discussed in Chapter 3.

The Sex Markets

This section outlines what the sex markets look like, the different types of markets where commercial sex is organized and how they are characterized by similarities and differences. The visible and hidden nature of different markets demonstrates the breadth of the sex industry and the varied sites and places where commercial sex takes place.

Types of sexual services: direct and indirect

Sexual services that are exchanged for money, gifts or other remuneration are divided in the literature between 'direct' and 'indirect' sex work. Direct sexual services refer more specifically to types of commercial sex where physical contact of a sexual nature is exchanged for money. This involves some aspect of genital contact, although does not always mean penetrative intercourse. Direct sexual services usually take place in a known and recognized sex market such as in a brothel or on the street.

Commercial sex on the street is distinctly different from that found in the indoor markets. Workers are usually with the client for a short amount of time (about ten minutes). The service is straightforward 'hand relief', fellatio or intercourse with little else on offer. Services are administered primarily outside or in cars and prices tend to be relatively cheap in comparison to indoor services. Services offered from indoor markets can take more elaborate forms such as domination and bondage and can last several hours. What is termed 'the girlfriend experience' – a service that involves kissing, cuddling and intimacy that is traditionally associated with conventional male–female interactions – has become a popular request by men who seek out escorts. However, evidence suggests that the most frequently requested service is fellatio (Monto, 2001).

It is important to set aside the assumption that the sale of sex involves just vaginal intercourse or strictly involves 'conventional' heterosexual activities such as 'the missionary position'. Commercial sex involves the exchange of a whole range of sexual activities, many of which do not involve the full removal of clothes. What services are available are usually dictated by the individual worker. Sanders (2005a: 150–3) explains how 'bodily exclusion zones' are determined by brothel workers and escorts who allow customers access to certain parts of their body but not others. There are a myriad of personal reasons that explain why that some body parts and sexual acts may be 'off limits'. O'Neill (2001: 84) summarizes this process: 'The body is the tool of the trade. The self is for one's family, partner, self'. Some sex workers prefer not to kiss as part of their commercial interactions, but other women who provide a more in-depth social, emotional and physical experience may include kissing as a natural element of the service. The level of intimacy provided by some sex workers to their clients takes the form of emotional labour and has led Lever and Dolnick (2000) to refer to sexual services as one of the 'listening occupations'.

Indirect sexual services refer to a whole range of other types of sexual services which do not necessarily involved physical genital contact but the exchange is sexual in nature and is characterized by money or gifts. Lap dancing, stripping, erotic telephone sex work, massage, and bondage are some examples of indirect sex work (see below).

Sites of sex work

The provision of sexual services for money is traditionally linked to the 'street'. The classic notion of the 'red light district' with women visible on street corners in deprived areas of towns and cities has been the dominant cultural imagery of the sex industry promoted by the media. In addition, official policy and policing practices as well as academic research have largely been concentrated on the street market. This has been because of an historical concern with female street sex workers as a 'risk group' (Lupton, 1999). Sexually transmitted infections, drug use and HIV/AIDS have often been associated with female street sex work which has meant that this site of sex work has been over-represented whilst other markets and characteristics have been reported and researched less frequently. The issue of sex workers and health is discussed further in Chapter 3.

Harcourt and Donovan (2005b: 202) present a typology of 'direct' and 'indirect' sex work, referring to different sites of commercial sex across the globe. Here, we simplify this typology and identify some additional characteristics that explain the main types of markets that exist (Tables 2.1 and 2.2).

Table 2.1　Sites of direct sex work

Type of market	Characteristics	Geographical prominence
Street	Visible soliciting. Use of car and public spaces for sex. Lower prices and basic sex acts.	Across the world despite illegality in many places.
Brothel (also known as sauna or massage parlour in some parts of the world).	Premises specifically for sex where several women work, with receptionist. Safer than the street. Regulated and licensed in some countries.	Across the world. Legalized in Germany, Holland, parts of Australia. Decriminalized in New Zealand.
Escort	Independent worker or through agency. Outcalls to hotels and homes. Internet advertisements. Higher prices and more elaborate sexual services.	Across the world but dominant in Western countries.
Private flats and houses	Premises rented for business. Informal setting, individual or collective workers. Range of services including domination.	Across the world. Private business usually legal.
Homes	Informal and ad hoc individual arrangements between sex worker and customer who may be from local community/networks.	Not formally in the sex markets. Ubiquitous across the world.

Table 2.2　Sites of indirect sex work

Type of market	Characteristics	Geographical prominence
Lap dancing	Specialist clubs or shows in hotels where erotic dancing takes place. Fantasy and party rooms in hotels.	Western cities and towns.
Bondage and domination	Specialist services often non-contact in specific venues, clubs, flats, private parties.	Western countries.
Erotic telephone sex lines	Expensive telephone lines where sexual fantasies are described.	Western countries.
Strippers	Men and women hired to attend parties and social venues. Time-limited and non-contact.	Western countries particularly around male rituals such as birthday and pre-wedding parties.

There are many more places where commercial sex is available but not necessarily advertised or considered part of the sex industry because it is not 'prostitution'. Swingers' clubs; bondage; domination and sadomasochism (BDSM) clubs; golf 'caddy' girls; and other female sexualized labour are staple parts of Western tourist hot spots such as Las Vegas. Geisha in Japanese cities; male 'beachboys' in holiday destinations such as the Caribbean (Allen, 2007); 'guesthouses' where male tourists can encounter prospective male sexual partners, sometimes in exchange for money (Hall, 2007); 'hospitality workers' in the registered bar system in the

Philippines (O'Connell Davidson, 1998: 26); 'beer girls' in African developing coun-tries. All these represent locally based activities where individuals exchange sex to sup-plement their income. Cusick, Martin and May (2004) identify 'survival sex' connected to the exchange of drugs for sex with other drug users or drug dealers as another aspect of the myriad of sex markets. There are many other types of opportunistic sex work that take place across the world where sexual services are exchanged in social venues, through social networks and local communities. In developing countries, in particular in areas of serious deprivation such as refugee camps, Harcourt and Donovan (2005b: 203) note that food and security can be a more desirable currency than cash.

Urbanization and rural settings

The spaces where sex is sold are not confined to these general markets indicated in Tables 2.1 and 2.2. Highlighting the cultural context of the sex markets means that there are many other arrangements that are made between sex workers and their clients which reflect the context of the environment. For instance, Harcourt and Donovan (2005b: 202) note that, in the United States, sex workers drive along highways and con-tact truck drivers through CB radios, using truck stops and parking areas to solicit and deliver services. In addition, the authors mention that in the 'transport' sector which is a male-dominated occupation, sex workers board ships, trucks and trains to 'service the crew or passengers or pick up clients at stations and terminals' (2005b: 202).

Using descriptive material from ethnographic observations in Spain, Agustin (2005) provides evidence of how each country includes many different aspects of the sex industry. Not claiming to present an exhaustive list of the localities where com-merce and sex merge in Spain, Agustin sketches out four dominant examples: large highway clubs; private flats; small houses associated with agriculture; and the inter-national costal zone. The example of the 'highway clubs' given by Agustin demon-strates the rich cultural context which sellers and buyers of commercial sex inhabit:

> Streams of cars and trucks roar along multi-laned routes that connect Spain with France, Germany and other states east and with Portugal to the West. For long-distance truck drivers, the backbone of European commerce, long stints of solitary driving must be broken up with places offering rest and recreation. The buildings strung along these superhighways, as well as along smaller, provincial roads, are known informally in Spanish society as *puticlubes* (whoring clubs), but to those that work there they are *hotels de plaza*, a term that refers to the employment system used, in which those offering sex for sale pay a daily rate for a place to live and work for three-week stretches ... These businesses may house 50 workers or more ... numerous clubs are located close together forming a veritable erotic shopping area. With multiple floors, luxurious decorations, videos, live shows, Jacuzzis and 'exotic' music ... these clubs have come to represent luxurious sites of conspicuous con-sumption. Here customers pay as much as ten times the ordinary price for drinks, and it is the job of the women working there to get them to buy as many as possible, since this is the owner's major source of income ... A large number of support personnel is needed to keep these high-overhead businesses going, and because they employ migrants, good ·public relations are necessary with local police and immigration inspectors. Workers move on after their three week stints, assuring the novelty will always be on offer. (2005: 623)

These qualitative examples illustrate how sex markets take different shapes depending on their urban, suburban or rural location. Speaking specifically of a less-researched locality, Scott (2006) examines rural prostitution in the outback of New South Wales, Australia. Scott found that sex workers who had once worked in urban settings had moved out to more rural locations due to competition and opportunities for greater business in areas where there were few sex workers but still a demand for sexual services.

Lap dancing, strip clubs and the night-time economy

The sex industry consists of many different types of sex products, imagery, services and entertainment that together form a huge and significant global industry made up from small retail and entertainment businesses as well as a few corporate companies. The industry of erotic dancing, also known as lap dancing and stripping, is one part of the indirect sexual services industry. This form of indirect sex work involves a personalized striptease dance where the dancer moves erotically, semi-naked or nude, to music for a fee. The customer can be an individual or a group. Whilst the over-whelming majority of this form of sex work is female to male, there is a minority of outlets that provide male strippers for female audiences. The classic 'Chippendales' theatrical performance for large crowds of female audiences for celebratory occasions such as 'hen nights', as well as nude men performing private erotic dance for individual women, are becoming easier to locate amongst adult entertainment options.

Jones, Shears and Hiller (2003) note that this form of 'entertainment' was transported from the USA to the UK in the 1990s as 'lap dancing clubs' became a licensed and regulated feature of the night-time economy. In 2002, these authors estimated that there were 200 lap dancing clubs in the UK. There is evidence to suggest that this part of the industry has grown and has expanded beyond major cities. At the time of writing, the website www.ukstripclubs.com has 313 clubs listed for England, 7 for Wales, 19 for Scotland. There are no clubs listed in Northern Ireland. There are some 'superclubs' which have high profiles and reputations across the country. American company Spearmint Rhino has emerged as the main player in lap dancing with 9 large clubs across England and Scotland, offering 'luxurious interior', 'an unforgettable evening' with 'beautiful dancers' (www.spearmintrhino.co.uk). This website states club etiquette protects the dancers through the following rules: customers must remain seated during the performance; prices must be agreed with dancers; dancers have discretion about who they dance for; photograph and video footage are forbidden; and dancers must not be propositioned. The industry has become increasingly organized with agencies recruiting and organizing workers across Europe as well as clubs gaining a collective and critical voice with industry regulators.[1]

The interactional order and dynamics between dancers and their male customers have been studied in many different ways. Researchers who adopt participant observation and ethnographic methods as dancers have produced some in-depth insights into the organization of lap dancing (Egan, 2003; Frank, 1998; Ronai and Ellis, 1989). For instance, Egan (2005) observed the interactions between customers and dancers and concluded that the dancers provide a service beyond that of sexual arousal and fantasy but emotional labour through their exotic service. Developing the concept of 'emotional consumption', Egan notes how regular customers engage in a commercial economic exchange that is deeply rooted in psychological desires and needs beyond the sexual.

Equally the power relationships and struggles between female dancers and male customers are complex and theorizing on the micro-interactional relationship between dancer and customer has been the preoccupation of sociologists. There are implicit gender inequalities that mean female dancers commodify parts of their body for economically privileged men. But the relationship is neither simply one of exploitation or empowerment but is more complex. Deshotels and Forsyth (2006) refer to 'strategic flirting' as an aspect of emotional labour that dancers employ to gain sexual power in the micro-interaction with customers. Egan (2003) describes how dancers actively engage in a trade-off by creating and fulfilling male fantasies for cash profits and regular custom.

Qualitative studies involving observation and interviews have reported the strategies dancers develop to manage customers. Spivey (2005) notes that nude dancers use resistance strategies such as spatial distancing, verbal one-liners, physical aggression and solidarity amongst colleagues to resist harassment from clients. Yet despite the empirical evidence of the empowerment and control that female dancers experience in their work, issues of stigma continue to affect women's lives. Thompson and Harred (1992) found that dancers who stripped for a living were stigmatized because of their involvement in a 'deviant' occupation. Asking this same question ten years later, Thompson et al. (2003) found that stigma was still prevalent in the lived experience of the dancers and clearly affected their identity and everyday lives.

Such evidence of stigma experienced by women who work in strip clubs is resonant amongst all sex workers irrespective of the market they work in. Day and Ward (2004) produce a three-stage model of stigma. Drawing on the concept of 'the whore stigma', they see this label typically evident in wider society that categorized women who sold sexual services as immoral, dirty and criminal. This 'whore stigma' soon became implicit in social and structural mechanisms, through the law, gendered policy, and the organization of work. Finally, stigma was experienced as a social oppression and affected women's life-chances and opportunities, reputations and identities. Scambler (2007) examines the 'whore stigma' further by using the experiences of migrant sex workers in London to demonstrate how stigma is structured by class and ethnic relations, and determined by gender relations. Increasingly, evidence on stigma and its effects on sex workers demonstrates that the negative images and attitudes attached to the sex industry are increasingly the most damaging aspects of the work. Vanwesenbeeck (2005) conducted a study of 96 female indoor sex workers in the Netherlands to assess levels of 'burn out'. Compared to a control group of female nurses, only on the factor of 'depersonalization' were sex workers significantly higher than the nurses. The study concluded that 'burnout' was not specifically associated with sex work *per se*, but with the conditions within which sex workers experienced the work and their stigma-related experiences. Amongst male sex workers who identify as gay, stigma as an everyday feature of their working lives creates the need for strategies of resistance (Morrison and Whitehead, 2005). As sex work becomes politically high profile and visible in society, stigma appears to be persistent and takes different forms.

Participants: Sex Workers and Beyond

Chapter 3 describes in detail the characteristics and experiences of sex workers. Here, the point to be made is that women who sell sex are not the only actors in the sex industry, as it is made up of many different types of sex workers (male, female and transgendered) as well as other people who work in the industry.

Rickard (2001) notes that sex workers usually have many other types of jobs before and after they work in the sex industry, and as more middle-class women opt for selling sexual services (Bernstein, 2007), women from all socio-economic groups can be found in the sex markets. Several studies describe how sex workers have left mainstream jobs to work in 'elite prostitution' as escorts or in expensive brothels (Lucas, 2005; Sanders, 2005a). To describe further the different types of sex worker and the various entrance routes into sex work, Scambler (2007: 1080) presents a six-category typology of different types of sex worker, ranging from the 'coerced' victim to the 'bohemian' who makes a lifestyle choice (Table 2.3).

Table 2.3   Scambler's (2007) 'Typology of sex work careers'

Career	Paradigmatic example
Coerced	Abducted, trafficked
Destined	Family, peers in trade
Survivors	Drug users, single parents, debtors
Workers	Permanent job
Opportunists	Project financing
Bohemians	Casual, without need

Scambler's typology goes towards demonstrating the complexities of different sex work careers and how people enter the industry for different reasons and with a myriad of intentions. O'Neill (2001: 83) notes that there are some central motivations for entering the sex industry: (1) economic need; (2) associated or involved in the subculture; (3) drug use; (4) vulnerable women and men involved in local authority care.

It is important to identify that sex markets extend much further beyond female sex workers, as male and transgender sex workers adopt both the same and sometimes different characteristics, working arrangements and patterns. As is discussed in Chapter 3, men sell sex to men who identify with different sexualities: 'gay', 'bisexual', 'straight' (West and Villiers, 1992). Browne and Minichiello (1995) note that the social meanings behind male–male sexual transactions can shift depending on the sexuality of the client and the sex worker. Where men who sell sex also identify as gay, the sale of sex becomes less demarcated by a commercial exchange but a transaction that takes place in leisure spaces, resulting in the blurring of work and play (Minichiello et al., 2002; Scott et al., 2005).

As already mentioned, men also sell sexual services to women as male strippers (Dressel and Petersen, 1982; Montemurro, 2003), and in various guises as 'gigolos' (such as dance teachers) in sex tourism sites like Cuba and the Caribbean (Cabezas, 2004;

Sanchez Taylor, 2001). In both developed and developing countries, transgender sex work is evident both on the streets and located in indoor sex markets (Slamah, 1999; Weinberg et al., 1999).

Yet, to examine the sex markets in their entirety and move the focus away from the sex workers, it is important to understand the other individuals, roles and industries that form the rich tapestry that makes up the sex industry. In an article on the informal economies of the sex industry, Sanders (2008c) reflects on observations and interviews that took place in the brothel scene of a British city and notes that there are several ancillary industries that support the brothel industry. Sanders divides these ancillary industries into six types which are all characterized by cash-in-hand payments and informal networks based in local communities:

- *Premises*: landlords/renting premises (flats, houses, rooms, etc.).
- *Advertising*: website managers/photographers/card 'boys'/printers and publishers/ Internet directories/specialist magazines.
- *Security*: CCTV operators/doormen/bodyguards/receptionists/maids.
- *Transport*: drivers/taxi operators.
- *Presentation*: suppliers of beauty products/laundry services/cleaners/sellers of stolen goods and clothing/hustlers/fittings and fixtures (especially for domination services).
- *Recreation and hospitality*: drugs/alcohol/tobacco/food/commodities 'out of hours'.

The Occupational Cultures

Under the title of 'working girls' in her book *Sex Work: A Risky Business* (2005a: 1), Sanders describes a visit to two female sex workers who operate from a house which they rent for the purposes of selling sexual services in the suburbs of a large English city:

On a dreary Wednesday mid-morning in February, I am visiting working premises. We stop outside a semi-detached house in an unspectacular tree lined street with rows of ex-council houses now donning private brightly coloured front doors. Alison [health outreach worker] and I gather bags of condoms, lubricants and some leaflets on Hepatitis B injections that are offered at the clinic, stash them in an unobtrusive white plastic bag and head for the door. This is my fourth visit to this particular house and the women's friendly acceptance means I am looking forward to seeing them. It takes Katrina and Leigh a few minutes to answer, grabbing something to put round them before checking through the peephole. Greeted with a genuine welcome Leigh, wearing a black bikini and knee length boots, ushers us into the lounge where Katrina is putting a sarong around her thong bikini. All four of us are in the lounge, curtains drawn over heavy nets, and the heat is stifling. In the middle of winter, wearing not many clothes, it needs to be red hot. Alison and I peel off layers as Leigh strolls to the kitchen to make coffee as we hug Katrina in a 'good-to-see-you-haven't-for-ages' way ... Alison has known these two women for several years and has a strong, open relationship with them. As an observer I'm very aware that I am cashing in on their lengthy acquaintance, listening intently to the conversation and occasionally chipping in.

Applying moisturiser to her legs, Leigh tells us with nervous excitement that she is expecting her favourite client – a six-foot fireman – with whom she breaks all the rules and enjoys every second of his company. The doorbell rings, Leigh checks her lip gloss in the full length mirror, bounds to the door and whisks the client up the stairs. Alison and I never see any clients, just their vague shadow as they walk up the path. A few minutes later Leigh returns to the lounge to stash her earnings and is gone for twenty minutes. Katrina chats with us about how business has been going, the landlord who is trying to put up the rent and hence, their search for a new property. Our chat is interrupted while Katrina takes calls from prospective clients, giving out directions, and slamming down the phone on timewasters. Eventually the phone is too distracting so she takes it off the hook, preferring to relay her news. Katrina tells us of a new business venture they are trying out after a client told them about their competitors who advertise online. The girls have had some arty photographs taken together and now have a website where they are promoting specialist services at a higher price. Katrina jokes that she has gone a long way in ten years when she started on the street. Leigh returns just as Katrina's client arrives, a friendly GP we are told, who walks stridently towards the door, doctor's bag in hand, no doubt disguising his reasons for visiting. (2005a: 1)

The reality of many indoor sex work premises, particularly massage parlours and women who work alone or in small groups, is that the 'everyday' nature of the business mimics similar systems, rules and organizational features of mainstream businesses. For instance, May, Harocopos and Hough (2000: 26) report that parlour owners operate through a set of house rules including: 'Never employ juveniles, no anal sex, condoms always to be used, no partners allowed in the workplace, no overcharging, no rudeness or unpunctuality, no drunkenness and no clients under the age of 18'. In qualitative research studies in Birmingham and Merseyside, Sanders and Campbell (2007) found these rules also existed. The use of drugs amongst sex workers and clients was a rarity in the massage parlours and independent flats. These rules, along with others such as organized shift rotas, using a set of screening strategies to assess clients and employing a receptionist to manage the day-to-day activities (see Whittaker and Hart, 1996), characterize the massage parlour setting as an ordered workplace with a distinct occupational culture.

Much of the occupational culture, rules and regulations of the sex work venue and routine are ordered around the management of risk. Lewis et al. (2005), commenting on the organization of a range of markets from escorts, exotic dancing, massage and street working, identify how the management of risk is affected by the location of the commercial sex exchange; whether the work is organized as 'in' or 'out' calls; and whether the person works independently or for an agency or venue. In the legal brothel system of Nevada, Brents and Hausbeck (2005) found that despite strict surveillance by owners, there were clear working rules around the negotiation process and that women formed alliances with law enforcers and each other to deal with problematic customers. Buddying systems took place between experienced workers and novices as individuals would become self-appointed trainers who would teach novices how to keep safe and deal with customers.

On the street there are also occupational rules and codes of conduct between workers but sometimes due to the public and policed environment, working rules and practices can be fragmented. Day (2007: 66), reflecting on over 15 years of anthropological studies with sex workers in London, notes how 'personalised economic relationships involving trust' have been a foundation of sex work networks. Individuals often work in pairs and have routines and rules to protect themselves and make informed decisions about which customer to choose. Taking down car registration numbers, taking the client to a set and known destination, rejecting vans or cars with groups of men are some generic street rules.

One national example of the occupational culture amongst sex workers is the system of Ugly Mugs (Penfold et al., 2004). This system is operated by specialist support projects who collect reports from sex workers of clients who have acted violently, robbed them, or other people who have caused nuisance or committed crimes. These reports are collated and distributed to other sex workers, venues and projects. These rules and working practices, which have the safety of the women at the core, are threatened when there is heavy policing that deters women from working together and causes anxiety and suspicion on the street (see Sanders, 2004).

Advertising

How sex workers make contact with those who want to buy sexual services is an area that has seldom been studied by social scientists. However, from reviewing the literature, it is evident that the communication and advertisements of sex workers to their customer base are taking many new forms with the rise of Internet technology and the mobile phone (see below). Advertising is an important aspect of the sex industry. In some American cities, even when prostitution is illegal, magazines and cards advertising how to find sex workers are publicly displayed on the pavement, on billboards, in newspapers and on mobile posters that are driven around the streets with seductive semi-naked models marketing availability. In the UK, the advertisements take more subtle forms. Despite the cost, independent workers use several different methods of advertising, from traditional newspapers to creative webpages. Most male sex workers use the gay press to make their services visible. Although street workers do not pay financially to advertise their body, physically parading their availability for hire on the public streets places women at risk of criminalization, violence including hate crimes, harassment from protesters and stigma. A common feature of advertising for all sex workers is the allure of the fantasy body, as a central marketing tool.

O'Connell Davidson recognizes that the legal constraints on advertising sexual services influence how clients and sex workers are matched:

> Since sex workers are prevented by law from stating the nature or price of the services they offer, advertising this form of prostitution does not and cannot centre on 'product awareness' but rests fundamentally on attracting the custom of men with existing knowledge. (1995: 2)

Jones and Pratten (1999: 39) suggest saunas and brothels rely on three types of advertising: word of mouth recommendations, small adverts in local newspapers and direct visits from those who see the establishment on the street. Advertisements in local and national tabloid newspapers, specialist magazines, even shop windows have often taken a subtle approach to stating what is available. During the 1980s, escorts in the UK advertised in newspapers and magazines under classified personal services, using phrases to signal what was on offer:[2]

French Polishing a Speciality
Large Chest for Sale
Swedish Massage by Helga
Wicker Seats Re-Caned
Construction and Demolition – by Appointment Only
Games Mistress for Hire
'O' Level Students Invited and Encouraged

Although these types of phrases have now been replaced with more explicit images on the Internet and in specialist magazines, conventional signals are still used to advertise different services using a sexual code. Customers who are interested in buying sex become aware of the code from their peers, websites, health-related literature and magazines. Only those interested in the sex industry would make sense of the code. For example, phone booth cards advertise 'French, Greek and Spanish' (fellatio, anal sex and breast relief), 'O' Level and 'A' Level (oral and anal sex), or DIY (female masturbation), AC/DC (bisexual), BBW (big beautiful woman), OWO (fellatio without a condom). The gay press, however, advertises specific sexual services more directly with explicit adverts and images (Connell and Hart, 2003).

In the city of London, placing cards with brief details and images in telephone booths has been a traditional medium of signalling to the tourist and local customer that 'sex in the city' is available. However, under the Criminal Justice and Police Act 2001, it became illegal to place an advertisement for commercial sex in a telephone booth. Hubbard (2002) analyses the introduction of this piece of legislation and equates the concerns of advertising sex in a public place to a classic moral panic as the cards have been characterized as a threat to community values and cohesion. Since this Act, and the consistent removal of sex advertisements from telephone booths, there has been a decrease in this form of advertisement since the 1990s. The introduction of legal constraints and the policing of this form of advertisement have coincided with the rise of the Internet and other more successful formats for attracting customers.

The role of the Internet and technology

Without giving attention to the active role of independent entrepreneurial sex workers who manage their business online, some commentators have connected the use of the Internet and other new technologies for prostitution purposes as a postmodern form of abuse and violence (Gillespie, 2000; Hughes, 2004). Speaking from an abolitionist perspective, Hughes (2001) describes the growth of Internet-facilitated sex markets as a 'global medium for men's sexual exploitation and abuse of women and children' that acts as a vehicle for normalizing men's abusive behaviours. There is undoubtedly a relationship between new technologies, sexual abuse and criminal activity that capitalizes on the exploitation and coercion of women and children. We hear of how the Internet has been used as a 'grooming' tool for men who seek out underage children for sexual activity and where sexual offending behaviour finds sympathy and networks (see Quayle et al., 2000; Quayle and Taylor, 2002). However, although there are such examples of exploitation via the Internet, the murky side of the use of new technologies is not *necessarily* extended to prostitution. There is another side to the interplay between the sex industry and the Internet that enables women and men to actively control the working environment, interactions with clients and, to some extent, impose regulations and standards on the sex work they perform. The changes that have taken place are a result of two factors:

- Sex workers who have used traditional methods such as advertisements in newspapers have made the technological transition onto the Internet.
- Sex workers entering the industry are opting to use only the Internet to advertise, market, negotiate and organize their business. This can be done independently, through a third party or as part of a sex work business such as an escort agency or sauna.

As Kilvington, Day and Ward (2001) note, the Internet provides the opportunity to work in the sex industry without the costs associated with physical visibility on the streets. O'Neill (2001: 150) recognizes the shift to the Internet is driven by the high costs of advertising space in contact magazines and telephone booths which are more open to surveillance and policing than the Internet which remains outside the capabilities of everyday law enforcement. Reflecting on the changes in the UK, Sharp and Earle claim

> In recent years, demand for commercially available sexual services had soared, and the nature of the relationships involved in the selling of sexual services is undergoing a significant transformation in a number of ways, owing to the emergence and near exponential spread of the Internet. (2003: 36)

Some independent workers, especially escorts, are ditching the traditional newspaper advertisements and telephone booking system in favour of websites and email to market and organize their business. Durkin and Bryant (1995: 180) call this 'computer erotica' and warn, 'just as the computer has begun to revolutionize social life, it may also revolutionize crime and the parameters of sexual deviant behaviour'. They go on to discuss why the virtual arena is so attractive for organizing illicit sexual activity: 'The sexual computer network offers a high degree of anonymity, protection and secrecy' (1995: 187). The difficulty of policing the Internet gives sex workers the freedom to advertise their services explicitly.

New technologies are offering opportunities for sex workers across the globe. Veena (2007) reports on a small qualitative study with ten freelance sex workers who all work from the Internet in Bangkok, Thailand. The opportunities that the Internet provides these sex workers can be generalized to the basic benefits of using technology as a tool to organize business for independent women. Sex workers in Veena's study reported that through the Internet women could maximize their earnings by reducing costs such as those incurred when arranging to meet clients through a third party who would be part of the organizational triangle. Alongside financial independence, women could charge higher prices. Beyond the financial benefits, the sex workers in Veena's study identified 'the privacy factor' (2007: 105) as a key benefit of using the Internet. Many of the sex workers were students and wanted to keep their sex work employment hidden from the university community. What was also evident and concurs with work from Sanders (2005a: 68) on independent Internet-based escorts, is that the Internet sex work community becomes a prime place where safety is discussed between women and strategies and advice are shared for choosing 'safe' customers.

Bernstein (2007) identifies the Internet and entrepreneurial activities as clear signs of how parts of the sex industry are becoming professionalized. An example of such professionalization, where the sex industry mirrors features of mainstream employment, is that of the website EscortSupport.com. Bernstein (2007: 482) explains how this is an example of 'a website for sex workers which extends tips and networking to a broad online community'. Evidence of entrepreneurialism and 'mainstreaming' show how the sex industries are embedded in consumption and work patterns in contemporary society.

Sexual Services in Late Capitalism: An Expanding Industry?

Consumption as a lifestyle, an economic force and a device for marketing and making profit all impact on sexuality, sexual behaviour and the sex industries. Brents and Hausbeck (2007: 427), writing from the point of the regulated, legalized Nevada brothel system and the sexualized tourism that thrives in Las Vegas, state: 'sex businesses as forms of commerce must be situated in local institutional fields of consumption as they intersect with global late capitalist culture and economy'. That is, to understand the existence and, some would argue, expansion of the sex industries on a global scale, the capitalist economic structures must be examined in conjunction with cultural practices. Bernstein (2001) has argued that the prolific and unabridged use of sex, in particular the female body form, in advertising and other mechanisms of cultural production have produced a greater acceptability of the erotic, a normalization of the desire for the erotic and an increasing acceptance for men (and increasingly women) to pursue these desires.

The state of late capitalism and the rise of Internet technology is a significant dynamic that has altered the nature and extent of the sex industry. The Internet means that the ability to advertise, seek out, negotiate and arrange sexual services has no barriers or boundaries. There are not limits imposed by time, space or geography, and the unregulated form of communication means that there are few state sanctions that can stem what Bernstein (2001) terms 'an unbridled ethic of sexual consumption'. Moreover, there is a convergence between mainstream tourism and entertainment sites with venues where sexual consumption is the main activity. Brents and Hausbeck (2007: 437) conclude 'it is no longer useful to position sex industries as "other" to late capitalism industry'. Sex is defined as a product in contemporary society and this is marketed, packaged and available like many other service products. The turn of 'professionalizing' erotic work is clear through websites and sex worker rights movements as we witness what Bernstein (2007: 475) terms a 'new "respectability" of sexual commerce'. This somewhat difficult reality of late capitalist society 'mainstreaming' the (mainly) female commodification of the body and sex as an acceptable consumer product is at the heart of contemporary gender politics.

Future Policy and Research

From a review of the literature on the cultural context of commercial sex, we can conclude that there need to be new directions in research and theory focused on the following areas:

- macro-analysis of the context of sex markets, regulation and informal/formal economies;
- the role of the Internet and communication technologies and the organization of the sex industry;
- women as consumers of male sexual services and adult entertainment products and services;
- male sex work: migrants, sexuality and customers;
- transgendered sex work: participants, buyers and the place of the market;
- globalization and the sex industries.

Notes

1 www.strip-magazine.com is an industry directory, offering a strip job service, forums for dancers and news from the industry as well as advertising routines, lessons, colleges and equipment.
2 These phrases were taken from the film *Personal Services* written by David Leland (1987).

Suggested Reading

Agustin, L.M. (2005) 'New research directions: the cultural studies of commercial sex', *Sexualities*, 8(5): 618–31.
Bernstein, E. (2007) 'Sex work for the Middle Classes', *Sexualities*, 10(4): 473–88.
Brents, B. and Hausbeck, K. (2007) 'Marketing sex: US legal brothels and late capitalist consumption', *Sexualities*, 10(4): 425–39.
Browne, J. and Minichiello, V. (1995) 'The social meanings behind male sex work: implications for sexual interactions', *British Journal of Sociology*, 46(4): 598–622.
O'Neill, M. (2001) *Prostitution and Feminism*, Cambridge: Polity Press, Chapter 5.
Sanders, T. (2004) 'The risks of street prostitution: punters, police and protesters', *Urban Studies*, 41(8): 1703–17.

Study Questions

Level one

- Describe the different types of sex markets and explain why there are differences between direct and indirect sexual services.

Level two

- To what extent does the cultural context of the setting affect the organization of different sex markets?

Level three

- Critically examine the impacts of late capitalism on the shape, nature and organization of the sex industries.

3

SEX WORKERS AND SEX WORK

The aim of this chapter is to provide an overview of up-to-date research and literature on the complex nature of the sex industry and those who work in and manage the industry. The chapter discusses female, male and transgendered workers and outlines many different types of sex work. Routes into and out of the sex industry are discussed as well as mobility within the markets. The chapter challenges some common stereotypes and opens up the diversity of those working in the sex industry and of others involved, such as partners, pimps and drug dealers who may draw people into the sex industry. Research is then summarized on the following key issues: health and drug use; violence and safety; managers, organizers and coercers.

Socio-demographics of Sex Workers

Participation in the sex industry

Traditionally, sex work is seen as a female occupation and the majority of academic studies and policy reports focus on girls and women in the sex industry, particularly on street-based sex workers, emphasizing a specific range of issues and problems. This by no means reflects the whole of the sex industry, however: not only does this focus largely ignore men selling sex, but it is also notable that street-based workers form a minority of both male and female sex workers,[1] with a far greater proportion being based in indoor locations. As Weitzer (2005) points out, new directions in research in the sex industry must also include examining the relationship between transgendered communities and commercial sex.

Historically, sex workers have been portrayed variously as purveyors of disease, a social evil, public nuisance and, more recently, as victims needing to be 'rescued' from their abject state. The identity of people working in the sex industry has become inextricably associated with their work selling sex in much policy debate, with little scope for considering them as individuals and rational agents. It is important to stress, however, that sex workers are 'ordinary' people and that the fact that they sell sex is a part of their lives rather than a single identifying characteristic. Day (2007) discusses the stigma that is attracted to sex workers' 'public' body, and the ways in which women use instrumental rationality to separate out their private and public lives. As for all men and women, sex workers' private lives are shaped by many factors, including their different sexualities; relationships with parents, friends and siblings; infertility; and, for some, being a parent.

There are no reliable statistics on the numbers of men and women working in the sex industry.[2] Similarly, there is no comprehensive study documenting the backgrounds of sex workers, although studies of different populations show that sex workers can come from a range of backgrounds, with different routes in to sex work (O'Neill, 1997). While it appears from some studies that a majority of adult sex workers were under the age of 18 when they first started working in the industry (e.g. Cusick et al., 2003; Davies and Feldman, 1997; Pearce et al., 2002), by no means all enter at a young age. There are many different reasons for entering into sex work, in addition to the common stereo-type of the young person who has been abused or exploited. These include: wanting to earn extra money or having few other options for income, being introduced by a friend, or deciding independently to start working. In Chapter 4 we review the routes into the sex industry amongst young people. Amongst adults, however, the routes into the sex industry are not necessarily about victimhood or coercion, as will be discussed below.

Female sex workers

Women working in the sex industry are a diverse group, not only in terms of where and how they work, but also in relation to their age, background, personal relationships and sexuality. As Perkins and Lovejoy (2007: 136) note, whether they identify as heterosexual, bisexual or lesbian, sex workers 'treat prostitution as "work" and not as an expression of their sexuality or sexual desires'. It can be seen from this section that women sell sex in a variety of ways. Chapter 2 defines the differences between and characteristics of types of sex markets and 'direct' and 'indirect' sexual services. The majority of women working in the sex industry are based in indoor locations and street-based sex work is seen to have been declining over recent years, although it still forms the most visible aspect of the industry and thus continues to be the main focus of much policy attention. While there is no defining set of characteristics that differentiates street-based sex workers from those working indoors, there are nonetheless certain issues that tend to predomi-nate for women working on the street compared with their indoor-based counterparts.

Street-based workers

Street-based sex work takes place in many cities and towns. There have been no national multi-site research studies of street-based sex work and thus it is hard to estimate the numbers of women selling sex on the streets. Figures cited from individual studies or statistical sources show that the number of women in the UK working in any one night has ranged from just a few in small towns to more than 100 in larger cities.[3] Police statistics may underestimate the total number of women working, as such official mea-surements are based on those workers who are known to the police, or on numbers of arrests or convictions for illegal activities. Individual project statistics and studies in specific locations suggest that the figure is likely to be considerably higher than indicated by the official measurements (Sanders, 2005a).

From small-scale local studies, a relatively large proportion of women who work on the street entered sex work before they were 18 years of age (Galatowicz et al., 2005; May et al., 1999, 2001; Pearce et al., 2002). Chapter 4 discusses the sexual exploitation of young people in greater detail. Women working on the streets in the UK and many other countries are more likely than indoor workers to use drugs, particularly 'Class A' drugs such as crack cocaine and heroin, as discussed later in this chapter. Studies also document additional problems, such as homelessness and debt (Campbell, 2002; Galatowicz et al., 2005; Hester and Westmarland, 2004; May et al., 2001; O'Neill and Campbell, 2001; Shelter, 2004).

It is important to highlight the fact that not all women who work on the streets are dependent on drugs or have other problems that may be associated with drug use, nor do they by any means all fit the stereotype of the woman coerced at a young age (Brooks-Gordon, 2006; McKeganey and Barnard, 1996). Some women prefer to work on the street rather than indoors, as they feel it gives them a greater degree of independence (O'Connell Davidson, 1998; Pitcher et al., 2006). The quote below from McKeganey and Barnard (1996) illustrates the typical conditions of street work in a UK city and a range of reasons women have given for their involvement in street-based working:

Compared to settings such as saunas, street work may seem more arduous as it involves standing outside in all kinds of weather for long or short periods of time depending on how long it takes to get the next client. Having attracted a client the streetworking woman has the increased hazard of going away to a place where sex can be provided in relative privacy. Often this will entail being in deserted car parks or ill-lit streets ... When asked why they did so, many women cited the flexibility in being able to decide when to work and for how long. Shift work, which is the norm in saunas and massage parlours, was viewed negatively, particularly where women had children and claimed they could not be sure of adequate childcare arrangements during the daytime. Another point made by those women who had tried working in the saunas related to the numbers of men using the service; women spoke of long periods of time spent doing nothing because of a lack of trade. On the streets in a similar situation women can leave the area and go and do something else. Streetworking women referred to the advantages of being their own boss: in particular they, unlike women working in the saunas, did not have to pay the sauna manager a fee or a percentage of their takings. (1996: 20)

Indoor-based workers

Women working in indoor locations work in a variety of settings. These include:

- licensed brothels, saunas and massage parlours;
- unlicensed saunas and other premises;
- private rented flats or houses, either alone or with one or two others;
- working in windows in some cities;
- working as escorts (independently or via an agency);
- working from own home;
- as lap-dancers, strippers or 'hospitality workers' in clubs/bars.

There are no global statistics for the number of female sex workers working in indoor locations and national figures tend to relate to small-scale or localized studies.[4] Provided that indoor working does not give rise to complaints from the public, this form of working tends not to be given the same degree of police scrutiny as street-based sex work.

Research shows a slightly older age profile for women working indoors than on the street (Sanders, 2006a). In major cities such as London there have been increasing numbers of migrant women working in the sex industry since the 1990s, sometimes reaching more than half of indoor workers in some areas (Agustin, 2006; Ward et al., 2004). It is important, however, to distinguish between migrant and 'trafficked' sex workers: there has been little research undertaken with migrant sex workers and even less is known about those who may have been trafficked (Agustin, 2006). Many migrants to the UK and elsewhere make rational choices to work in the sex industry, as an alternative to other, lower-paid and sometimes more abusive forms of labour, yet this is not portrayed in many accounts. Much of the research that does exist supposedly on 'trafficking' into sex work does not clearly separate out the issues (Agustin, 2006, 2007a), but instead conflates migrant labour with coerced trafficking (Butcher, 2003; Outshoorn, 2004).

The reasons women have given for working in brothels include the presence of a third party who provides additional security and facilitates sex worker/client exchanges. The manager of the brothel also takes a fee: for example, a percentage of the sex worker's income/shift fee, in exchange for renting a space or a room in a similar way to a hairdresser or taxi driver making arrangements with an employer. There are usually set hours in brothels and the expectations of the work routine are explored in Chapter 2. There may often be fixed rates but sex worker and client may also negotiate over the rate (O'Connell Davidson, 1998).

For some women, independent work is preferable to 'employed' sex work. Independent sex workers may be seen in a number of settings, including working from home and escorting services. A number of 'window' sex workers are also self-employed (Ousthoorn, 2004). The type of woman working as an independent worker in her own property is often in a very different situation from that of many other sex workers, in terms of economic circumstances, degree of choice and control over her working life (O'Connell Davidson, 1998; Sanders, 2005b). As an example, O'Connell Davidson considers the experience of a British sex worker in her thirties, 'Desiree', who started to work as a sex worker from her own home in order to supplement her regular income as a clerical worker and is now self-employed and financially successful:

> Desiree regularly earns between £1,500 and £2,000 per week. She has already saved more than £150,000 and owns several thousand pounds' worth of jewellery as well as three (immaculately renovated) properties after only five years in the business. Her aim is to save £250,000 by the time she is thirty-six, at which point she intends to stop working as a prostitute. Her financial success distinguishes her not only from most other prostitutes, but also from the majority of wage workers in Britain. Furthermore, Desiree, unlike most prostitutes

and most wage workers, has chosen, designed and owns the physical environment in which she works. She plans and controls all aspects of her business: where and how to advertise, whom to employ and what tasks to assign to them, the pricing system, what services are and are not on offer, the hours and days of business. (1998: 90–1)

The degree of control Desiree has over her working circumstances, as described above, is by no means typical of the majority of sex working women, but this example illustrates that work at the 'top end' of the sex industry can be markedly different not only from that of street-based workers, but also of the many women working in the 'employed' sectors of the industry. Vanwesenbeeck (2005) notes that amongst female indoor sex workers there is an expressed and identifiable 'hierarchy' of markets amongst workers based on working conditions, characteristics of the sex work and generalizations about 'types' of workers.

In some locales, lap-dancing clubs, massage parlours and hostess clubs may be the main spaces of sex work. Exotic dance tends to be viewed differently from other forms of sex work, although there are also hierarchies within this section of the industry, with some dancers perceiving their work as 'higher class' than others, depending on their working environment (Murphy, 2003). Dancers are also able generally to set boundaries regarding the amount of sexual and emotional contact they have with customers (Barton, 2002; Frank 2007), although there may be differences in the degree of control exercised by dancers according to the type of club they work in (Trautner, 2005). This is discussed further in Chapter 2.

Male sex workers

There is far less policy attention paid to male sex workers than to female workers and a smaller amount of literature on this group. The main types of male sex worker have been identified as: escorts, independent workers and street workers (Connell and Hart, 2003). Although much early research focused on street-based sex work, the evidence shows that selling sex on the street is less prevalent for men than indoor work, except in certain urban centres and known outdoor spaces for public sex.

Many men admit to having started selling sex before the age of 18. Nonetheless, this also needs to be balanced against the fact that many also engaged in consensual sex before the age of 16 (Davies and Feldman, 1997; Gaffney, 2007). For some, the first exchange of sex for money or other incentives was seen as part of 'the experimentation of youth'. Contrary to some early stereotypes, many adult male sex workers, certainly in the UK, but also more widely, identify as gay or bisexual (Davies and Feldman, 1997; Gaffney, 2007; Hall, 2007). Some may have non-paying male partners. Not all male sex workers are gay, however, and not all clients are male. In the case of 'sex tourism', for example, while men may form the majority of purchasers, there are also comparatively affluent heterosexual women who purchase sex from men or boys in certain countries, generally those with a high rate of poverty (O'Connell Davidson, 1998). Female sex tourism, also known as 'romance tourism' is a growing area of research in tourism destinations.

Street-based workers

Male street-based workers (also sometimes known as 'rent boys' in the UK) form a minority of male sex workers. Unlike female street sex work, most street-based male sex work takes place in the centres of large cities, often in busy areas with bars and cafés, which may also be known 'cruising' areas for gay men (Gaffney, 2007). Many clients approach on foot rather than traditional kerb crawling in cars, although sexual transactions may take place away from the cruising area, in clients' cars or homes, in saunas or in quiet areas such as parks or woods (Connell and Hart, 2003). As for women, the risk of violence is also greater for street-based male workers than indoor workers. Violence may also be related to homophobia (Marlowe, 2006). Street-based male sex workers are more vulnerable than those working indoors to sexually transmitted infections or HIV, which may be linked to their drug use (Connell and Hart, 2003). Some street-based workers in London are also engaged in criminal activities such as robbery and shoplifting to fund their drug use (Gaffney, 2007).

Indoor-based workers

The majority of men selling sex do so indoors, in brothels, or bars in some countries, independently in flats, or as agency or independent escorts, often advertising through the gay press, over the Internet and on websites such as Gaydar (Gaffney, 2007). Independent escorts may work from their own premises, or partly from home and partly in hotels, saunas and other public venues. Some may also visit their clients' homes. Brothels tend to be relatively discreet and located in areas with busy street scenes. Adult men working in them tend, in the main, to be there voluntarily. According to Gaffney (2007: 31): 'the organised, commercial scene is self-regulating around the protection of young people', although Connell and Hart (2003) found some younger men in brothels in their study.

Some men have reported becoming involved in pornographic films as a result of being involved in sex work (Connell and Hart, 2003). Other forms of indoor work, for men as well as women associated with the sex industry, include exotic dancing or stripping (Frank, 2007). While many men have their first exchange of sex for money or other incentives at a relatively young age, others may enter into escorting or other types of indoor work because of financial reasons such as debt or redundancy later on in life (Connell and Hart, 2003). Reportedly, many male workers in London are also migrants from outside the UK (Gaffney, 2007). Project statistics suggest that the proportion of migrant male sex workers working indoors in London is similar to that of women (Agustin, 2006).

Transgendered sex workers

Less is known about transgendered sex workers, partly because this is not a recognized category in much policy. Dixon and Dixon (1998) interviewed 'she-male prostitutes' who are publicly visible in the alternative sex scenes in San Diego, California. This micro-community involves men who dress and behave as women (including cosmetic surgery) but have not taken the step further for full gender reassignment surgery for genital changes so are not transsexuals. They were involved in professional sexual activity including massage, stripping, modelling, domination as well as oral sex and most worked from apartments. The majority of their customers were male who were aware of the workers' male sex. Interviewees described advantages of the sex work as an 'ego boost' to their own sexuality.

In relation to transgendered sex workers, Leichtentritt and Davidson-Arad (2004) identify that in Israel there is a link between the desire for gender transformation, accumulating the necessary financial resources and using commercial sex to do so. This builds on existing knowledge amongst Brazilian male-to-female transgendered communities, that sexual labour can be a means of gaining self-worth and recognition for those engaging in gender reassignment surgery (Kulick, 1998).

Entering, Mobility and Leaving the Sex Industry

This section looks at routes into sex work, the extent to which people move around different jobs in the industry and routes out of sex work. While men and women working in the sex industry may encounter different circumstances and patterns of entry, these circumstances may also be interlinked with their ability to control their working lives and exercise a degree of choice over remaining in sex work.

Routes in to sex work

The popular stereotype of entry into sex work for women is of the young girl being enticed or coerced by an older man (the traditional 'pimp'). While this may be the case for some sex workers who enter the trade, particularly at a younger age, it is by no means the only route into sex work. As O'Neill (1997) notes, women have many different reasons for entering sex work and do so under different circumstances. While for many the prime reason is economic need, some women make independent rational choices to enter the sex industry and some may 'drift in' through being introduced to the option by friends who are already working, either as sex workers or in other jobs associated with the sex industry, such as receptionists or maids in indoor establishments (O'Connell Davidson, 1998; O'Neill, 1997, 2001; Sanders, 2005a). For many sex workers, their decision to enter sex work is based on considerations of the limited alternative options available to them, particularly if they have few skills and thus only access to lower-paid work (O'Connell Davidson, 1998). Those with skills, qualifications and a history of work in the mainstream employment sector also make rational 'cost–benefit' choices to enter into the sex industry to earn more money for less time. Earning a minimum wage for many hours even in a semi-skilled profession is less favourable than working two or three days a week for greater pay. The pressures of single parenthood, living on low welfare benefits and pressures of debt are also factors that can spark trained women to turn to the sex industry as an option for making financial profit within a shorter amount of time. For street-based workers in particular, sex work may be a means of supporting their own or their partner's drug use (O'Neill, 1997). As was discussed earlier, there are examples of women who have left lower-paid professional jobs or have started to work in the industry to supplement other income, for example, to pay off debts or to support college and university education (Roberts et al., 2007). Bernstein (2007) notes an increase in middle-class women (and men) entering sex work.

While many women may take an informed decision to enter the sex industry, it is important not to downplay circumstances of coercion that occur for some women, particularly younger girls. Research documents a range of 'vulnerability' factors impacting on young people's entry into sexual exploitation, including grooming, coercion or abuse by adults, experience of the 'looked after' care system, running away from care or home and childhood abuse (Coy, 2007a; Cusick et al., 2003; Drinkwater et al., 2004; O'Neill et al., 1995; Pearce et al., 2002). Darch (2004) notes a similar range of factors amongst young men working on the street in London, with confusion about sexuality often being a complementary issue. Further discussion on young people and sexual exploitation can be found in Chapter 4.

For men as well as women, the motivating factor for entry into the sex industry is economic need and for many this is a conscious choice, as it offers them more money than they could earn in mainstream employment. Some of the main reasons given for entering sex work include recognition of the potential earning opportunities, being introduced to sex work by a friend or partner, or being approached by an older man. Some young men may be coerced into sex work, particularly those who enter at a young age, who may have a history of abuse or family breakdown. Some male sex workers may have become homeless as a result of running away from home due to bullying and exclusion from the family because of their sexuality. Some have also been in local authority care. Most respondents in Davies and Feldman's (1997) study saw sex work as a part-time job which they had entered through choice. As Gaffney (2007: 28) notes: 'most would not consider themselves as victims or having been abused'.

For some, recruitment also takes place through pimps, paedophiles or money lenders, although Gaffney (2007) notes that indoor male sex work does not have the same 'pimping' role as for female sex workers. Some male sex workers are recruited into agency or brothel work through 'couch testing' by recruiters (Connell and Hart, 2003).

Mobility within the sex industry

There are sometimes shifting boundaries between indoor and street-based sex work. Some women sex workers are 'occupationally mobile' and may move between indoor and outdoor working (Hubbard and Sanders, 2003). Street-based sex workers, for example, sometimes turn to indoor activities such as working from home or a private rented flat in response to police crackdowns, aggravation from communities, or increasing levels of violence on the street. Connell and Hart (2003) also describe mobility between different sectors of male sex work, such as from renting to escorting and vice versa. It is becoming increasingly popular to combine on-street work with some indoor work by using different forms of contact, such as mobile phones and the Internet (Sanders, 2005a). Not only is there mobility between sub-sectors of the sex industry, but some men and women work for relatively short periods of time or at particular times of year (Agustin, 2005; Gaffney, 2007; McKeganey and Barnard, 1996). For instance, with the financial burdens of Christmas, this period often results in an increase in sporadic workers in all types of markets.

There is occasionally an upward transition from street-based to indoor work, particularly where harm reduction services have supported sex workers to make changes in their lives. Indoor working may not be a feasible option for all street-based workers, however, particularly if they experience problems such as homelessness and drug use. The strict rules and anti-drug culture of the brothels and saunas (further described in Chapter 2) make the indoor work environment hostile to drug-using street sex workers. Furthermore, some sex workers may move from indoor to street working as a result of increasingly problematic drug use (Galatowicz et al., 2005), whereas others may prefer to work on the streets as it gives them relative independence (Pitcher et al., 2006). While there is sometimes evidence of dispersal of women to off-street locations as a result of enforcement activities, equally some initiatives, such as evictions of women selling sex from council property, have meant that some women move to working on the streets. In some areas with geographically close street sex markets, workers may move periodically to different areas to avoid police crackdowns in some towns and cities (Pitcher et al., 2006). Independent escort work displays a wider range of geographical mobility than some other forms of sex work (Connell and Hart, 2003).

Routes out of sex work

What has come to be known about how women leave the sex industry has been pieced together from research into employment histories and social work practices and interventions to assist women to leave. As the political agenda in Northern Europe has moved towards the aim of eradicating the sex industry, theories on 'exiting' have developed. To support the Swedish project of eradicating the sex industry, Mansson and Hedin (1999) developed an 'exit model' that highlights the influence of structural, situational, interpersonal and individual factors when women attempt to leave. This model concludes that it is the 'emotional commitment' of individual women that determines whether removal from the sex industry is achieved, advocating that the 'responsibilization' of sex workers should be at the core of any support services. In criticizing this model, however, others have highlighted the fact that it is not only the individual's ability to make changes that is critical in how women leave the sex industry but making transitions out of sex work also relies on social and environmental factors and influences.

Cusick and Hickman (2005) have identified strong connections between being 'trapped' in 'outdoor/drift' sex work, drug use and having criminal convictions. Drug use presents a serious barrier to moving out of sex work (Surratt et al., 2004; Williamson and Folaron, 2003). Cusick et al. (2003), in their UK study, identify 'trapping' factors that have the potential to mutually reinforce sex work and drug use, particularly for outdoor workers. These are discussed further in Chapter 4. Street-based workers who are 'pimped' may find this an economic constraint on their ability to move out of sex work and, where abuse is involved, may find themselves denied the freedom to make choices for themselves and forced into remaining in sex work (May et al., 2001; O'Connell Davidson, 1998).

Research on juveniles involved in prostitution in Taiwan found that young people expressed four main reasons for remaining in prostitution: financial, emotional, drug issues and identity-related factors (Hwang and Bedford, 2004). Hester and Westmarland (2004) evaluated 11 multi-agency projects across the UK and found amongst women who used outreach services that 69 per cent (128 out of 186) of street workers had attempted to leave on one or more occasion (2004: 85). Sanders (2007) concludes from a small-scale qualitative study with 30 sex workers, all of whom had made transitions out of the sex industry, that there are four types of routes out:

1   *Reactionary* – a sudden impulse to a crisis or critical issue (such as ill-health, severe violence, pregnancy, drug overdose).
2   *Gradual planning* – alternative career planned or training; successful drug treatment and re-housing.
3   *Natural progression* – older women slowing down, seeing fewer clients, finding other ways to make money; age as a factor for leaving.
4   *Yo-yoing* – failed package of support results in re-entering; process of stopping and starting any of the above routes out fails and leads to a return to make quick money; patterns of working on and off.

From this study, Sanders (2007) concludes that the criminalization of sex work has also become a trapping factor for those wanting to make a move out of selling sex. A criminal record for soliciting, loitering or anti-social behaviour offences will prevent anyone from getting a secure footing in the mainstream labour market. In addition, the transformation process where official agencies do offer support, is understood in a rigid framework without any flexibility or expectation that there will be some yo-yoing as a reaction to making significant changes which include identity change and removing oneself from old networks (see McNaughton and Sanders, 2007).

Connell and Hart (2003) found that most of their male respondents wanted to leave sex work. For many, this was seen as a gradual process, for example, through a reduction in the number of clients over time. Stopping sex work for a short time and then recommencing was also a common pattern for many men. Many male sex workers returned to sex work because of the need to earn money. For some, sex work supported their drug use. Some also described sex work as a 'habit' and felt that they might be tempted to participate on an opportunistic basis. Yo-yoing in and out of sex work for both male and female sex workers appears to be a natural and perhaps necessarily inevitable part of making significant changes to lifestyle, economic sustenance and identity.

Many projects provide support for men and women wishing to leave the sex industry. This is generally accompanied by other forms of support and harm minimization, although a few projects have 'exiting' as their main focus (Pitcher, 2006a). Where sex work is principally a means to fund drug use, successful drug treatment has led to exiting (Cusick et al., 2003). It is important for projects to recognize that both male and female sex workers will only access services when they are ready to do so and thus they need to be flexible to their circumstances and lifestyle stages (Darch, 2004; May et al., 2001). Support is also necessary on a long-term basis for many and services must be able to deal with a range of complex needs (Surratt et al., 2004).

Violence and Safety

The global research picture suggests that those involved in the sex industry experience a high degree of violence as part of their work (see Sanders and Campbell, 2007, for a review). While only a small number of studies have focused specifically on violence against sex workers, many research studies have collected data about violence amongst a range of other issues. Much of the literature focuses on harassment or violence against street-based workers, which is seen as being much more prevalent than for indoor workers and can include verbal abuse, slapping or kicking, through to serious physical assault, kidnap, sexual assault, rape and murder (Campbell and Kinnell, 2001; Church et al., 2001; Hester and Westmarland, 2004; May et al., 2001; McKeganey and Barnard, 1996; O'Neill and Barbaret, 2000; O'Neill et al., 1995). Violence may be perpetrated by clients, pimps or managers, drug dealers, robbers, other sex workers, passers-by or sometimes local residents, whose activities can sometimes tip over into vigilantism (Kinnell, 2006a; O'Neill and Campbell, 2004; Pitcher et al., 2006; Sanders, 2004). Some street-based sex workers have experienced intimidation by police (Campbell, 2002). As is discussed later, drug-using sex workers may be more vulnerable to violence than non-drug users.

While some indoor workers, particularly those working alone or in vulnerable circumstances, may experience work-related violence, on the whole, this is far less prevalent than for street-based workers (Church et al., 2001; Kinnell, 2006a). Evidence from the regulated brothels of Nevada demonstrates that where there is a system for protecting sex workers and the state is involved in monitoring and registering venues, violence is limited (Brents and Hausbeck, 2005). Similarly, in brothels in the UK, indoor workers experience much less violence compared with those on the street, although robbery is a factor as well as other forms of violence such as verbal abuse and disrespectful client behaviours (see Sanders and Campbell, 2007).

Many male sex workers have also experienced a considerable degree of abuse and physical or sexual violence, particularly those working on the street, but also men involved in organized sex work in brothels (Connell and Hart, 2003). Perpetrators of violence are mainly clients and organizers of sex work. For street-based workers, members of the public may also be abusive or violent as homophobic hate crimes and harassment affect this community. Men working on the street are more likely to work in cruising areas, some of which may be poorly lit (Connell and Hart, 2003). 'Gay bashing' from members of the public may also be common in these areas.

Deaths by homicide are more likely amongst the female sex worker population than for women in most other occupations. Kinnell (2006a) in her analysis of the international literature found that street-based sex workers were particularly vulnerable, although some indoor workers, particularly those who work alone or in isolated situations have also been victims of murder. Ward et al. (2005) note that sex workers are twelve times more likely to be murdered than other women their own age. Gaffney (2007: 31) also notes the murder of a male masseur, which highlights that male lone workers are also vulnerable.

While clients are the most commonly reported perpetrators of violence against female sex workers, Kinnell (2006a) suggests that a *minority* of clients commit violence against sex workers and that often men who attack or murder sex workers frequently have a past history of violence against sex workers and other women. Kinnell (2006a: 151) identifies four types of 'trigger factors' that spark off violence from male clients. First, sex workers refusing to perform types of sexual services; second, disputes over money; third, the sex worker finishing the service before the client has ejaculated; and finally, the client's failure to get an erection. However, it must be remembered that the majority of commercial transactions take place without violence or incidence.

Many sex workers have strategies or mechanisms for averting or dealing with violence from clients. For those working indoors with other indoor workers or a maid, the presence of others can act as a deterrent, as can CCTV and locks (Brooks-Gordon, 2006). Other forms of 'risk management' for avoiding customer violence for indoor workers include spyholes in doors for screening clients, making some assessment of clients' potential for violence, employing verbal mechanisms for diffusing potentially violent situations and building up a clientele of regular customers (Kinnell, 2006a; Sanders, 2005a). Certain sexual positions are seen as riskier than others, such as a sexual position where the man is on top of the sex worker.

Street-based sex workers, while they do not have access to the same range of mechanisms for safety as groups of indoor workers, also have strategies for reducing the threat of violence as much as is possible within the environmental circumstances. These include soliciting near to other sex workers, keeping an eye out for one another, for example, taking down registration numbers of cars used, watching from the end of an alley, working with partners nearby or, in some cases, carrying a weapon (McKeganey and Barnard, 1996; O'Neill and Campbell, 2004 and Figure 3.1). They also employ similar mechanisms for assessing clients and intuiting the potential for violence as indoor workers (Connell and Hart, 2003; Kinnell, 2006a). Some female street-based workers prefer to solicit close to residential areas as this is seen as a safer option than more isolated areas (Pitcher et al., 2006). Nonetheless, the general public may be unsympathetic and ignore instances of violence towards sex workers (Brooks-Gordon, 2006).

The majority of studies have found substantial under-reporting to the police of crimes of violence against both female and male sex workers (Church et al., 2001; Connell and Hart, 2003; Kinnell, 2006a; May et al., 1999; McKeganey and Barnard, 1996). The reasons for this may include that sex workers do not expect sympathetic treatment, particularly if they had prior experiences of negative attitudes, or that they may be in fear of arrest for prostitution-related or other offences (Connell and Hart, 2003; Kinnell, 2006a). Indoor workers are more likely than street-based workers to report certain crimes against them, particularly non-violent crimes and robbery (Brooks-Gordon, 2006). Some studies have found that the persistence of harassment and/or violence can mean that certain levels of violence may be treated as 'part of

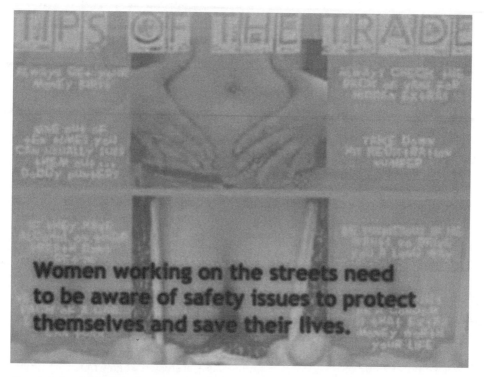

Figure 3.1 O'Neill and Campbell (2001) Participatory Action Research Project 'Safety SoapBox: Sharing our true colours'. Image created by female sex worker.
Source: www.safetysoapbox.co.uk/gallery2.htm

the job', which can be a further factor contributing to under-reporting (McKeganey and Barnard, 1996; Pearce, 1997).

Strategies of enforcement against street-based sex workers and their clients may often increase the dangers of violence to sex workers. They can force workers to solicit in less well-lit and more isolated areas because of fears of being arrested; sex workers may take less time to negotiate transactions with clients to avoid being seen; and clients caught up in kerb-crawler initiatives may take out their anger on sex workers (Kinnell, 2006a; Pitcher et al., 2006).

Health and Drug Use

Sex workers and use of drugs

The connection between drug use, particularly of Class A drugs, and sex work is well-documented for street-based workers, although the causal links are not always easy to disentangle (Campbell, 2002; Hester and Westmarland, 2004; May et al., 1999;

McKeganey and Barnard, 1996; Pearce et al., 2002). Evidence from several studies suggests that drug-using sex workers may start to engage in sex work to fund their drug use (Epele, 2001; May et al., 2000; Pearce et al., 2002). Use of crack cocaine, either replacing or in addition to heroin, may lead to increased risk-taking and working hours and increase sex workers' vulnerability to violence (Becker and Duffy, 2002; May et al., 1999, 2001; Surratt et al., 2004). McKeganey and Barnard (1996) also note that drug-injecting sex workers tended to work longer hours than those who did not inject drugs. Women working from home or in indoor establishments, however, are generally far less likely to be dependent on drugs and more in control of working (and personal) lives (Galatowicz et al., 2005; Sanders, 2005a).

Although drug use is reported as less problematic for male sex workers than for women, many street-based male sex workers are dependent on drugs or use alcohol (Connell and Hart, 2003; Gaffney, 2007). For some men who were already drug users, sex work may exacerbate their use of drugs and some may start using drugs as a result of participation in sex work. Recreational drugs such as ecstasy, cocaine and speed are more common amongst male sex workers (Davies and Feldman, 1997). There is some indication that use of Class A drugs such as heroin and crack cocaine is increasing amongst men working on the street (Gaffney, 2007).

Many women sex workers are reluctant to approach services because of the fear that they will be judged (Becker and Duffy, 2002; Pitcher and Aris, 2003). Drug-using women may face particular barriers to accessing drugs services (Hester and Westmarland, 2004; Shelter, 2004; Sondhi et al., 2002). The problem is exacerbated when women are homeless, which is a particular issue for street sex workers (Galatowicz et al., 2005).

Sexual health

Prostitute women were constructed as a danger to public health in the nineteenth century, in response to moral panics about sexually transmitted diseases. This led to the introduction of legislation in the UK designed to control prostitutes, particularly the Contagious Diseases Acts of 1864, 1866 and 1869 (Scoular, 2004a; Ward and Day, 1997). While the laws targeting prostitutes for mandatory testing have been repealed in the UK (Ward and Day, 1997), from time to time there has been a resurgence in concerns that sex workers are responsible for spreading infection, particularly following the increase of HIV/AIDS, and the issue of compulsory testing continues to be raised. In many parts of the world, sex workers are required to have health checks (Day, 2007).

The prevalence of HIV is also related to the degree to which sex workers use condoms with their clients. McKeganey and Barnard (1996), reviewing international studies, found relatively high levels of condom use amongst sex workers in many European countries, including the UK, as well as in parts of North America, New Zealand and Australia. The rates of HIV transmission were also relatively low in these countries compared with parts of Africa and Asia and the evidence suggests that with an insistence on safer sex, the risk of transmission amongst sex workers may be even lower. Connell and Hart (2003) reported increased awareness of sexual health issues and safer sex practices amongst their male respondents, although condom use sometimes varied, for example, according to the type of sexual act or in response to client preference.

Vulnerable groups which may need particular guidance include young sex workers, who may have less experience of health issues than adult sex workers; and drug-using sex workers who may take greater risks and be less cautious about practising safer sex (Europap, 2003). May and Hunter (2006) note the increased health risk posed by problematic drug use, particularly for those injecting drugs, who may be at risk of contracting blood-borne viruses such as HIV or Hepatitis B or C. Migrant sex workers may go without health checks for fear of deportation, which may put them at greater risk, although Day and Ward (2004) found that rates of sexually transmitted infections amongst migrant sex workers reflected the relatively low rate in the sex worker population generally in cities such as London.

Mental health

Depression and anxiety may often be associated with problematic drug use, particularly crack cocaine (May and Hunter, 2006). Day (2007) also notes a range of mental health problems reported by sex workers, including depression, stress, panic attacks, insomnia, eating disorders and manic depression. These problems may reflect the stress of leading a complex life, but also may result from the stigma encountered by sex workers.

Connell and Hart (2003) found that the majority of their interviewees felt that sex work had had a negative impact on their mental health, with depression, anxiety, apathy, low self-esteem, emotional detachment and isolation being experienced by many. It should be borne in mind that their research was predominantly with street-based sex workers and Marlowe (2006) presents a rather different picture for escorts, although Gaffney (2007) also reports that isolation is a problem for many men working in indoor locations.

Brewis and Linstead (2000a, 2000b) draw on research with female sex workers in the UK and Australia to examine the type of tactics that women employ to negotiate and construct their sense of self and manage the relationship between professional and personal identity. Elsewhere, Sanders (2005b) notes how sex workers create clear barriers between sex as work and sex as pleasure in their personal lives by deciding which parts of their bodies can be used for sexual services; using the condom as a psychological barrier; using a pseudonym; and applying different meanings and feelings to sex at work. Also, sex workers who decide to work as 'entrepreneurs' sometimes create a 'manufactured identity' which consists of a separate persona and character for the normal 'self' in order to maintain a division between work and home/leisure (Sanders, 2005b). However, as Brewis and Linstead (2000) and others identify, the difficulties and trials of maintaining divisions between identities can be a strain whilst Vanwesenbeeck (2005) clarifies how indoor sex workers suffer 'burn out' from the pressures of sex work. For some, the pressure of managing different identities may impact on their relationships and self-identity even after they have moved out of sex work.

Physical health

High levels of violence, particularly over a period of time, can have a considerable impact on the physical and mental health of sex workers (Connell and Hart, 2003; Cusick and Berney, 2005; McKeganey and Barnard, 1996). Drug-using sex workers may face a number of physical as well as mental health problems associated with their drug use. These can include significant weight loss, chest pains, and abscesses; and for women, unwanted pregnancy, miscarriage or irregular periods (May and Hunter, 2006; Ward et al., 2000). There is also the possibility of drug overdose, particularly for sex workers who inject, in some cases leading to death (McKeganey and Barnard, 1996). For some men and women participation in sex work can lead to an increase in alcohol consumption, which can impact on their health and exposure to danger (Connell and Hart, 2003; Sanders, 2004).

Managers, Organizers and Coercers

The traditional notion of the woman working on the street is of someone who is 'controlled' by a pimp, who lives off her earnings and coerces her into staying in sex work. While some women may be managed by pimps, however, this is far less common than is supposed (May et al., 2000; McKeganey and Barnard, 1996). Nonetheless, for the minority who are 'pimped' in the traditional way, there is considerable risk of physical or mental abuse from their pimp. Young people and women working in street markets are the most at risk of being pimped, although there are also many women working on the street who would consider themselves to be independent (May et al., 2000; McKeganey and Barnard, 1996; Pitcher et al., 2006). Chapter 4 has further discussion on the issue of sexual exploitation and coercion of young people. Traditionally, those who are involved in pimping street-based sex workers are male. Women do not always remain with one pimp and it is quite common for some to move from one pimp to another. Sometimes women may choose to 'hire' a pimp for company or protection (Day, 2007).

Drug use is often also found to be prevalent among pimps, who also sell on to sex workers (May et al., 2000). In some cases, drug dealers have become organizers of street-based workers in place of the traditional pimp and there is evidence to suggest that, while violence is used as a strategy of control by some, in other instances the relationship has become more one of covert control through using the worker's reliance on drugs (Pitcher et al., 2006).

The situation is complicated by the fact that some women working on the street are accompanied by their boyfriend or partner, sometimes for reasons of safety, who may be seen by outsiders as being in a pimping relationship with the sex worker, although accounts from adult sex workers themselves often present a different picture which is more one of co-dependency (May et al., 2000; McKeganey and Barnard, 1996). Partners may be dependent on Class 'A' drugs and some women work on the streets to fund their partner's drug use. The boundaries between different relationships may also be blurred in many instances. Day (2007: 129), in her research with sex workers over a number of years, makes the point that relationships with partners may change as the sex worker starts to earn more than her partner or other associates: 'Money was even credited with the capacity to foster "pimping" or "poncing" and to corrupt what were previously private relationships based on friendship and love'. In some countries, street children involved in prostitution are themselves drawn into pimping as a survival mechanism (O'Connell Davidson, 1998).

Indoor establishments such as saunas and massage parlours generally have someone who is in a position of manager, with whom there is some form of contractual agreement (May et al., 2000; Sanders, 2005a). Some escorts may be self-employed but have a contractual arrangement with a third party, who facilitates transactions (O'Connell Davidson, 2006). Third parties, managers or agents, also need to establish some mechanism for benefiting financially from their role and thus may devise strategies of control to maximize their own income. Third parties may be male or female.

Male sex workers may also be recruited by pimps, although sometimes the pimping is indirect, through other sex workers (Connell and Hart, 2003). Generally, however, male sex workers are more likely to work independently of pimps (Marlowe, 2006). Young men may also be coerced into sex work by paedophiles or money lenders. Brothel owners or managers, or their associates, may threaten or perpetrate violence as a means of ensuring continued participation in sex work, as well as enforcing silence about their business (Connell and Hart, 2003).

Thus it can be seen that the role of the 'pimp' and the relationship between pimps and sex workers is far more complex than popular stereotypes would suggest. O'Connell Davidson argues that the term 'pimp' should be restricted to

individuals who secure a benefit from prostitution either because they exercise some form of direct control over one or more person's prostitution (articulating specific demands that she or he prostitutes and surrenders some or all of the proceeds from prostitution) or because they perform some identifiable function on behalf of one or more prostitutes and receive payment in exchange for these 'services', or because they combine the two. (1998: 46)

Under this definition, O'Connell Davidson (1998: 47–58) considers specific patterns of pimping, which depend on factors such as the relationship between sex worker and pimp, the mode of exploitation and the way in which compliance is enforced. In summary, these are:

- *Pimping as a form of 'street hustling'*: which may include the stereotypical image of 'pimps – usually male – who play an active role in the reproduction of – usually female – street prostitution', but also situations where street workers and their male or female pimps may be more interdependent, although 'the relationship between a pimp and a street prostitute is never genuinely reciprocal'.
- *Child 'pimps' and 'survival sex'*: generally amongst street children, where older children in a group will protect younger entrants and take a proportion of their earnings in exchange. In some cases this will be enforced through violence and other 'tactics used by street-hustling pimps'.

- *Pimping as an 'extension of sexual abuse'*: where the financial gain is of secondary importance.
- *'Entrepreneurial' pimping*: for example, acting as 'agents' for sex workers, working as manager or sometimes maid/receptionist in indoor establishments.
- *'Customary' pimping*: for example, through family members.

With the increase in migrant sex workers in the UK, there are also concerns about the role of the 'trafficker', although as for other sex workers, the nature of the relationship with intermediaries may not always be as clear-cut as that of coercer and coerced and in some cases third parties may form a part of the worker's own networks (Agustin, 2007a).

Future Policy and Research

Drawing on the literature examined here about the people who are involved in selling sex, we suggest that there needs to be further examination of the following aspects of the sex industry:

- people who are involved in organizing the sex industry;
- partners of sex workers;
- transgendered sex workers;
- mental health and psychological well-being in relation to sex work;
- reporting of and responses to violence against sex workers.

Notes

1 For example, female street sex workers in the UK and elsewhere are estimated to form no more than 10–12 per cent of all types of women working in the sex industry (see, for example, Perkins and Lovejoy, 2007; Sanders, 2005a).
2 The Home Office (2004) estimated that there were as many as 80,000 people involved in the UK, but this figure was extrapolated from a relatively small-scale survey of 17 well-established projects in urban locations and thus is likely to significantly under-estimate the total numbers (Sanders, 2005a). A study in the Netherlands in 1998 esti-mated between 20,000 and 30,000 sex workers in that country, of whom around 5 per cent were male and 5 per cent transgender or transsexual (Outshoorn, 2004).
3 A study in Scotland (Scottish Executive, 2005) identified around 1,400 women involved in four cities, of whom approximately 180 were likely to be on the streets on any night. Matthews (2005), drawing on police statistics in 2004 in 18 towns and cities in England and Wales (excluding London), found that numbers of women who had been identified as involved in sex work over a 12-month period ranged from 30 in one town to 300 in another, with between 10 and 150 per site believed to be currently active. The total number across 18 towns was 905 seen as currently active (i.e. whom the police had come into contact with over the past three or four weeks), although there may be some double-counting as some women may move from one area to another. The average numbers of women seen to be working on any one night ranged from 4 in one town to 25 in a large city. Additional figures based on the Metropolitan

Police 'prostitutes index' showed that 635 women had come to the attention of the police over a six-month period during 1997, with 115 women estimated to be working on the streets in London in any one night (Home Office, 2004).

4 For example, Sanders (2005a) cites a figure for 1859 which shows as many as 80,000 women working indoors in London. Perkins and Lovejoy (2007), drawing on a study in Sydney, estimate around 2,400 working as 'call girls' in Australia at any given time, out of a total figure of approximately 9,500 women working nationally (including brothel and street workers). Outshoorn (2004) demonstrates the wide variation between estimates in parliamentary debates in the Netherlands and those made by researchers (which were much lower than the estimates cited by politicians).

Suggested Reading

Campbell, R. and O'Neill, M. (eds) (2006) *Sex Work Now*, Cullompton: Willan.

Connell, J. and Hart, G. (2003) 'An overview of male sex work in Edinburgh and Glasgow: the male sex work perspective', MRC Social and Public Health Sciences Unit, Occasional Paper, June. Available at: www.sphsu.mrc.ac.uk (under publications, occasional papers).

Day, S. (2007) *On the Game: Women and Sex Work*, London: Pluto Press.

Phoenix, J. and Pearce, J. (eds) (2008a) *Regulating Sex for Sale: Prostitution Policy Reform in the UK*, Bristol: Policy Press.

Sanders, T. (2005) *Sex Work: A Risky Business*, Cullompton: Willan.

Study Questions

Level one

- What are the differences between sex workers based indoors and those working on the street? What are the relative advantages and disadvantages of the different forms of working?

Level two

- 'Violence is an inevitable consequence of the job for sex workers'. Discuss.

Level three

- What are the differences, if at all, between male and female sex workers and the environments in which they sell commercial sex?

4

CHILDREN, YOUNG PEOPLE
AND COMMERCIAL SEXUAL
EXPLOITATION (CSEC)

This chapter contextualizes the involvement of children and young people in sex markets by providing an overview of global issues, historical discourses, and policy contexts before moving on to explore the contemporary experiences of young people selling sex gathered through research projects in the UK. The chapter also discusses the emerging politics of the commercial sexual exploitation of children (CSEC) including the differing theoretical approaches and perspectives to young people selling sex. The chapter reviews international legislation and protocols as well as the UK policy context.

The Concerns for Children in the Sex Industry

The phenomenon of young people and children selling sex is an emotive as well as a complex social issue. As an issue of public and governmental concern, it is linked to child sexual abuse, sex tourism, trafficking and the organization of sexual exploitation on a global scale (Shaw and Butler, 1998). The not-for-profit organization ECPAT[1] states: 'ECPAT UK believes that the sexual exploitation and abuse of children is a global outrage that requires urgent action in order to protect children everywhere' (www.ecpat.org.uk/0).

This in turn gives rise to rhetorical claims by campaigns and journalists reflecting the anxiety experienced by linking childhood (connoted by vulnerability, care and being looked after) to prostitution, exploitation and selling sex. This is reflected in the following quotation and related article: 'More than 5,000 children are being forced to work as sex slaves in the UK, including thousands trafficked to this country by criminal gangs', *The Independent on Sunday* can reveal. (Goodchild and Thompson, 2007). Some theorists working in this area say that anxiety and outrage over children and young people's involvement in prostitution lead to the representation of children as 'victims' of evil purchasers and the purchasers as 'paedophiles and monsters', and that this actually masks the true complexity of the issue by creating binaries (victim/villain) that reinforce a homogenous view of the young people and children who sell sex; and does not reflect the diversity of young people's lived experience (O'Connell Davidson, 2005).

Research evidence provides complex stories and shows that routes in to selling sex for children and young people are very clearly related to poverty, debt, homelessness, running away, being in or leaving local authority care and are described as a 'survival strategy' for youth. The research documented in this chapter on young people and prostitution is about listening to young people in order to better understand the reality of their lives in order to offer meaningful responses through policy and practice (Green et al., 1997; Melrose et al., 1999; O'Neill et al., 1995; Pearce et al., 2002). Selling sex is a global phenomenon and evidence suggests that whilst children and young people sell sex in all nations, the majority takes place in South-East Asia and South America. What then, are the global dimensions to young people selling sex?

––––––––– **The Global Commercial Sexual Exploitation of Children (CSEC)** –––––––––

Lin Lean Lim (1998: 175) writes that 'globally, child prostitution is estimated to net US$5 billion annually and is reported to be more serious in Asia and South America'. A United Nations report in 2001 estimated that 1.2 million children are trafficked each year. Moreover, prostitution (defined as providing sexual services for material gain – money, food, a roof)

> has strong economic foundations as well social bases involving unequal relations between men and women and between parents and children ... we can justifiably speak of a commercial sex sector that is integrated into the economic, social and political life of these countries. (Lim, 1998: 1)

In Indonesia, 60 per cent of registered prostitutes are aged between 15 and 20 years old and include children selling sex for survival and boys selling sex in tourist resorts. Lim writes that the CSEC is 'not just an intolerable form of forced labour but a contemporary form of slavery' (1998: 150). International policy responses can be found in the work of the UN, ECPAT, the Council of Europe[2] member states, as well as national governments.

In reports by the UN, ECPAT and Council of Europe the CSEC is discussed in relation to child sexual abuse, child prostitution, child pornography and trafficking for the purposes of prostitution. Research by ECPAT, the UN and key researchers (Bishop and Robinson, 1997; Lim, 1998; O'Connell-Davidson, 2005) maintains that poverty and globalization combine to facilitate the CSEC in South-East Asia and that children are:

- more likely to be victims of debt bondage and trafficking;
- more vulnerable to being sold by guardians;
- tricked, coerced, kidnapped;
- more susceptible to group/peer pressure;
- more likely to contract HIV/AIDS.

Children in orphanages and street shelters are especially vulnerable. Psychological trauma both in the short and longer term is one outcome including post-traumatic stress, impairment in forming relationships and attachments, low self-esteem and dissociation.

Theoretical approaches (especially in South-East Asia) show a commercial sex industry embedded in processes of internationalization and globalization as well as the combined impact of both the social and economic bases of prostitution (Lim, 1998). Collating research conducted in South-East Asia, Lim argues that children experience a greater level of physical and sexual violence than their adult counterparts and uses Muntarbhorn's (1996) concept of a 'spiral factor/chain effect' to document the apparent spiralling trend towards younger 'victims'. This spiralling effect is due, in part, to the disturbing belief that 'customers' can 'rejuvenate' themselves 'by having sex with very young virgins' (Lim, 1998: 176). The chain effect refers to the links (that make a chain) between child sexual abuse, running away and routes into selling sex as a means of survival to fund drug use, leading to dependence on selling sex in order to 'get by'.

Research by the World Health Organization highlights the fact that children pose a greater risk to health than adults because of their increased vulnerability to STDs as well as their lack of power to negotiate 'safe sex' (Belsey, 1996: 29, cited in Lim 1998: 176).

In 1997, fuelled by frustration at the relative invisibility of male sex work in research, service provision and policy, coupled with a concern about the specific problems and forms of discrimination experienced by (young) men, the European Network of Male Prostitution (www.enmp.org) was formed.[3] Across many countries there was evidence that service provision specifically for male sex work was the exception and not the rule. The taboos around male sex work and the complexities of homosexual identities meant that many agencies refused to address the issue of male sex work.

The network is organized into regional groups that develop specific cooperation and support relative to need within and between regions. The international policy context for CSEC is examined below.

International legislation and guidance

States parties undertake to protect the child from all forms of sexual exploitation and sexual abuse. (Article 34, UN Convention on the Rights of the Child)

This statement from the UN Convention on the Rights of the Child has become a benchmark for tackling exploitation in prostitution of young people. 'Efforts to eradicate child prostitution have become most salient since the development of the United Nations 1989 Convention on the Rights of the Child' (Mayorga and Velásquez, 1999: 178). Key international legal instruments include:

- the UN Convention on the Rights of the Child;
- the 'Optional Protocol to the Convention on the Rights of the Child on the sale of children, child prostitution and child pornography';

- the 'Protocol to Prevent, Suppress and Punish Trafficking in Persons, Especially Women and Children', supplementing the 'United Nations Convention against Transnational Organized Crime' (Trafficking Protocol).

It is interesting to note that not all member states have signed up to the protocols. The UN Convention for the Suppression of the Traffic in Persons and the Exploitation of the Prostitution of Others (1949) declared that both trafficking and sexual exploitation are 'incompatible with the dignity and worth of the human person and endanger the welfare of the individual, the family and the community'.

In 1996, the first World Congress against CSEC took place in Stockholm. Here it was agreed that child prostitution constitutes a form of coercion and violence against children, and amounts to forced labour and a contemporary form of slavery. The Stockholm Agenda for Action against the commercial sexual exploitation of children (CSEC) was adopted by 122 countries at the Congress.

In 2006, ECPAT International launched its 'Global Monitoring Reports on the Status of Action against Commercial Sexual Exploitation of Children' (GMRs) for 54 countries. The GMRs analyse the actions taken and identify the remaining gaps and priority actions recommended in addressing CSEC and protecting children.

In July 2007, the new Council of Europe Convention on the Protection of Children against Sexual Exploitation and Sexual Abuse was adopted by the Council of Europe's Committee of Ministers following 10 months of negotiations. The main aims of the Convention are to prevent and combat sexual exploitation and sexual abuse of children, and to protect the rights of child victims. It also aims to promote national and international cooperation against abuse (NSPPC, 2007: 2).[4]

ECPAT, the UN and the Council of Europe are very clear in the language they use to define the involvement of children and young people selling sex. Young people are victims of child sexual exploitation and young person/child covers young people under the age of 18 as per the relevant international instruments. It is useful to explore the politics involved in defining the CSEC.

The politics of definitions

How do we define the involvement of young people and children in sex markets? Shaw and Butler (1998: 180) tell us that definitions are always the product of a process of social construction and identify tentative boundaries between organized abuse, ritual abuse, child pornography, paedophilia and child prostitution. This chapter is concerned with young people and children who sell sex, although there may be overlaps with these other categories in the individual lives of young people. Participants at the first World Congress against CSEC took a human rights approach to the issue and defined the category 'child' as being under 18 years as defined in the UN Convention on the Rights of the Child – Article 1 which defines 'child' as 'every human being under 18 years unless under law applicable to the child, majority is attained earlier'.

In the UK, legal instruments such as the Sexual Offences Act 2003 demarcate the legal boundary between child and adult prostitution. The Act introduced specific legislation for dealing with the commercial sexual exploitation of children. This covers children of both sexes aged under 18 years and includes the offences shown Table 4.1.

Table 4.1   Sexual Offences Act 2003

- Legislation dealing with commercial sexual exploitation of children and paying for the sexual services of a child under 18 years: penalty 7 years' to life imprisonment depending on type of sexual act and age of the child.
- Causing or inciting a child to become a prostitute or to be used for pornography: up to 14 years' imprisonment and/or an unlimited fine.
- Controlling the activities of a child in prostitution or pornography: up to 14 years' imprisonment and/or an unlimited fine.
- Arranging or facilitating the prostitution of a child or the use of a child in pornography: up to 14 years' imprisonment and/or an unlimited fine.

The UN, ECPAT and the Council of Europe (including the UK) take an abolitionist approach to 'child sexual exploitation' and would like to see the eradication of CSEC. However, O'Connell-Davidson (2005: 3) challenges the distinction between adult–child prostitution because the 'social categories "adult" and "child" refer to monolithic and homogenous groups, and so overlook the realities of many people's lived experiences'. She asks, why do we limit our concern to those under 18?

> A crack addicted 38 year old is not necessarily better positioned than a non-drug-using 17 year old to make choices about prostitution, and equally we should recognize that some children like some adults are faced with such a forlorn set of alternatives that they can and do decide that selling sex is their least-worst option. (O'Connell-Davidson, 2005: 3)

Campaigning groups such as ECPAT would say that adults are in a position to make informed choices whereas children are not. A key problem for O'Connell Davidson is 'if children are in the sex trade because they will starve if they are not ... then to identify their commercial sexual exploitation as the factor threatening their development seems rather to put the cart before the horse' (2005: 42).

Despite this cautionary note that flags up the broader issue of the economic and social bases for selling sex and asks us to reflect upon adult and child prostitution as being on the same trajectory, international organizations such as the UN and ECPAT, as well as the Parliamentary Assembly for the Council of Europe and the UK government, make a clear demarcation between adult prostitution (which may be voluntarily chosen) and child prostitution (under the age of 18) which is deemed sexual exploitation.

Theoretical Approaches

There are two main lines of analysis in relation to policy and practice. On the one hand, researchers such as O'Connell Davidson (2005), Kempadoo (1999) and Mayorga and Velásquez (1999) suggest that we need to look at the issue of child prostitution and child sexual exploitation as part of a trajectory that may lead to and includes adult sex work. This is not to deny the vulnerability of children and the need to protect those under the age of consent (and older) from abuse, exploitation and harm. Separating children from adults, however, and focusing upon sexual exploitation as the main issue to address in their young lives, takes the emphasis away from the structural, economic, environmental and socio-cultural contexts that lead to routes in, and the prevalence of child/adolescent prostitution.

On the other hand, organizations such as ECPAT and the UN demand the eradication and abolition of child sexual exploitation because children and young people are under the age of consent and their childhoods should be protected. The focus here is on ending child sexual exploitation by addressing eradication through a specific focus upon child sexual exploitation and the legal instruments, research and monitoring that might help to achieve abolition.

A third line of analysis steers a middle path through this binary and includes the work of the UK National Working Group[5] led by Jenny Pearce and research that puts young people in centre stage, valuing their experience and works towards influencing policy and practice by creating the space for the voices of children and young people to be heard and listened to – such as in participatory, action research and ethnographic projects (Coy, 2007a; Mai, 2007; Melrose et al., 1999; O'Neill 2001; O'Neill et al., 1995; Pearce et al., 2002; Pearce 2006). This research uncovers and works with complexity. The politics of defining young people's involvement in sex work in the UK has its roots in historical analysis and the framing of the problem of child prostitution.

CSEC in the UK: Is History Repeating Itself?

Young people and children's involvement in selling sex is an historical fact and social historians state that the Victorian period (where we witnessed the making of an outcast group regarding women selling sex) is also where the cultural trope of the child prostitute/victim emerges (Self, 2003; Walkowitz, 1980). Involvement in prostitution by 'innocent' children (female children) is defined as abhorrent and the children and young people themselves are defined as both victims *and* corrupting, despoiled *and* out of control, deviant (Brown, 2004). As Brown documents:

> Child prostitution first became a subject of national public attention and indeed alarm following publication of a, now well-known, series of sensationalist articles written and published by W.T. Stead in the *Pall Mall Gazette* (1885). These 'Maiden Tribute' articles and their emotive presentation of innocents betrayed and sexually abused provided the crucial force to ensure the final passage of the Criminal Law Amendment Act 1885, which increased the age of consent from 13 to 16 years of age and augmented police powers to deal with vice. (2004: 347)

The journalist W.T. Stead documented the process of buying a 13-year-old girl (virgin) for £5 through a series of newspaper articles in the *Pall Mall Gazette* in 1885. The articles are described as:

A *tour de force* of late Victorian journalism, it exposed in graphic detail the entrapment, abduction and 'sale' of young under-privileged girls to London brothels. Written in successive instalments, Stead's 'infernal narrative', as he called it, revealed to respectable Victorians a criminal underworld of stinking brothels, fiendish procuresses, drugs and padded chambers, where upper-class gentlemen could revel 'in the cries of an immature child'.[6]

On the other hand, as Self (2003), Roberts (1992) and Walkowitz (1980) argue, many girls and young women were involved in selling as an economic necessity (akin to their older female counterparts) and parents and guardians were also implicated because of extreme poverty and economic necessity due to limited choices and not necessarily as 'the "passive, sexually innocent victims" depicted by Stead' (Brown, 2004: 347).[7]

Self argues that fears of 'white slavery' and for their middle-class daughters led to 'moral panic' and the changes in law. Moreover, Self (2004: 6) states that

Looked at historically, certain reoccurring themes related to prostitution stand out clearly ...

• the protection of children, rather than women
• the contradictions raised by a combination of the need for public order and the protection of vulnerable individuals. (2004: 6)

Social historians are very clear that the social attitudes and values during this period (Victorian–Edwardian) established the framework in which the problem of prostitution is organized, perceived and regulated in the UK. Within this historical context we see certain themes emerging: definitions of childhood; issues of coercion and 'choice'; moral censure and anxiety about the links between childhood and prostitution; a focus on girls (not boys) and how this impacts upon the law; cultural constructions of selling sex linked to disease, dirt, abjection; and slippages between being the victim of evil purchasers and being a 'corrupting' force, as abnormal children/ young people.

Young People Selling Sex in the UK: Victims or Villains?

The problem of child prostitution in contemporary times is heavily influenced by these historical constructions and discourses. This is most obvious in the work conducted by children's charities in the 1980s and 1990s leading up to the Sexual Offences Act 2003. A report by the Children's Society, *The Game's Up* (Lee and O' Brien, 1995) highlights the criminalization of young people involved in prostitution and their pathways through the criminal justice system, emphasizing the need for child protection from sexual exploitation and abuse. Further to this, the report highlights the links between involvement in prostitution and running away, unemployment, school problems, neglect, sexual abuse and living in, or leaving local authority care. The risks to young people include violence, murder, rape, sexual assault, involvement in pornography and organized prostitution. Associated risks are sexually transmitted diseases, HIV/AIDS, drug and alcohol abuse, depression, self-mutilation, attempted and actual suicide, physical injuries, problems in sleeping and failure at school (Lee and O'Brien, 1995: 15).

Prior to the Sexual Offences Act 2003, children and young people were more likely to have the legal framework used against them. They were more likely to be perceived and treated as 'criminalized' villains rather than exploited victims (Barrett, 1997). At that time a young woman who could not legally give consent for sex could be prosecuted under the Street Offences Act. This anomaly gave rise to a series of campaigns by children's charities, academics and researchers.

The Children's Society and Barnardo's[8] argued that young people involved in prostitution should be treated as 'victims not villains' and that the clients should be dealt with by the law as child abusers. For example, Brown (2004) states: 'Patrick Ayre and David Barrett note that child prostitutes may not be adequately provided for by welfare agencies, largely because of challenges they pose to the victim concept.' As Barrett and Ayre (2000: 55) argue '[a]ggressive, streetwise, anarchic young people who steal and do drugs as well as prostitution do not conform obviously to our idealised image of a child in need'. As a consequence of research, debate and campaigns, policy guidance was issued by the Department of Health and Home Office in 2000: 'Safeguarding Children Involved in Prostitution'; the Sexual Offences Act came into being in 2004; and following the publication of *Every Child Matters* in 2003 (which provided an overhaul of child protection procedures and established a national assessment framework), local authorities had to develop protocols and create local 'Safeguarding Boards' for working with children sexually exploited through prostitution.

Overwhelmingly, as in Victorian times, the focus on child/prostitution was predominantly on girls and young women.[9] Boys and young men were relatively absent from debates and discourses – prostitution was seen as something women do. *No Son of Mine!*, a Barnardo's report (Palmer, 2002) drew attention to this anomaly. Yet, it was not until the Sexual Offences Act 2003 that the law was made gender neutral.

Boys and young men

Despite the relative dearth of research on boys and young men there is a reasonable amount of research that engages with young men and provides complex stories about routes in and prevalence. Research in the UK by West and de Villiers (1992), Gibson (1995), Gaffney and Beverley (2001), Palmer (2002) and Gaffney (2007) highlight how leaving care, running away, survival, and sexual experimentation are key precipitating factors to routes into selling sex. Both globally and in the UK young men (and women) become trapped in socio-economic and cultural circumstances that perpetuate their involvement in selling sex (Mai, 2007; Mayorga and Velásquez, 1999).

What we do know is that the social organization of male and female prostitution in the UK is both different and similar. Differences include ideologies around 'homosexuality', and the way the criminal justice system deals with young men involved in prostitution. McMullen (1987: 37) states that he was 'reliably informed by a magistrate that when such young people come before the bench – girls are invariably fined, whilst boys are sent for psychiatric reports'. On the other hand, there is evidence to suggest that girls who are in the care of the local authority are more likely to be sent to secure units and seen to be in need of moral guidance (Coy, 2007a; Soby, 1994).

The majority of service provision is for (young) women, although some projects also cater for young men. There are a few separate young men's projects. Overall, less is known about the service and support needs of boys and young men (Melrose and Barrett, 2004; Palmer, 2002). Some of the risk factors are the same as for girls and young women (e.g. running away from home). Some (but not all) young men who are involved in sexual exploitation identify as gay, but it is important not to treat commercial sexual exploitation of boys as a 'gay' issue, as some evidence shows that only a minority of 'punters' identify as gay (Palmer, 2002). While street-based sex work is more common amongst women than men, some boys do work on the street and are often likely to have experienced a range of vulnerability factors. Patterns of drug use or types of drugs taken may differ between young women and men, although Darch (2004) identifies a high proportion of young men using Class A drugs including heroin and crack cocaine. There may also be differential *modus operandi* of adults who abuse them, although the grooming or 'conditioning' model identified by Swann (1998) can apply to both young men and young women, as can Pearce et al.'s (2002) more diverse model of risk-taking behaviour.

Thus routes in for young men follow a similar trajectory overall: social dislocation and alienation from significant others such as families and carers; sub-cultural drift; economic need linked to poverty, homelessness, running away; routes in from care and/or a background of physical and sexual abuse; globalization and sex tourism. However, the strong association in the public imagination between prostitution and girls/women has meant that young men have not been a focus of concern, added to which male prostitution is not so visible: it is hidden, taking place in bars, flats, saunas and public spaces that are not visible – due in part to the taboo on homosexuality. (See Chapter 3 for further discussion on male prostitution.)

In the past two decades we have witnessed a shift in discourses about young people selling sex from villains to victims, and there is much greater awareness about the involvement of young men. These shifting discourses have also impacted upon the legal and policy context. We have seen a re-framing of the issue as child sexual abuse and a concomitant shift from enforcement to welfarist policing (Matthews, 2005) moving from 'prosecution to protection' (Melrose and Barrett, 2004). This entails a significant shift from criminalizing the young people involved to treating them under child protection procedures as victims of sexual abuse and exploitation (Lee and O'Brien, 1995).

Trafficking of young people

Recently we have witnessed a return to discourses of slavery in relation to the trafficking of young people.[10] The UK Human Trafficking Centre based in Sheffield was set up in response to the draft UK National Action Plan on Human Trafficking published in 2005. In 2006, Operation Pentameter was launched in order to tackle 'trafficking for sexual exploitation. It involved all 55 police forces in the United Kingdom, several other policing agencies and also non-governmental organisations. 12 of the 84 victims rescued during Pentameter were minors (aged 14–17)' (UKHT, 2006: 1).

As with discourses of child prostitution/CSEC, discourses around the trafficking of minors are fraught with complexity. Agustin focuses upon the economic and social bases of 'travelling to work in the sex industry' (Agustin, 2007a: 124) and provides clear accounts of the economic and cultural dynamics of 'trafficking'. As O'Connell Davidson writes:

> In Moldova, for children and adult alike labour migration is viewed as the only alternative way to improve one's life chances, and remittances from migrants amount to 50% of Moldova's state budget (UNICEF 2001) … to paraphrase William Faulkner (1961), is that left with a choice between grief and nothing, some people will choose grief, and this is true of children as well as adults. (2005: 84)

This highlights the fact that there is a slippage between economic migration for survival and 'trafficking' for the purposes of prostitution.

The UK Policy Context

The current policy and legislative framework for dealing with children who are commercially sexually exploited is outlined in

- *Safeguarding Children Involved in Prostitution* (Department of Health and Home Office, 2000);
- the Sexual Offences Act 2003;
- the Home Office's *A Coordinated Prostitution Strategy* (2006).[11]

Table 4.2 outlines both the relevant legislation and policy guidance.

Young People's Voices

Routes in, risk factors and survival

The issue of young people (male, female, transgender) selling sex is relatively under-researched in the UK compared with adult female sex work. Research that engages with young people raises some important findings. Melrose et al. argue that young people are not passive victims but are responding to conditions created for them by global economic forces (Melrose et al., 1999). Gibson (1995) argues that the young men she worked with lacked the basic needs defined by the NSPCC and that their lives were marked by destructive relationships. McMullen (1987) developed a two-pronged analysis, that routes in to selling sex are marked by: (1) a poorly developed sense of personal power, a feeling of being/inconsequential; and (2) a lack of economic power, which forms the motivating agent. O'Neill

Table 4.2   Legislation and policy guidance for children under 18 years

Legislation	Date	Main points
Sexual Offences Act	1956	Has offence for a man to solicit or importune in a public place for immoral purposes: does not distinguish between men and boys
Street Offences Act	1959	Has offence of loitering and soliciting, applying to young women and adults involved in prostitution
Sexual Offences Act	2003 (became operational in May 2004)	Covers children of both sexes aged under 18, and covers new offences of commercial sexual exploitation of a child; causing or encouraging a child into commercial sexual exploitation; facilitating the commercial sexual exploitation of a child; and controlling the activities of a child involved in prostitution or pornography
Guidance		
Safeguarding Children Involved in Prostitution	2000	Obligates responsible authorities in England and Wales to develop local protocols to more effectively identify and respond to children abused through prostitution, shifting focus from prosecution to protection. Still leaves provision for using criminal justice system for 'persistent' young offenders
Every Child Matters	2003	Signifies overhaul of child protection in England and Wales, through better prevention; stronger focus on parenting and families; earlier intervention; improved accountability and integration; and workforce reform. Includes creation of Local Safeguarding Children Boards in 2006.
Solutions and Strategies: drug problems and street sex markets	2004	In terms of young people, recommends value of local protocols, early warning systems and preventive work; good practice principles to guide service provision for sexually exploited young people, including holistic approach, specialist facilities, a named key worker and regular training for project staff and other practitioners.
Tackling Street Prostitution: towards a holistic approach	2004	Contains a number of recommendations relating to under-18s involved in selling sex. Highlights the need for specialist provision.
A Coordinated Prostitution Strategy and summary of responses to Paying the Price	Jan. 2006	A key focus is on prevention, including: • key messages to challenge attitudes • updated guidance on *Safeguarding Children Involved in Prostitution* • updated resource site for schools • increasing the proactive identification of sexually exploited children • targeted intervention for those particularly at risk • a strategic response to the use of the Internet as a tool for child sexual exploitation • a holistic approach to support and protection, including ways to manage the transition to adulthood. Other elements of the strategy include effective investigation and development of a UK Plan on Trafficking.

et al. (1994, 1995, 2001) and Coy (2007a) examine routes in from local authority care. Pearce et al. (2002) established three categories of 'risk' of involvement in selling sex for young women:

> *Category 1 – at risk*: running away from home or care, prolonged periods of truanting from school/going missing. Beginning to engage in emotional and sexual relationships with older, abusive men.
>
> *Category 2 – swapping sex*: increasing engagement in sexual relationships with older, violent men, increasing use of drugs and returns 'in kind'.
>
> *Category 3 – selling sex*: spending extended periods of time on the street, living in temporary accommodation or homeless, selling sex and intermittently identifying as working in prostitution.

The UK research literature that engages with young people shows the following key factors or vulnerabilities linked to routes in to selling sex:

- substance misuse
- exploitation, coercion and sexual abuse
- homelessness
- depression
- running away from care or home
- peer networks and pressures
- economic need – debt, poverty
- family breakdown and problems.

'Routes into prostitution happen within the context of complex lived relations' (O'Neill et al., 1995). Hence research suggests that there is usually not one factor or experience that leads to selling or swapping sex for under-18s. Young people will have a number of experiences which may make them vulnerable to exploitation.

In O'Neill and Campbell's study in Walsall (2001),[12] 62 per cent (n = 28) of participants said that they had started selling sex when they were under 18. The youngest starting age was 11. Examining the life histories of some of the women and men who started selling sex as children clearly illustrates profiles of socio-economic disadvantage.

Social exclusion

Many researchers have documented the socio-economic disadvantages experienced by young people involved in prostitution and increasingly they have argued that they form a socially excluded group (Cusick et al., 2003; Gibson, 1998; Jesson, 1993; Lee and O'Brien, 1995; McMullen, 1987; O'Neill, 2001; O'Neill et al., 1995; Pearce et al., 2002; Shaw and Butler, 1998; West and de Villiers, 1992). Social exclusion here is not just defined as poverty and economic need but also as emotional exclusion or alienation. Young people experience psychological and social alienation as part of social exclusion. Alienated from parents, carers and schools Pearce et al. found that 'isolation from support runs through the analysis of material presented by the young women who experience severe problems with drug and alcohol abuse and are often in established, abusive relationships with adults' (2002: 55).

Sexual abuse

Sexual abuse is an aspect of some young people's lives. Some young people talk of being sexually abused at young ages. The meanings associated with sex, with love and affection are often coloured by these early experiences of abuse. For example, O'Neill and Campbell's (2001) study found that for 'J' getting involved in prostitution was 'to better herself' but also as a rebellion, against the abuse she experienced as a child:

> I can't say I did it for the money because I was, it was like to better myself I think. And maybe as well to rebel. I mean I was abused as a baby and then I was adopted ... I got put back into care when I was fourteen ... And I think subconsciously ... I think subconsciously I don't like men ... But I always go into abusive relationships as well. It's what you deal with as well. My concepts of love is like abusive relationships, rejections, you know, rejections and things like that. (2001: 102)

Substance misuse

Many studies of young people and sexual exploitation identify problematic drug and alcohol use as a factor that shapes young people's entry into selling sex, or that contributes to continued involvement. Cusick et al. (2003) explore the complex relationship between drug use and routes into prostitution. They found that sex work and drug use may be mutually reinforcing, so much so that exiting becomes difficult. 'Their mutually reinforcing potential is strengthened where individuals are exposed to "trapping factors"' (2004: v). These trapping factors are:

- involvement in prostitution and/or hard drug use before 18;
- sex work 'outdoors' or as an 'independent drifter';
- experience of at least one other vulnerability indicator, such as being 'looked after' in local authority care or being homeless.

The most vulnerable women in the study were exposed to all three of these 'trapping factors' and they shared these characteristics:

- They were young – the mean age for first prostitution was 13.8.
- They were problematic drug users and continued to sell sex to fund their habit.
- They were girls.
- They were likely to have been 'looked after' – 71 per cent were living in or had run away from local authority when they first prostituted.
- They had supported the problematic drug use of at least one boyfriend.

Homelessness and running away

Lee and O'Brien (1995) found that young people often sell sex as a survival strategy when they are homeless or have run away from home or residential care. This is supported in research by Melrose et al. (1999), who found that those with a history of going missing from home or care became involved in prostitution at the youngest age. Over 50 per cent of those who had been looked after had a history of going missing. O'Neill and Campbell (2001) found that, amongst the young women they interviewed, homelessness was connected to leaving home, running away from home or foster care, or leaving care. Pearce et al. found that, for young people who run away from home or care,

> The combination of poverty, familial abuse, drug misuse and social exclusion/marginalisation places young people running from home in specifically vulnerable conditions. With few, if any, personal or financial resources for support, they are highly susceptible to exploitation. (2002: 45)

For some young men who have become involved in selling sex, their sexuality may be a key factor relating to their leaving care or home, for example, feeling isolated from family and friends, being bullied because of their sexuality, or being told by family members to leave (Connell and Hart, 2003).

Running away from home or care and then having no place to stay is identified by researchers as a clear risk factor in terms of vulnerability to sexual exploitation. Pearce et al. (2002) suggest that running away itself is linked to young people's confusion and distress, then through running, young women become increasingly vulnerable to poverty, hunger and drug and alcohol addiction, which all place them at risk of sexual exploitation.

One young woman in Pearce et al.'s study ran away from home and then had to develop strategies to survive, including the need to find accommodation, which involved sex with men:

> I ran away for three months, when I couldn't take it no more out there. I had no food, nothing ... I got tempted to do prostitution. I've slept in men's houses that I don't know ... I'd sit in a pub, act like, you know I'd just come in from work or something. (2002: 45)

She would wait for a man to approach her and accept a drink. Then, lying, she would explain that a friend with whom she was staying had not shown up and the man would offer to let her stay at his house for the night. The same pattern would then occur the next night. Some of these 'relationships' or 'arrangements' can become increasingly exploitative. Pearce et al. report the case of 'K' aged 16:

> K aged 16 also talks of using a man's flat, being given a key and staying there in exchange for sex when running from her residential placement. She was desperate for a place to stay and spoke of the man as her boyfriend to whom she turned during periods of stress. After having encouraged her to use the flat, he locked her in, raped her and tried to force her into having sex with his friends. (2002: 46)

Routes in from local authority care
In a recent paper Coy (2007a) asks why young women who have experienced the care system are so disproportionately likely to become involved in prostitution. Coy explores the psycho-social dimensions to young women selling sex and argues that the specific habitus of local authority care 'and the key principles of

frequent and unplanned placement moves, deny young women the chance to establish a healthy sense of self that is based on meaningful relationships with others' (2007a: 14).

> The only reason I'm out on the streets now is cos I was in care. They let you down. They say they're gonna do this and gonna do that and they're not. My life now is down to them (Christina, aged twenty-one).

> I never got nothing, no support, no money, so I had to turn to the game because of the life I've been through, it's all I could turn to (Jackie, aged nineteen). (Coy, 2007a: 7)

Campbell and O'Neill (2004) document a whole range of risk factors that have been identified as reasons for the disproportionate number of young people with care backgrounds involved in street prostitution and selling sex:

- the targeting of young people in and leaving care/coercion from exploiters including pimps;
- problems that brought young people into care;
- pre-care experience and abuse;
- use of untrained care staff;
- needing money to support drug use;
- the experience of the 'care' system (multiple placements, social stigma, marginalization);
- peer association and peer pressure;
- homelessness;
- poverty.

They argue that the complexity of young people's lives means that for some, coercion and association lead to their entry into prostitution, but economic need keeps them there as well as a sub-culture of similar and significant others. For others, economic need leads to their involvement but coercion and sub-cultural entrenchment keep them there. For others selling or swapping sex is a temporal activity and they would not self-define as 'prostitutes'.

—— Understanding Politics and Making Policy: What Do Young People Want? ——

The following two research case studies provide examples of participatory research with young people, and provide a clear account of the voices of young people. They also raise awareness about the needs of young people selling sex. In the first research case study, the Voices Heard Group used peer researchers to access a hidden and hard-to-reach group to raise awareness about young people 'hidden for survival' in the North-East. The second case study is an example of a preventative project that emerged from the recommendations of a participatory action research project that used visual methodologies.[13] 'Sex, Lies and Love?' incorporated drama, art and research to prevent and minimize the harm to young women at risk of or involved in selling sex.

Hidden for Survival (2007)

This is a study into hidden sex markets within the Sunderland, Newcastle, Gateshead, North Tyneside and South Tyneside area by the Voices Heard Group. Voices Heard 'are a group of peer led researchers who all have exited problematic drug use and/or work within the sex industry. This is the first piece of research undertaken by the group and we know it will be the first of many pieces of research to be undertaken with follow up studies already being planned' (Voices Heard Group et al., 2008: i).

Peer researchers accessed young people who are identified as a 'hard to reach'.

Demographics

- The majority of respondents are in their twenties.
- Mostly on benefits.
- High levels of crime.
- High incidence of homelessness or temporary accommodation.

Drug use

- Higher daily drugs-spends than other sections of the drug-using community (men spend more than women).
- Evidence of child protection and domestic abuse deterring women's involvement in drug treatment.
- High levels of intravenous drug use (63 per cent). Intravenous use of heroin, cocaine, crack and alcohol.
- A number do not inject themselves and many use risky injecting methods.

Health

- High reporting of physical pain through violent punters (57 per cent).
- High reporting of mental health problems and the emotional impact of sex work.
- Low level of use of family planning services (24.5 per cent).
- Low level of use of GUM clinic (43 per cent have visited GUM).
- One quarter believe they have caught an STD through their work.

Sex work

- Respondents travel all over the North-East to work.
- Two main markets identified: low end markets which include sex workers working from bed and breakfasts and hostels, and upper end market respondents employed by agencies.
- Low levels of condom use.
- Evidence of risky sexual behaviours.
- High reporting of physical and sexual assaults largely unreported by respondents.

The landlady takes all the bookings for me. She takes her cut for the rent and that, I get my cut and a free bed.

People know where to come, we're all young lasses in here so men know where to come and know what they'll find, everyone is doing it whether they admit it or not.

The lads in the pizza shop are no bother, if you're starving they give you a pizza and if you need a client they always find them for you ... I give the owner £20 a night and he lets me see punters in the back room while they wait for their scran [food].

The next case study, 'Sex, Lies and Love?' was a collaborative project planned and delivered during 2003 by Empowerment Theatre (Walsall Youth Offending Service and Breathing Space Ltd), Street Teams and Walsall Youth Arts. It was a response to referrals of under-age young people to social services for selling sex and the recommendations made by a previous study *Working Together to Create Change* (O'Neill and Campbell, 2001). Between June 2001 and January 2004 there had been a total of 37 referrals to social services. The majority of referrals were girls (n = 36). The project was funded by the National Youth Agency and was a preventative project designed to address the 'grooming' of young people for prostitution, and more widely to prevent sexual exploitation and to explore healthy and unhealthy relationships. The project worked with young women and used community drama and arts to address these issues. The project gained national recognition as a finalist for the Community Care Awards 2003 in the category of Protecting Children and Young People.

The partner agencies that delivered the initiative were keen to further develop their work, building on the strengths of 'Sex, Lies and Love?' but wanted to ensure that any future interventions were effective and needs-based. To assess the effectiveness of the initiative, consult participants, and to produce the evidence base to inform a strategic approach to the future development of preventative interventions, an independent evaluation of 'Sex, Lies and Love?' was commissioned.[14]

Sex, Lies and Love? (2003)

Aim

The aim of 'Sex Lies and Love?' was to: 'use drama and art workshops to educate and debate with young women on the risks of prostitution and the partners who "groom" women' (Campbell and O'Neill, 2004). Intended outcomes were to:

- raise awareness of the realities of abuse through prostitution and the nature of 'grooming';
- prevent young women from putting themselves in risky situations;
- raise awareness and understanding about healthy and unhealthy relationships, enabling young women to make choices and avoid exploitative relationships.

The programme was aimed at young women aged between 13–17 years who were at risk of becoming involved in exploitative relationships.
  Three Peer Educators were recruited and 28 participants joined them.

Structure and content of the programme

'A two-day interactive workshop using drama, the arts and multimedia to enable young women to explore the relationships they encounter. There will be a focus on grooming within relationships, how to avoid this and how to form healthy relationships.'

DAY 1: Interactive work groups and drama workshops raising awareness and highlighting issues.
DAY 2: Expression of the issues presented on day through the use of creative arts.

Participants' responses

The programme was effective in raising awareness and increasing knowledge about:

- Grooming and sexual exploitation: 89 per cent (n = 25) of participants said that after taking part they had a better understanding of grooming.
- Where young women could seek help: 78 per cent of participants reported that they would know where to go if they or someone else was experiencing grooming.
- The arts and drama elements were welcomed by participants and peer educators with drama being the most popular.

Peer educators' responses

The project achieved:

- confidence and self-esteem building;
- improved communication skills;
- building trust;
- gaining skills in planning and team work;
- the opportunity to help and/or teach other young people;
- a safe environment to deal with their own issues;
- personal development;
- gaining knowledge about issues related to grooming, sexual exploitation and prostitution;
- gaining relevant experience.

The arts-based outcomes were exhibited at the launch of the report in the Walsall New Art Gallery.

The evaluation report concluded that:

> Future preventative work should build in peer involvement. This not only enriches the project but provides a vehicle to further build the capacity of, and empower, young people who have been at risk of, or who have experienced, sexual exploitation and abuse through prostitution. 'Sex, Lies and Love?' provides a model for other agencies who wish to develop work with young people in the field of sexual exploitation. (Campbell and O'Neill, 2004)

The following images were created by the young people involved in the project. Figure 4.1 shows both sides of an information card produced by young people to help prevent grooming. Figures 4.2 and 4.3 represent some of the key issues and feelings young people talked about in the arts workshop, especially regarding grooming and unhealthy relationships.

Future Policy and Research

From the research with and for young people documented above we can conclude that they want help with drugs; access to education, employment and safe housing; emotional support and someone to talk to. Moreover the complex needs of young people should be the basis upon which strategy and service provision are provided – according to need and including harm prevention, support, therapeutic services, and safe accommodation, care and other relevant provisions.

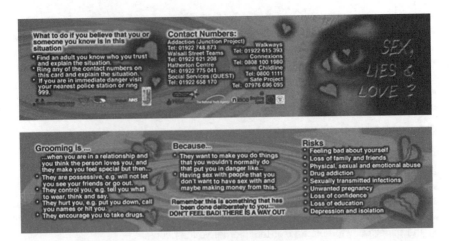

Figure 4.1   Prevention of Grooming Information Card

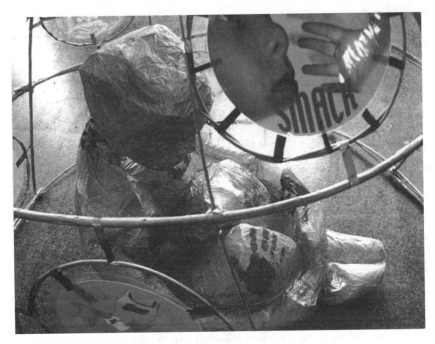

Figure 4.2   Trapped, hands all over me, being smacked and hit

Drawing together the recommendations from the various research projects considered in this chapter, we can conclude that future policy and research needs to do the following:

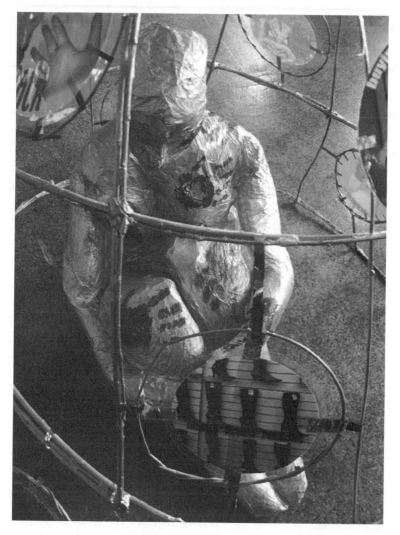

Figure 4.3 **The symbols on the cage include statement such as 'buying me expensive things'**

- Address the *structural factors* that alienate and damage young people including restricted opportunities such as 'shit jobs and govvy schemes' (Melrose et al., 1999). Otherwise young people will inevitably 'carve out a path in the spaces between family, the state, and the formal economy' in order to survive and 'get by'.
- Address the *social/cultural factors* that precipitate entry and sustain involvement in selling sex. Here there is a role for education and welfare agencies to work together, such as schools; the statutory and voluntary sector; the 'looked after' sector; the law and regulatory framework, the benefits system and the Home Office. There is also a need, however, for these agencies to develop a deeper understanding of the different factors relating to young people's involvement in selling sex.

- Address *participation* in drugs and risky behaviour. What becomes clear when listening to young people is that doing drugs and selling sex makes sense in the context of the 'restricted material and structural conditions in which they live have loosened the bond to the conventional social order and left them in a state of 'drift' (Melrose et al., 1999). Their identity is found in street cultures, sub-cultures marked by poverty and disadvantage – they are the 'hidden voices'.
- There is also a need for research to develop new knowledge, raise awareness and challenge the social construction of CSEC as a problem of sexual exploitation. Research that uses participatory action research methodologies and creates space for young people's relatively hidden voices can help to impact upon policy measures.

On a broader scale, ECPAT, the UN and the Council of Europe are working to eradicate CSEC within the context of globalization, poverty and the dynamics of migration (often defined as trafficking). If we accept that young people and adults migrate for work both in and out of the sex industry as a compelling alternative to absolute poverty, then we must surely focus upon the socio-economic and cultural bases for entry and prevalence rather than solely focus upon 'sexual exploitation as the factor threatening their development', whilst assessing those over the age of 18 by different standards and measures.

The adult–child binary needs to be re-framed as a trajectory so that holistic and multi-stranded approaches regarding policy and practice can be developed according to need instead of the current approach which ignores the diversity of young people's lives and socio-economic and cultural bases and separates children from adults. Most importantly, young people's agency and autonomy should be respected and in addition to recognizing them as victims, we should also see them as survivors.

Notes

1 ECPAT is a network of organizations and individuals working together to eliminate the commercial sexual exploitation of children. It seeks to encourage the world community to ensure that children everywhere enjoy their fundamental rights free from all forms of commercial sexual exploitation.
   The ECPAT acronym stands for 'End Child Prostitution, Child Pornography and Trafficking of Children for Sexual Purposes' (www.ecpat.net/EI/main/front/index. asp).
2 http://europa.eu/scadplus/leg/en/lvb/l33138.htm
3 In 1997, the AMOC/DHV Foundation launched the European Network Male Prostitution (ENMP), with partners from 19 different countries, financed by the European Commission and the Dutch Aids Fund. The ENMP started its second phase in November 2000. The network now consists of 18 different agencies, engaged in the fields of HIV and STI prevention with male sex workers. Justin Gaffney is the regional co-ordinator for Northern Europe and participants in this regional network are Ireland, Denmark, Norway, Finland, Sweden and the UK.
4 Available at: www.nspcc.org.uk/Inform/policyandpublicaffairs/Europe/Briefings/councilofeurope_wdf51232.pdf (accessed 17 February 2008). A change in UK legislation will be required: 'in relation to dual criminality. The UK should be able to convict a UK national for a crime committed overseas, which is a crime according to UK law, even if this is not a crime in the country where it was carried out'. This will require amending Section 72 of the Sexual Offences Act 2003/ (NSPCC, 2007: 3).

5 The National Working Group for Sexually Exploited Children and Young People (NWG) has developed as a support group for individuals and service providers working with children and young people who are at risk of or who experience sexual exploitation. Membership covers voluntary and statutory services including health, education and social services.

6 www.attackingthedevil.co.uk/pmg/tribute/index.php (accessed 4 February 2008).

7 This is mirrored in global research. The following quotation is from 'The State of the World's Children' (2002: 52), available at: www.unicef.org/soc02/pdf/sowc2002-eng-full. pdf_ (accessed 17 February 2008):

> Imagine in a family where there is a boy and a girl, the girl will do all the work in the house. If there is any sacrifice to be made it will be the girl that will suffer, for instance, when the family income is down the girl will be sent to go and hawk, that is to sell things in the streets and along the highway. Most times they will push her out to an old man or introduce her into prostitution. Even our mothers are also guilty of this act. This is very wrong, people of the world should change their attitude towards girls and women. (Taiwo, 13, Nigeria)

8 Two key reports by Barnardo's were *Whose Daughter Next? Children Abused through Prostitution*, authored by Sara Swann in 1998, and *No Son of Mine! Children Abused through Prostitution*, authored by Tink Palmer in 2002.

9 This mirrors the situation with adult prostitution, that the moral panic was predominantly focused upon women – and indeed see the case law on prostitution.

10 For more information on trafficking, see www.ecpat.net/eng/index.asp and for the UK – the UK Human Trafficking Centre: www.ukhtc.org/

11 The Home Office Strategy (2006) was informed by a range of research and policy documents on the involvement of under-18s in selling sex. These include: (1) *Solutions and Strategies: Drugs Problems and Street Sex Markets, Guidance for Partnerships and Providers* (Hunter and May, 2004). This guidance is aimed at police, DAATs, PCTs, CDRPs, local authorities, commissioners, service providers and other bodies. The guidance makes specific reference to services for under-18s who are experiencing abuse through prostitution and have substance misuse issues. (2) *Tackling Street Prostitution: Towards an Holistic Approach* (Hester and Westmarland, 2004). The evaluation overview document contains a section entitled 'Providing Support to Young People' and a number of recommendations relating to under-18s are made. (3) *Paying the Price: Home Office Review of Prostitution*. A consultation paper from the Home Office Review of all legislation and policy relating to prostitution was published on 16 July 2004. The review included under-18s as well as adults, indeed a large part of the review related to under-18s.

12 See www.safetysoapbox.co.uk for the executive summary and full report.

13 See the www.safetysoapbox.co.uk website and gallery.

14 Nacro, Crime and Social Policy Section were commissioned to carry out the rapid evaluation in partnership with Staffordshire University. The evaluation was carried out by Rosie Campbell and Maggie O'Neill.

Suggested Reading

Brown, A. and Barrett, D. (2002) *'Knowledge of Evil': Child Prostitution and Child Sexual Abuse in Twentieth Century England*, Cullompton: Willan Publishing.

Cusick, L. (2002) 'Youth prostitution: a literature review', *Child Abuse Review*, 11(4): 230–51.

Mai, N. (2007) 'Errance, migration and male sex work: on the socio-cultural sustainability of a third space', in S. Ossman (ed.), *Places We Share: Migration, Subjectivity, and Global Mobility*, Lanham, MD: Lexington Books, pp. 97–120.

O'Connell Davidson, J. (2005) *Children in the Global Sex Trade*, Cambridge: Polity.

Pearce, J. with M. Williams and C. Galvin (2003) '*Is Someone Taking a Part of You*': *A Study of Young Women and Sexual Exploitation*, London: National Children's Bureau for Joseph Rowntree Foundation (available at: www.jrf.org.uk/knowledge/findings/social policy/513.asp).

Study Questions

Level one

- 'If children are in the sex trade because they will starve if they are not … then to identify their commercial sexual exploitation as the factor threatening their development seems rather to put the cart before the horse' (O'Connell Davidson, 2005: 142). Do you agree or disagree with this statement?

Level two

- Critically explore routes in to selling sex for young people and outline some policy objectives that you would like to see put into practice.

Level three

- To what extent is the CSEC embedded in practices and processes of globalization?

5

BUYING SEXUAL SERVICES

This chapter explores the different groups of people who buy commercial sexual services. The first section looks at who actually buys sex: women from male escorts; men who buy sex from men and more traditionally, men who buy sex from women working in the sex industry. Next, summarizing the evidence and literature available, this chapter examines the motivations for buying sexual services, the heterogeneity of the population of men who buy sex and the meanings attached to buying sexual services. The complexities of relationships between sex workers and clients are explored, which challenge some of the notions of what happens in the relationship, by examining emotions and intimacy as part of the commercial exchange. While some clients perpetrate violence against sex workers, the majority show responsible behaviour in how sex is purchased. The male purchaser is discussed in relation to the government's concerns about the supposed rise in male 'demand' for female sex workers. This claim is contested and critically discussed. Finally, the move to criminalize men who buy sex is explored. 'Tackling demand' as a priority in the UK strategy for prostitution is explored in relation to wider issues of regulating sexual services.

Who Buys Sex?

When considering who buys sexual services it is common to think of men buying sex from women, and often the classic example of the male 'kerb-crawler' cruising the streets to find a street sex worker under the dark of night in a well-known urban 'red light district'. This scenario is made popular by repeated media images of street prostitution, and high profile cases of male celebrities arrested for buying sex on the street. Popular culture is awash with *Pretty Woman* images of a rich man 'saving' a down-trodden street prostitute from a life of poverty and misery (see Hallgrimsdottir et al. 2006). This idea that commercial sex is purchased mainly by men from the female street sex market is a myth, however, as there are many different groups of people who buy a range of commercial sex in many different settings. The diversity and complexities of who buys sexual services will be demonstrated below.

Women who buy sex

There is some information on women who engage in different forms of the sex industry such as buying toys and material from sex shops (Malina and Schmidt, 1997; Storr, 2003), consuming pornographic material and choosing lifestyles that include different aspects of the sex industry in increasing numbers (Comella, 2008). Recent work has been done on the female gaze on male strippers as they perform for crowds of women who gather for staged shows of erotica and nudity (Smith, 2002). There have been less academic accounts of women purchasing male escorts, although some good journalism in the print media offers an insight into professional women buying the company of a male escort for entertainment and sex. Equally, there is clear evidence of male escorting services online in major cities that offer a range of social activities and companionship. Women who buy sex from women, often to try out a same-sex experience whilst not identifying as lesbian, is also evident in the gay press and advertising. O'Connell Davidson (1998: 181) comments that it is 'unusual but not unknown' for Western lesbians to engage in sex tourism.

Academic studies that have focused on how women buy sexual services have tended to concentrate on 'female sex tourism'. There have been several commentaries on the difficulties of the general concept of 'sex tourism' (Jeffreys, 2003; Ryan and Hall, 2001) and where women are the purchasers of commercial sex the gendered dynamics have been recognized by the term 'romance tourism'. Sanchez Taylor (2001) argues that gender and heterosexuality blur the dynamics of female sex tourism and that the sexual exploitation and victimhood of the male sex workers need to be understood through the lens of racialized power, usually between white privileged women and poor black men. In this regard, Sanchez Taylor (2006: 43) claims that the term 'romance tourism' detracts from the reality of the situation and feeds into the 'double standard' applied to women who buy sex that makes it appear more acceptable.

O'Connell Davidson (1998: 181) describes how female sex tourists in destinations such as the Caribbean, Goa, Costa Rica, Cuba and Venezuela use their economic privileges and power to purchase romantic and sexual relationships with local men. She argues that white Western women use their different positions of power to racialize local men and secure sexual access for their own fleeting pleasures. O'Connell Davidson (1998: 182) rejects the assertion by some theorists that female sex tourists are pushing the boundaries of their traditional gendered identity and seeking alternative means of expressing their femininity and sexuality. Instead, she argues that female sex tourists who revel in being defined and 'adored' as beautiful, feminine and sexy by men and boys, are actually using their economic power to affirm a certain kind of traditional female role, rather than challenging gender assumptions: 'The Western female sex tourists we observed and interviewed did not want to stop playing the gender game any more than their male counterparts did; in fact, I am not even certain that they wanted to change the rules so very much' (1998). Here we see how simply exchanging the gender of the client from male to female raises different questions, but potentially the same race, class and gender-based dynamics are still the essence of the commercial sex relationship.

Men who buy sex from men

Any real estimate of the numbers of men who buy sex from other men is very difficult to obtain as they are spread across the population, age brackets and different types of sexualities and relationship status (see Minichiello et al., 2002; Scott et al., 2005). Groom and Nandwini (2006) analysed responses to a standard health screening questionnaire from 2,265 men, of whom 267 (10 per cent) said they had paid for sex. The majority of these men had bought sex from females, but 4.3 per cent of this sub-sample had purchased sex from men. Gaffney and Beverly (2001) describe the extent of the London-based male sex markets and note that the majority of sex workers identify as gay even if their customers do not (see Chapter 3). Men purchase sex from several different markets and sources including escorts, gay pornography, stripping (Boden, 2007), and exotic dance in male-only bars (Escoffier, 2007), Internet work and other specialist services (also see Bimbi, 2007, for a review). In addition, it is mainly men who buy sex from the transgendered commercial sex scene (see Chapter 3).

Whowell (2008) describes the spatial politics of the male sex work scene where 'economies of exchange' involve all kinds of bodywork. In detail, Whowell (2008: 13) describes how male sex work happens through anonymous encounters in 'country roads, shops, toilets, canal paths, swimming pools, parks, cinemas, clubs, bars, beaches and car parks'. Gaffney (2002) notes how 'public sex environments' are places where younger gay men and those experimenting with their sexuality can find a common space to do so. Yet the breadth of types of relationships that customers of male sex workers have range from the casual, anonymous sexual encounters to 'regular' relationships that develop into caring friendships and beyond (see Browne and Minichiello, 1995; Davies and Feldman, 1999). Yet, as documented in Chapter 3, Connell and Hart (2003) note that there is a subsection of more sinister clients who specifically seek out young boys for sex.

There is a range of literature that documents the lives, experiences and sexualities of men who sell sex to other men in tourist destinations around the world. Aggleton's (1999) collection documents the cultural, social, political and religious contexts in which male sex is sold and exchanged in 16 different countries of the world, giving a flavour of the complexities and structural dynamics of this form of sex work. Male-to-male sex tourism is decidedly a larger phenomenon compared with female sex tourism, and involves a range of relationships between men where sexual identities and lifestyles are not defined or separated out. An excellent example is provided by Padilla (2007) who conducted a multi-sited ethnographic study in the Dominican Republic of the informal labour economy that forms the local (and economically significant) pleasure industry. What Padilla (2007: x) terms 'the new brand of sweetness', that takes the form of black male bodies that are temporarily sold to white tourists (both male and female), reflects the colonial histories of the slave trade when sugar rather than sex was the desired commodity. The relationships between the male seller and male buyers are complex because often neither identifies as gay or bisexual but is in a normative heterosexual relationship. Padilla explains the stigma management strategies adopted by the male sex workers and the daily struggles to guard their same-sex encounters from public view or to actively deflect suspicion. Just as authors have argued how (white) female sex tourists erotize the black bodies of local men in holiday destinations, Padilla describes how male clients' fantasies of black men transpire to an 'exoticization and commodification of difference that is culturally and historically particular' (2007: 208).

Men buying sex from women

Although there are clear methodological problems with estimating the proportion of the population that purchases sex, the recent statistical evidence suggests there has been an increase in buying sex. Ward et al. (2005) note there has been an increase from 1990–2000 from 2.0 per cent to 4.2 per cent of the male population men buying sex. In Greater London, the figure rose to 8.9 per cent. In this survey the most notable change was an increase in men in the age group 25–34 years, although there was no association with ethnicity, social class, homosexual contact, or injecting drug use.

The first thing to say about the largest group of purchasers of sex is that there is no 'type' and that men who engage with the female sex industry are from all walks of life across the population. Sullivan and Simon (1998: 147) collected 3,432 responses to the National Health and Social Life Survey in 1992 in the USA and found some interesting conclusions:

- Men who go to religious services regularly are just as likely to have paid for sex as those who do not.
- The household income of a man makes no difference to their habits, suggesting that men across socio-economic groups buy sex.
- There was an equal likelihood of buying sex whether someone lived in rural, suburban or urban areas.
- Sexual attitudes had little bearing on behaviour: those men who considered sex before marriage, sex amongst teenagers and extra-marital sex to be wrong were as likely to buy sex.

Other studies have suggested there could be some demographic features that potentially separate men who buy sex from those who do not. Pitts et al. (2004) found from a survey of 143 Australian men that clients were more likely to be older, less likely to be educated beyond high school, less likely to have a regular partner and more likely to have had recent casual sex. A recent comparative study of men who buy sex in the USA with men in the general population by Brewer et al. (2008) found that there were few differences between the men who visited the street markets and those that frequented off-street venues. Nevertheless, there are no conclusive defining features that can predict which groups of men are more or less likely to pay for sex.

Types of male clients

From various studies on men who buy sex, it is clear that there are different types of purchasing habits, as men buy sex in different ways.

- *Occasional customers* – infrequent entertainment, often around 'celebrations' (birthdays, stag parties, etc.) and opportunistic scenarios.
- *Repeat customers* – men who regularly engage in the sex industry but visit different markets, use different geographical locations and usually visit different sex workers.
- *Regular clients* – men who visit the same sex worker(s) over a prolonged period of time.
- *Sugar daddies* – sex workers meet a single man and they are 'kept' by him. He pays rent, utilities and pocket money, often in return for stopping sex work and having sexual relations only with him.

Day (2007: 172) describes how regular clients provide street sex workers with 'stability to the working routine' in addition to guaranteed income which could cover overheads relating to work as well as everyday bills. Regulars are crucial to business as they enable a steady stream of customers, custom that can be relied on when times are quiet, and can be contactable when the worker decided to move to a different area, or work from home. Day (2007: 174) notes that sex workers also receive valuable other work opportunities from regular clients, professional advice and also friendship as relationships build up over time. However, regular clients also have their negative and stressful aspects. A common theme amongst qualitative research with male clients is how those that 'fall in love' with the sex worker can cause problems of obsession, stalking, jealousy and even violence (Day, 2007: 186; Sanders, 2008a: 104). Over-attachments from regular contacts, emotional connections, intimate sexual relations, growing friendships and trust often end up with the male client wanting to change the terms of the relationship. In addition, some sex workers manipulate customers' emotions, vulnerabilities and needs to extract financial gain, expensive gifts, cosmetic surgery, cars and other material goods in exchange for special treatment, reduced prices or simply 'friendship' and attention (such as phone calls and very regular visits). Sometimes these relationships move away from the explicit commercial exchange as conventional relationships emerge or these relationships turn sour and end.

Sanders (2008a: 48) suggests a five-point typology of men's involvement in buying sex that attempts to explain how there are different types of engagement with the female sex industry across the life course (Table 5.1).

The many different forms of engagement with the sex industry demonstrate that there is a wide range of clients who will buy commercial sex at different points in their life stage (see Soothill and Sanders, 2005). Men are often involved in various forms of conventional relationships such as marriages and long-term relationships whilst commercial sex runs parallel to these 'ordinary' relationships.

Motivations for Buying Sex

The research findings on why men buy sex could be a useful point on which to think about the role of prostitution in a modern society. There is a plethora of reasons why men buy sexual services from women. Some reasons are obviously linked to sexual fantasy, gratification and the desire for sex. The research does suggest that certain sex

Table 5.1   A typology of male involvement in buying sex across the lifecourse

Pattern of involvement	Lifecourse stage	Characteristics
Explorers	Any	Start at any stage; sexual experimentation/curiosity/fantasy; single or in relationship; short-term involvement; becomes dissatisfactory; filters out.
Yo-yoers	30s +	Pattern-forming behaviour; reduces when conventional relationship starts; involvement subsides when in relationship; starts when relationship becomes dissatisfactory; repeated pattern; attracted by 'danger', excitement and the process rather than sex or interaction.
Compulsives	Any	In or out of a conventional relationship; compulsion is the planning/arranging/Internet rather than sexual experience. Unpleasant and uncontrollable consequences. Usually ends with satisfying conventional relationship or change in relationship and/or therapeutic help.
Bookends	Beginning (20s) and end (mid 50s–60s +) of lifecourse	Initial sexual experiences and experimentation; incompatible with relationship; long period of absence during marriage; returns to buying sex in later life; widower/final chance for sex life; companionship not just sex; often regular clients to one sex worker; romantic courting rituals.
Permanent purchasers	Throughout the lifecourse	Sporadic over lifetime; abroad; travelling with work; away from home; long-term partner; not usually regular clients; driven by sexual needs.

acts, such as fellatio (Monto, 2001) have been cited as a key reason for men to buy sex. For instance, Perkins (1999) surveyed 667 Australian clients and 74.8 per cent (n = 499) said they always purchased oral sex. But with changes in sexual attitudes and behaviours (such as a reduction in the age of first sexual intercourse, the increased acceptance of pre-marital sex and oral sex becoming an acceptable and popular part of sexual interactions), buying oral sex may become less of a motivator for purchasing sex (Gagnon and Simon, 1987; Scott, 1998). Directly relating the desire to buy sex as a physical sexual urge, Mansson (2006) uses data from Scandinavian research to suggest there are five motivational themes that attract men to buying sex: 'the whore fantasy'; 'another kind of sex'; 'image of the kind-hearted comforter'; 'image of sex as a consumer product'; and 'fantasies of another kind of woman'. Wider analysis of motivations for buying sex looks beyond just physical and sexual desires to a range of social reasons for wanting temporary commercial relations. For instance, the ethnographic study of prostitution in bars in Peru by Nencel (2001) unpicks how men's motivations to buy sex are deeply connected to their sexual stories and stories about the self.

Others motivations are located in wider social structures and cultural manifestations of leisure and the commodification of sex (for a review, see Brooks-Gordon, 2006: 80–6). McKeganey and Barnard (1996) conducted research with 143 male clients in Scotland and concluded that there are five key motivations for purchasing sex: the ability to buy different types of sex acts; access to different women; the ability to have sex with women with different characteristics; the attraction of temporary relationships; and the thrill of engaging in an unconventional activity. Campbell (1998) and Warr and Pyett (1999) note how men buy sex because they are lonely (usually working away); find it difficult to form sexual or social relationships (because they are disabled, involved in caring for elderly parents, etc.); seek intimacy that they do not find in conventional relationships; seek emotional support and friendship; or prefer to pay for sex rather than have an adulterous affair that could result in devastating the family home. Plumridge et al. (1997) argue that for some men there is an attractive discourse of paying for sex as a means of removing themselves from the larger obligations of traditional, family-based relationships.

Sanders (2008a) categorizes the motivations for buying sex into 'push' factors, which stem from an individual's own life experiences and circumstances, and 'pull' factors which are associated with the wider culture of sex and the organization of commercial sex. Some push factors are associated with the sexual motivations already stated, including unsatisfactory existing sexual relationships or unease with conventional dating etiquette which involves alcohol consumption and rituals in nightclubs, which men in her study described as intimidating and disappointing. For the group of older men she interviewed, there were specific narratives around wanting to have more sexual experiences, wanting to have a sex life after a partner (for widowed or separated men), and also using new medicines such as Viagra to continue their sex lives in older life. For a group of men who could be described as professionals who spent many hours at work, relaxing and 'time out' in an 'overworked' culture was cited as a reason for seeking paid-for pleasure.

Brents and Hausbeck (2007) and Bernstein (2007) argue that the pull factors are related to the social environment that presents the opportunity to engage with the sex markets, learn about them, explore and access them more readily through new technologies. With what has been called the 'mainstreaming of the sex industry' (Brents and Hausbeck, 2007), especially through the Internet and the merging of sex work venues (such as lap dancing bars and strip clubs) with the everyday adult entertainment industry in the high street, there is less stigma and more acceptability about engaging in the sex industry (see Hubbard et al., 2008b). Changes are taking place within the sex industry as services move from the routine, predictable, ordinary sexual exchange, what Hausbeck and Brents (2002) called the 'McDonaldization' of the sex industry, to an 'upscaling' of venues, premises, services and presentation of women. In the modern sex industry, that must compete with other kinds of adult leisure activities, fantasy becomes a corporate strategy as more venues compete for trade. One way in which there has been a marked change in the marketing of sexual services is in what is termed 'the girlfriend experience' (GFE) (Bernstein, 2001; Sanders, 2008a: 93). The GFE service incorporates a more holistic experience which may include intimate acts such as kissing and more tactile interactions, but may also involve socializing, eating out, other more normalized activities as well as regular contact outside of the bedroom activities.

These pull factors can be explained by the wider changes in the sexualization of popular culture, what Hawkes (1996) terms 'sex as leisure' and McNair (2002) describes as the commonplace 'striptease culture' that is on display in all urban cultural centres.

Although the city is not a new place for sex and sexual 'deviance', these authors argue that there has been a normalization of the commodification of sex and sexuality on display and for consumption. Enlightening historical accounts of 'sporting guidebooks' that list brothels and bawdy houses in the 1800s in London and New York demonstrate how 'the city' has always been associated 'with a "sporting" male culture of sexually predatory men and an ideal city of male sexual opportunity' (Howell, 2001). Yet in late capitalism, Bernstein (2001) and others have argued that the demand for sexual services is intricately meshed to the many different features of economic structures. For instance, new technologies are intricate to the shape of the modern sex industry, as reported by Sharp and Earle (2003) and Sanders (2005c). The Internet has had a profound effect on the accessibility of commercial sex, as websites advertise individual escorts, saunas and a range of activities that can be ordered online, through email and by the telephone. The ease with which these advertisements can be found and services negotiated to be delivered to the hotel door has changed the way that men can interact with the sex industry from the privacy of their own computer at a convenient time of the day or night.

There are other more specific reasons why some groups of men seek out commercial sex. Research shows that men who live with physical impairments sometimes buy commercial sex to find sexual fulfilment, intimacy and emotional connections. Sanders (2007b) found that men who lived with physical disabilities and were receiving state support in the form of Disability Living Allowance were using this cash payment to purchase sexual services with an escort. Organizations such as Touching Base (www.touchingbase.org/about.html) in Australia and the Outsiders group (www.outsiders.org.uk/) in the UK demonstrate the centrality of commercial sex to men (and sometimes women) who are disabled by the social environment.

Patrons of lap dancing

It is useful to separate out explanations of why men visit lap dancing bars and strip clubs as a group of men who purchase indirect sexual services.[1] This demarcation is useful because, first, there is a separate sociological and feminist literature that attempts to make sense of this sex market, and also, these men who buy exotic dancing may not necessarily be the same group of men who buy direct sexual services.

Again, researchers have attempted to understand the types of men who visit lap dancing bars by categorizing them. Erickson and Tewksbury (2000) suggest a six-category typology based on their observations in lap dancing bars: the lonely; socially impotent; bold lookers; detached lookers; players; sugar daddies. Brewster (2003) also suggests there are two types of customers in exotic dancing bars: 'monetary regulars' who frequently buy dances and spend money; and 'frequency regulars' who often attend the bars but do not pay unless they deem it 'necessary'. Although these categorizations are useful in enabling the reader to think about why and how men purchase exotic dance, research that is conducted in lap dancing bars that claims to be participant observation from the customers' perspective, yet is not reflexive in terms of the researcher's dual role (as both a researcher and participant in purchasing sex), has been criticized. Egan and Frank (2005) point out that where participant observation is part of the research, it should be explicitly reflected on in order to locate the position of the researcher. In using reflexive methodology, the position of the researcher is understood in relation to power, gender, privilege and how the data are mediated and interpreted through this lens.

Customer practices when they attend strip clubs have been the focus of sociological investigation from participant observers who have been dancer–researchers. Notably the works of Katherine Frank (1998, 2002) and Danielle Egan (2005, and also Egan et al., 2006) have highlighted the micro-relationship between dancers and customers. Examining the customer from the dancers' perspective provides opportunities to understand the appeal of this culturally hegemonic group. The commodified relationships between dancer and customer become more complex when habits move from being an occasional customer to that of 'the regular'. Egan (2005: 87) notes how this relationship intensifies as extensive time and money is spent by the customer on an individual dancer: 'These relationships are saturated with power, sexual desire and fantasy'. Egan (2003) describes how 'love' and 'narcissism' become powerful defining aspects of the emotional and erotic bonds that customers feel for the dancers they visit.

Yet it is not simply the case that in the lap dancing bar the relationship is one where the male customer has all the power to purchase the body and sexual performance of the female dancer, leaving the woman powerless. Egan (2005) notes that the erotic setting becomes the place where agency and resistance are performed, in addition to the male customer adopting a particular script which is infused with expectations of heterosexual masculinity, affected by race and class dynamics as well as expectations around sexual fantasy and performance. Egan reconceptualizes consumption in exotic dancing so we come to understand what happens as a dynamic rather than a one-sided activity where the client has complete power over the sex worker.

What Do They Buy? Intimacy, Emotions and Sexual Services

There is generally a taboo about the types of sex involved in a commercial contract. The idea of time-limited, unemotional sex between strangers is what is often conjured up when commercial sex is imagined. Anything other than this image would challenge the notion that 'good sex' is that which exists only in the confines of a heterosexual reproductive relationship that is sanctioned by the state and is bound by positive emotions and commitment, and that 'bad sex' is something which is outside of this. The 'seedy' idea of commercial sex preserves the notion that only emotional, intimate sex can be found in long-term conventional relationships, and that other forms of sex (casual, group, masturbatory, BDSM, etc.) are unsatisfying, abnormal and also immoral. All other forms of sex are compared to a normative premise of Victorian morality which produces stigma and disgust towards anything that is other than this.

Various accounts of the 'missing voice' of the client demonstrate that these predictable expectations of the substance of commercial sex are not always the case (Korn, 1998). Recent reflections on normative male sexual scripts that are made up of romantic courtship, mutual satisfaction, friendship, emotional connections and sexual satisfaction were mapped onto the relationships that regular clients have with sex workers over a period of time (Sanders, 2008b). Here the argument is that general understandings of sex work and prostitution are based on false dichotomies that distinguish commercial sexual relationships as dissonant from non-commercial ones. Sanders (2008b) shows that there is mutual respect and understanding between regular clients and sex workers, dispelling the myth that all interactions between sex workers and clients are emotionless. There is ample counter-evidence (such as Bernstein, 2001, 2007) that indicates that clients are 'average' men without any particular or peculiar characteristics and increasingly seeking 'authenticity', intimacy and mutuality rather than trying to fulfil any mythology of violent, non-consensual sex. This information needs to be considered alongside the fact that sex workers, particularly those on the streets, experience significant violence from clients (see Church et al., 2001; and Chapter 3 for further discussion of violence) and that there are dangerous, predatory clients that have histories of violence and directly target sex workers because of their vulnerability.

Further, investigations into the micro-dynamics of the relationships between sex workers and clients demonstrate that the sexual services often go well beyond sex in markets other than the street. Lucas (2005: 531) interviewed 'elite prostitutes' who worked as escorts who stated that the sex was often a pretext for engaging in commercial sex as emotional needs were primary. Even amongst escorts interviewed by Lucas (2005: 533) who put more emphasis on sexual gratification as the key motivator for men, there was an acknowledgement that commercial sex was not just about a physical relationship but was a combination of sexual, interpersonal and emotional skills that met the needs of the client. This supports previous research by Holzman and Pines (1982) that established how the construction of the commercial exchange that 'johns' experience featured verbal exchange and communication as important parts of the relationship, as well as the construction of romantic liaisons, social flirting and courting behaviours. These levels of perceived intimacy may have an impact on consistent condom use in developing countries as the boundaries of 'regular' sex can change the nature of the transaction making 'safe sex' less consistent (Murray et al., 2007; Voeten et al., 2007).

These reports of the extended services that are part of the commercial sex exchange support other research on the sexual labour and work that the sex worker provides (see Chapter 2). Literature on the emotion work that the dancer must perform for customers who are looking for 'the real thing' demonstrates how tiresome and demanding the work can be (Ronai, 1992). In addition, the strategies are used to ensure regular customers in the bar are met with other strategies to resist the objectifying gaze of the male customer (Barton, 2002; Deshotels and Forsyth, 2006; Wood, 2000). Brewis and Linstead (2000a, 2000b) note clearly how sex workers manage their work in order to separate out sex work from other aspects of their lives. O'Neill (2001) discusses the performativity of the sex work role. Sanders (2005b) notes how a 'manufactured identity' is constructed by some sex workers to create a working persona and characteristics which is used just in their sex work jobs. This evidence suggests that any thorough account of the motivations for buying sexual services, both direct and indirect, needs to take into account the emotional aspects of the interactions. Nonetheless, it is also important to question, as O'Connell Davidson (1998: 209) does, whether there is something that distinguishes the motivations for purchasing sexual services from the desire to enter into a more mutual relationship that brings with it 'certain obligations and duties' which are not present in the commercial sexual transaction.

The attraction of sex tourism

It has been documented how purchasing sex abroad may have other attractions outside the general motivations for wanting sexual relationships that people are not finding in conventional forms of relationships. Sex tourism has different dynamics because of the power differentials in the race and ethnic background of the purchaser compared to the seller. Piscitelli (2007) describes from empirical findings of the sex industry in a beach area in Brazil, that the mainly white male foreign tourists who buy sex from local women and girls, are purchasing a racialized form of sexuality. Piscitelli (2007: 494) evaluates how foreign tourists are attracted to 'tropical sexuality': sexual encounters with certain women of skin colour as certain ethnic types are constructed as the embodiment of femininity. Further, the interviews she conducted with white male tourists who were openly racist, note how the tourists distanced themselves from buying sex from very dark-skinned women as they were associated with poverty and deprivation, while the lighter-skinned brown women were considered more feminine and with greater social status.

The racialized connotations to the attractions of sex tourism support O'Connell Davidson's observation work in sex tourism destinations. Here, she notes how the ability to purchase a woman for many tourists who visited alone, also became a symbol of status and masculinity to other men in the destination. O'Connell Davidson (1998: 172) concludes that men who may be considered social outcasts can attain a sense of inclusion in the expectations of masculinity by purchasing sex and demonstrating they are a 'normal', heterosexual male. There are significant links between buying sex and affirming masculinity. These findings highlight that when white tourists purchase sexual services and other forms of companionship from women in poorer countries, these dynamics are tainted by race, class, gender and sexuality inequalities which permeate the economic privileged position of mainly white men over poor non-white women. There is also the attraction of more relaxed laws in relation to the age of sexual intercourse in comparison to Western countries. The age disparity is another reason why older men visit sex tourism destinations in order to buy sex 'legitimately' from young boys and girls.

The Responsible Client, 'Fair Trade Sex' and the Sexual Contract

Attempts have been made to make causal links between male use of the sex industry, particularly watching pornography, with violence against women (Dworkin, 1981).

Although the debate is inconclusive, there have been more recent attempts to connect men who buy sex with domestic violence and controlling behaviours. Simmons, Lehmann and Collier-Tenison (2008) asked women who were in a shelter for domestic violence if their partners were involved in buying sex. The researchers conclude that men who domestically abuse women and also buy commercial sex are more likely to show controlling behaviours than those perpetrators who do not buy sex. However, overcoming the methodological difficulties of relying on accounts from third parties, Monto and Hotaling (2001) conducted a survey of 'rape myth acceptance' with 1,286 men who were arrested for trying to hire a street prostitute in Portland, Oregon; Las Vegas and San Francisco. Attitudinal questions rated to what extent attitudes that support sexual violence against women (rape myths) were held by men who used the street sex markets. The results demonstrate that there were very low levels of 'rape myth' acceptance amongst the sample and that only a very small number of respondents had high levels of acceptance of negative gender-based attitudes. Also, a Canadian study by Lowman and Atchison (2006) notes that from a survey of 70 clients, 80 per cent reported that they had not committed an offence against a sex worker. Of those that reported they had, this was usually refusing to pay for sexual services (n = 10) or robbery (n = 6). They conclude that 'sex-buyer violence appears to be empirically overestimated and theoretically underspecified' (2006: 292). Although not denying the importance of the issue of violence against sex workers, it is the nuances of who conducts the violence that is important in order to not cast all men who buy sex as sexually dangerous. Kinnell (2006a) reviews a range of data on the murder of sex workers, and although the majority of perpetrators of homicide against this group of women are clients (or men who pose as clients), this level of violence is committed by a very small number of clients.

Although a recent British study (Coy et al., 2007) found that some men held derogatory views of sex workers, the majority of evidence does not suggest that most men who buy sex are of this disposition. Most buyers conduct their business without the intention of being violent, aggressive or committing any offence and most commercial sex exchanges take place without incident. The majority of commercial sexual interactions are between consenting adults who negotiate a sexual service and a fee for that exchange. In addition to the consenting nature of most of the sex industry, there is also other evidence that demonstrates that male clients engage in the sex industry with a set of morals, etiquette and codes of conduct. In the research by Sanders (2008a), most men demonstrated a clear sense of where exploitation happened, the coercion from boyfriends for some women and the danger associated with the street sex market. They actively took steps not to visit sex markets where there was possible overt exploitation. For instance, there was a strong whistleblowing ethic and practice on the message boards when men became aware of establishments that were 'employing' under-age girls or women who seemed to have very little control over their activities. Clients were also concerned about women who were potentially trafficked and there was an ethic of being wary of establishments that had only migrant sex workers. Some men stayed away completely from these establishments as they could not tell whether migrant women were working by choice or whether there was someone controlling their activities. Internet message boards provide a space where benchmarking and etiquette were outlined as best practice that should be followed: this included condom use, not arguing about payment, and respecting the woman's sexual rules. The Internet forums were seen as places where standards could be passed on and maintained by the wider sex work community.

The Law and Buying Sex: Criminalizing Male Sexuality

Generally, the purchase of sex by men has not been criminalized in the same way that the sale of sex by women has been in most efforts to control prostitution. There are some notable examples which demonstrate extreme attempts to eradicate prostitution (which have failed). Chinese policy illustrates a model where it is a crime to pay for sex and men face considerable penalties which make shaming inevitable if not a desired outcome of compulsory rehabilitation programmes. Ren (1999) describes how sex workers are subject to mandatory rehabilitation and men who pay for sex can be arrested and sent to labour camps for re-education. Sweden has been an interesting case in Europe as it pioneered the criminalization of paying for sex while removing any sanctions against female sex workers as they are always considered victims.

The Act Prohibiting the Purchase of Sexual Services 1999 was introduced by the Swedish government amidst a range of measures to address violence against women (Ekberg, 2004). Gould (1999) notes that this extreme law was introduced as a result of the success of the prohibitionists that used evidence relating to violence, drug use, and the problems faced by sex workers in a one-sided and unproblematized way. Swedish contemporary legislation that began in the 1980s was based on arguments that selling sex was essentially 'the commercialization of women's bodies'; 'counter-productive to equality'; and showed 'contempt for women' (Svanstrom, 2004: 230). There was little room in the debates for anything other than an analysis that proposed prostitution as violence against women and the definition of prostitution moved from that of individual to structural violence against women (Leander, 2005: 118). Scoular (2004b) notes that this punitive policy was made for symbolic reasons to send the message that a civilized society does not tolerate commercial sex. Kulick (2005) identifies how the Swedish laws were the result of greater fears relating to the national identity of Sweden in a time of European nation-state and boundary re-configuration, and the fear of 'flooding' from immigrant women moving from Eastern European countries to the most affluent and stable Scandinavian countries. This trend has been adopted by other Scandinavian countries and more recently the UK has considered this approach as a way of managing the sex industry.

These moves to criminalize men who buy sex need to be considered in a wider context (Brooks-Gordon, 2005; Phoenix 2007/8; Scoular and O'Neill 2007). Referring to England and Wales, Phoenix and Oerton (2005) document how the 'problem of sex' has been defined as the 'problem of men' with an increase in legislation against men who buy sex since the 1980s. Kantola and Squires (2004) note from parliamentary debates on prostitution in the late 1980s and 1990s that concerns over the public nuisance of the kerb-crawler overshadowed any other discussions of the sex industry. The 'kerb-crawler as nuisance' discourse was tightly connected with a concern that prostitution was linked to organized crime and 'trafficking'. This has been an argument that Weitzer (2006) claims has been responsible for spreading myths and illusions about the reality of the sex industry, but has produced scaremongering about the nature of who is involved in selling and buying sex and exaggerate the criminal elements.

In England and Wales, at the time of writing, it is illegal to solicit a person for the purpose of prostitution in a public place (known as kerb-crawling), which was made an arrestable offence under the Criminal Justice and Police Act 2001 (Brooks-Gordon, 2006: 32). This trend signals a wider approach by UK governments to focus on men who buy sex. In October 2007, the policing minister in Northern Ireland announced that kerb-crawling would be introduced into law as a specific offence. In Scotland, the Prostitution (Public Places) Scotland Act 2007 came into force in October 2007, which criminalized 'loitering or soliciting in any public place for the purpose of obtaining the services of someone engaged in prostitution'.

'Tackling demand': UK policy responses

Despite it being legal to buy commercial sex between consenting adults in the UK, the British government's intention to 'eradicate street prostitution' and further to 'disrupt the sex markets' has seen increasing policy and policing attention to male clients. In Home Office documents there has been a strong undertone of disapproval, notably through the use of language such as 'the user', implying that those men who buy sex are implicitly abusers of women. For instance, in the Home Office consultation document, *Paying the Price* (Home Office, 2004: 12), men who buy commercial sex are conflated with those who perpetuate criminal activities in the statement: 'going to a prostitute can mean supporting the illegal drugs industry'. This simplistic assertion ignores many facts relating to both the nature of men who buy sex and the organization of the sex industry. The picture painted of men who buy sex is in contradiction to their own research evidence. 'The user' is described as a 30-year-old male who is married, in full-time employment and has no criminal record (Home Office, 2004: 17). This suggests that men who buy sex are ordinary citizens who are upstanding members of the community in terms of employment, contributing to society, obeying the law and family obligations.

There is implicit tension between the policies and approaches used to manage the sex industry. There is a burgeoning sex industry which is being promoted legitimately through the economic mainstreaming of various venues (see Brents and Sanders, forthcoming). To a lesser extent, but still significant, there is a growing cultural acceptance of buying commercial sex as the stigma is reduced and it is acceptable to purchase time and intimacy with women as a lifestyle choice. Equally, the majority of men who consume sex are not criminals and do not have criminal intentions. Yet governments are opting to eradicate certain types of sex markets as unwanted and problematic and this now includes targeting the purchasers of sex.

Scoular et al. (2007) note that it is the street sex market and the street sex worker that are being labelled as 'uncivil' and 'anti-social'. In the same way, it is men who buy sex from the street markets who are being targeted by 'kerb-crawler crackdowns', which include naming and shaming of personal details in the media, and encouraging individuals to attend shaming schools in the form of a one-day 're-education' programme.

In *A Coordinated Prostitution Strategy* (Home Office, 2006), the war against 'demand' continues through the overarching aim to 'disrupt the sex markets' by criminalizing sex workers and re-emphasizing the enforcement of laws against kerb-crawlers. 'Tackling demand' is notably a response to community concerns and informal warnings, court diversion schemes (re-education programmes), and prosecution (including the removal of driving licences) are promoted alongside 'naming and shaming'. This attention to 'kerb-crawling' in the British government escalated in 2008, when at the end of 2007 Labour MP Harriet Harman made false links between the 'demand' for sexual services as the sole reason and cause of human trafficking into the sex industry.[2] This sparked a new review of 'demand' and the Home Office decided to investigate the implications of making it a crime to pay for sex in 2008. In September 2008, the Home Secretary announced proposals to make it a crime if someone pays for sex from a person who is 'controlled for gain'. While this is intended to protect those people who are coerced and trafficked into prostitution beyond their will, the ambiguous and slippery term 'controlled for gain' would mean that men who are buying sex from those who are voluntarily involved in a third party arrangement to organize their business would become perpetrators. The implication would be that the majority of purchased sex in England and Wales would become a crime, which, it has been argued, would lead to a wide range of negative consequences for the safety of sex workers, the informal regulation of the sex industries and the delivery of sexual health services (see Brooks-Gordon, 2005; Sanders and Campbell, 2008).

Deterrence from 'deviance'

To deter men from using the street market as a legitimate place to buy sex, the British government promoted a campaign to warn men of their wrongful and potential damaging activities. The 'Kerb crawling costs more than you think' campaign ran in 2007. The 'marketing message' was aimed at 'potential' clients who went to the street through posters in the media and radio 'warnings'. Listeners were told that kerb-crawling will result in an arrest, a court appearance, letters sent to their home, a £1,000 fine, a driving ban and shame to their families and employer. Beer mats forewarn: 'Turn over to find out how much it costs to pick up a prostitute', the answer on the other side replying: 'Your driving licence. Your job. Your marriage. A £1,000 fine'. The slogan 'Kerb-crawling costs more than you think' that punctuates all of these gimmicks is intended as a deterrent and gives off a strong moral message that in reality is a mechanism of social control. There is a clear message about the disgust of buying sex from the street which is aimed at middle-class men who are supposedly risking everything important to them by seeking out commercial sex. There are three stories written on posters that reinforce this message. Here is one example:

> Alan Davis has been married for 8 years, has four great kids and a vibrant social life which centres on his local pub, the Crown & Goose. In 2002, Alan realised his ambition to set up a courier company. Alan and wife Sandra sacrificed much in order to ensure the success of their fledgling business. They remortgaged the family home, worked 18 hour days and took no holidays for the first three years. Last Saturday Alan was returning from the pub when he was arrested for kerb-crawling.

There is an underlying narrative that 'respectable' men should not be risking their livelihoods and family stability by taking part in such a sexual misdemeanour. The stories also suggest that buying sex would result in the end of precious relationships, implying that marriage is the only 'right' form of relationship. Other local authorities created their own campaigns to send the signal that men who cruise the streets are unwanted. Strong emotive language is used in such campaigns which is suggestive of hatefulness and disgust. The clearest case of hatred for the kerb-crawler is in a poster campaign issued by Wolverhampton City Council with the statement: 'Kerb crawling belongs in the gutter. Wolverhampton hates kerb crawlers'. This poster, which appeared on large billboards around locations known for street prostitution, pictured the face of a white man, under a drain gutter in the pavement. This imagery of the 'dirty rat in the gutter' was symbolic of the council's particular attitude towards this group of men and the intolerance towards the street sex industry in general (see Sanders and Campbell, 2008).

The unequal targeting of certain sex markets highlights the contradictions of the government's aim to 'disrupt the sex markets'. O'Connell Davidson remarks:

> It is difficult to image any government enthusiastically applying legal penalties to middle-class men who use 'discrete' forms of prostitution such as escorts agencies or high-class hostess clubs, and still harder to imagine governments intervening in the consumption of forms of commercial sex that are more closely linked to mainstream businesses in the print, film, leisure and tourism industries. (2003: 61)

These contradictions of government interventions based on class and 'respectability' are evident in the wave of 're-education' programmes for kerb-crawlers that have been imported from North America into the UK.

Rehabilitating the kerb-crawler

When the Coordinated Prostitution Strategy endorsed support for the court diversion scheme in the form of re-education or rehabilitation programmes, there was renewed criticism of the lack of evidence for the effectiveness of such programmes. Brooks-Gordon (2006: 16) notes how these 'shaming schools' are dangerous for sex workers as they create an intensification of policing the street, diverts resources from women's safety and generally create more difficult scenarios for sex workers. These criticisms echo previous warnings from Campbell and Storr (2001) who point out the futility of the first programme in the UK, based in Leeds, West Yorkshire, in 1998. Official bodies have tended to support these 'quick fix' programmes on the basis that men who attend the one-day workshop (where the content usually tells them about how wrong their behaviour is as well as health information, legal information and sometimes psychological profiling), do not appear in the re-offending statistics. Instead, low re-offending statistics are used as evidence that the programmes are effective.

Sanders (2009) identifies a range of flaws with these programmes based on the evaluation literature that demonstrates how re-offending rates cannot be counted as a valuable measure of success because of the significant problem of displacement (Monto and Garcia, 2001; Van Brunschot, 2003). If a man buys sex, is arrested and sent on a programme, the likelihood is that he will not commit the same behaviour in the same patterns that would get him caught, but would go to different areas and different markets. The lack of re-offending does not suggest there has been a change in behaviour or attitudes, but simply that the person has not been re-arrested. In addition, Brooks-Gordon (2005) makes strong arguments that indicate how the offer of attending a programme or going to court is not voluntary and that shaming becomes implicit in the policing tactics.

The futility of these types of 're-education' programmes which have a fundamental moral basis is an example of how some types of sexual behaviour are labelled as 'deviant', whilst other forms of commercial sex which appear to be more sophisticated (usually because they are less visible), are allowed to flourish. O'Connell Davidson notes how the state is clearly involved in promoting the sex industry:

> The state plays an important role in shaping the consumption of commercial sex, not simply by permitting or tolerating certain types of consumption, but also by endorsing, perpetuating or promoting the social divisions and status hierarchies that are so central to clients' choices as consumers. (2003: 60)

The Commodification of Sex

The breadth of literature on who buys sex indicates that the sex industry caters for many different groups of people and sexualities rather than just men buying sex from women. With a growing sex industry which is becoming specialist and catering for a range of tastes and desires in as many different settings, the possibilities of buying sex reflect diversity of sexual expression and identity. Yet despite the extent of the demand for sexual services, there are increasing pressures to target men who buy sex as scapegoats for broader economic and social structural changes and issues. Governments are trying to 'do something' about prostitution, and in the twenty-first century this intervention has taken the form of trying to stem the amount of 'demand' for sex. These interventions are inappropriate in terms of effectively managing the sex industry. As Bernstein (2001: 409) poignantly describes, the demand for sexual services needs to be located and understood through the key features of capitalism. Bernstein describes these features as: the merging of the public and the private; the extension and breadth of the service sector; the individualization of sex (the idea that we should all experience sexual satisfaction); and what Bernstein terms the desire for 'bounded authenticity'. This concept essentially means that there is a desire amongst some people for a neatly compact sexual and emotional experience which is protected by the boundaries of the commercial exchange. The 'bounded authenticity' is preferable for some compared to the messiness of non-commercial relationships which have other expectations. One other feature of late capitalism that needs to be taken into account is the normalization of the sex industry on the one hand, and yet increasing attempts to eradicate certain parts of the sex industry and render it wrong and immoral on the other. Sanders and Campbell argue that

> Supporting policies for further criminalization of clients fails to address the impact of such policies on sex workers themselves, their rights, social inclusion and safety. This means there are contradictions between such shifts in policy and other objectives of policy which are supposedly intended to reduce the victimization and vulnerability of sex workers. (2008: 164)

The regulation of the sex industry needs to take into account the vibrant dynamics of the market of the sex industry: that is, how the supply and demand mechanisms interact, and understanding how one does not exist without the other. Laying the 'blame' for the rise in the sex industry just at the door of certain types of heterosexual men is missing the point that the commodification of sex is prolific and entrenched in capitalism and consumption.

Notes

1 Broadly, the literature on exotic dance falls into three distinct bodies of knowledge: dancer–customer relations; emotional and sexual labour; and managing stigma and identity (Bradley, 2007; Thompson and Harred, 1992; Thompson et al., 2003). Qualitative studies involving participant observation and ethnographic methods (Egan, 2003; Frank, 1998; Ronai and Ellis, 1989) and interviews have reported the strategies dancers develop such as 'strategic flirting' (Deshotels and Forysth, 2006); resistance strategies (Murphy, 2003; Wood, 2000); and psychological boundary setting strategies (Barton, 2007) to control the sexual work.
2 http://news.bbc.co.uk/1/hi/uk_politics/6188203.stm

Suggested Reading

Bernstein, E. (2001) 'The meaning of the purchase: desire, demand and the commerce of sex', *Ethnography*, 2(3): 389–420.

Brooks-Gordon, B. (2006) *The Price of Sex: Prostitution, Policy and Society*, Cullompton: Willan.

O'Connell Davidson, J. (2003) '"Sleeping with the enemy"? Some problems with feminist abolitionist calls to penalise those who buy commercial sex', *Social Policy and Society*, 2(1): 55–64.

Sanchez Taylor, J. (2001) 'Dollars are a girl's best friend? Female tourists' sexual behaviour in the Caribbean', *Sociology*, 35(3): 749–64.

Sanders, T. (2008) *Paying for Pleasure: Men who Buy Sex*, Cullompton: Willan.

Study Questions

Level one

- Why is the traditional image of the buyer of sex a man and to what extent can this be challenged?

Level two

- What arguments have been put forward for making it a crime to pay for sex and what are the implications of this approach?

Level three

- What differences are there between conventional and commercial sexual interactions?

6

SEX WORKERS, LABOUR RIGHTS AND UNIONIZATION

Susan Lopez-Embury[1] and Teela Sanders

This chapter will explore the rise of the sex workers' labour movement across the world. In doing so, an examination of the rise of the 'sex as work' movement, from the late 1960s, will be traced. The development of the labour rights movement which includes the World Charter for Prostitutes' Rights and the more recent Declaration of the Rights of Sex Workers in Europe explain the human rights basis of the movement. Global organizing is examined with country-specific examples from Australia, the USA, India and Brazil. The individual country successes and the global impact of the sex worker rights movements are discussed in conjunction with the acknowledgement of the difficulties and limitations of the movement. Finally, the chapter concludes with a discussion of the recent unionization of sex workers to gain employment rights and recognition as workers.

───────────── **The Rise of the 'Sex as Work' Labour Movement** ─────────────

The history of prostitution is littered with examples of sex workers organizing together to resist stigma and oppression. For example, in 1790, in response to violence by police, 2,000 prostitutes from Palais Royal in Paris staged a protest (Bassermann, 1993), and the courtesans of Lucknow, India, in the mid-nineteenth century resisted British rule and social exclusion (Oldenburg, 1990). Guatemalan prostitutes during the same period fought for their rights (McGreery, 1986, cited in Kempadoo and Doezema, 1998), and colonial Kenya's prostitutes also resisted oppression in the 1920s and 1930s (White, 1990, cited in Kempadoo and Doezema, 1998).

The sex-positive aspect of certain radical feminist movements of the late 1960s and 1970s gave way to a new consideration of women's sexual choices in both public and private spheres. Women were becoming more sexually intrepid and autonomous and enjoying new freedoms denied to their mothers, largely due to the revolutionary achievements gained through the contraception pill which finally separated reproductive sex from sex for pleasure. During this era, traditional feminine roles were being challenged and new expressions of sexuality and orientation were being experienced openly. This political and social climate provided the backdrop for a radical sex profession to agitate for recognition and change.

In 1973, Margo St. James created COYOTE (Call Off Your Old Tired Ethics) in San Francisco, California, to draw attention to and speak out for the rights of women in the sex industry (see Jenness, 1990). The idea of prostitutes speaking out and demanding their rights was an unprecedented and direct challenge to the long-held beliefs that prostitutes were either passive victims of male sexual aggression or morally defunct, drug-addicted 'vectors of disease'. St. James believed that prostitutes deserved the same rights that other workers in the USA enjoyed, and that the criminal status of prostitution worked to prevent them from being realized. The general goals of COYOTE were to decriminalize all voluntary adult prostitution, to educate the public about the abuses and problems inherent to its criminal status, and to work towards eliminating stigma by normalizing commercial sex as work. Towards these ends, COYOTE embarked on a campaign to raise consciousness in the USA to recognize prostitutes' issues.

Integral to the aims of COYOTE was the celebration of prostitution as an employment choice. St. James believed that to make real changes, prostitutes' self-esteem must be raised and they must be able to take pride in their work. COYOTE's campaign included the Hookers' Film Festivals, Hookers' Congresses (Weitzer, 1991), and gala masquerade parties called 'Hookers' Balls' which were attended by up to 20,000 people (Pheterson, 1989: 4), and largely funded the campaigning.

COYOTE succeeded in 1974 in eliminating a law in San Francisco that required prostitutes who had been arrested to be quarantined in jails while awaiting results of mandatory gonorrhoea tests. The organization successfully argued that it was illogical and unfair to arrest and quarantine prostitutes, who were not a significant source of sexually transmitted diseases, while customers were not arrested and never quarantined and tested (Weitzer, 1991: 30). Following the formation of COYOTE, similar organizations sprang up throughout North America. These included Prostitutes of New York (PONY), Hooking is Real Employment (HIRE, Atlanta, Georgia), Prostitution Education Project (PEP, Ann Arbor, Michigan), and many others.

Meanwhile, prostitutes had been making themselves heard in other parts of the world. In Montparnasse, France, in 1974, Parisian prostitutes who had become tired of harassment by police and courts demonstrated to bring attention to their grievances (Mathieu, 2003). In 1975, a group of 150 prostitutes took over a church in Lyons, France, to protest at police inaction in solving the recent murders of several prostitutes, the lack of police protection in the face of such dangers, and to address abuses they suffered at the hands of the police, such as exorbitant fines, violence, and increased incarceration. The Lyons protest lasted seven days during which sympathetic protests and church takeovers took place in other cities throughout France. The public was very supportive of the group, who called themselves the French Collective of Prostitutes. Their actions spurred a growth in the development of organizations throughout Europe and the rest of the world between 1975 and 1985, including among others, the English Collective of Prostitutes (ECP), HYDRA in Germany, ASPASIE in Switzerland, CORP in Canada, and De Rode Draad in the Netherlands.

In 1975, Margot St. James and other sex workers from the USA and France met Simone de Beauvoir in Paris to plan for an international prostitutes' rights organization (Pheterson, 1989: 6). It would take ten years before this vision was realized. Back in the USA, St. James and Priscilla Alexander, a lesbian feminist, formed the National Task Force on Prostitution (NTFP) in 1979. The purpose of the NTFP was to bring together under a national network the various prostitutes' rights organizations throughout the USA, and it was officially recognized as an NGO by the United Nations.

Activism and mobilization continued across North America and Europe, culminating in the First World Whores' Congress held in Amsterdam in February 1985. As a result of this congress, the International Committee for Prostitutes' Rights (ICPR) was born, and together the participants developed the first international instrument for sex workers' rights: the World Charter for Prostitutes' Rights.

World Charter for Prostitutes' Rights (1985)[2]

Laws

- Decriminalize all aspects of adult prostitution resulting from individual decision.
- Decriminalize prostitution and regulate third parties according to standard business codes. It must be noted that existing standard business codes allow abuse of prostitutes. Therefore special clauses must be included to prevent the abuse and stigmatization of prostitutes (self-employed and others).
- Enforce criminal laws against fraud, coercion, violence, child sexual abuse, child labor, rape, racism everywhere and across national boundaries, whether or not in the context of prostitution.
- Eradicate laws that can be interpreted to deny freedom of association, or freedom to travel, to prostitutes within and between countries. Prostitutes have rights to a private life.

Human rights

- Guarantee prostitutes all human rights and civil liberties, including the freedom of speech, travel, immigration, work, marriage, and motherhood and the right to unemployment insurance, health insurance and housing.
- Grant asylum to anyone denied human rights on the basis of a 'crime of status', be it prostitution or homosexuality.

Working conditions

- There should be no law which implies systematic zoning of prostitution. Prostitutes should have the freedom to choose their place of work and residence. It is essential that prostitutes can provide their services under the conditions that are absolutely determined by themselves and no one else.
- There should be a committee to insure the protection of the rights of the prostitutes and to whom prostitutes can address their complaints. This committee must be comprised of prostitutes and other professionals like lawyers and supporters.

- There should be no law discriminating against prostitutes associating and working collectively in order to acquire a high degree of personal security.

Health

- All women and men should be educated to periodical health screening for sexually transmitted diseases. Since health checks have historically been used to control and stigmatize prostitutes, and since adult prostitutes are generally even more aware of sexual health than others, mandatory checks for prostitutes are unacceptable unless they are mandatory for all sexually active people.

Services

- Employment, counselling, legal, and housing services for runaway children should be funded in order to prevent child prostitution and to promote child well-being and opportunity.
- Prostitutes must have the same social benefits as all other citizens according to the different regulations in different countries.
- Shelters and services for working prostitutes and re-training programs for prostitutes wishing to leave the life should be funded.

Taxes

- No special taxes should be levied on prostitutes or prostitute businesses.
- Prostitutes should pay regular taxes on the same basis as other independent contractors and employees, and should receive the same benefits.

Public opinion

- Support educational programs to change social attitudes which stigmatize and discriminate against prostitutes and ex-prostitutes of any race, gender or nationality.
- Develop educational programs which help the public to understand that the customer plays a crucial role in the prostitution phenomenon, this role being generally ignored. The customer, like the prostitute, should not, however, be criminalized or condemned on a moral basis.
- We are in solidarity with workers in the sex industry.

Organization

- Organizations of prostitutes and ex-prostitutes should be supported to further implementation of the above charter.

Almost 150 attendees from 18 countries around the globe attended the Second World Whores' Congress. This single event registered and recorded the issues facing prostitutes worldwide, and highlighted the growing pains of a movement formed from disparate cultures. These problems continue today, and the story of the Second Congress forms a prologue to current policy discourse at the governmental and NGO levels, and a roadmap from which today's movement can further the journey towards sex workers' rights. The Second World Whores' Congress happened at a time when the AIDS scare was in full swing, so the double stigma of prostitution and AIDS was responsible for many abuses of prostitutes (from mandatory AIDS testing to incarceration if found HIV-positive) who were seen as 'vectors' of the virus. The participants discussed these issues at length in the health session of the Congress.

The significance of the two World Whores' Congresses cannot be underestimated. For the first time in modern history, a maligned and often despised group of people were making their stand for rights and recognition. The movement was officially more organized, recognized, and stronger than ever. Communication among prostitutes from around the world galvanized determination to demand respect as human beings, rights as workers, and representation as taxpayers and citizens.

Global Organizing: Solidarity Beyond Borders

As Kempadoo and Doezema (1998) explain, the movement had gained traction and media attention in the global North, yet workers in the South, unrecognized internationally and undocumented in their efforts, were busy organizing themselves and staging their own resistance to oppression. In 1982, the Association of Autonomous Women Workers in Ecuador was established; in 1987, Silvia Leite organized a national conference for prostitutes in Brazil, which resulted in Davida, the National Network of Prostitutes; and, in 1988, Uruguayan prostitutes appeared at the annual May Day march as AMEPU, and opened a child care centre and new headquarters.

The age-old view of prostitutes as vectors of disease in conjunction with the new AIDS epidemic meant that during the 1980s and 1990s funding was being channelled into research and healthcare projects aimed at prostitutes. Due to concerns that this work potentially stigmatized sex workers and further violated their rights, as well as the fact that prostitutes saw themselves as best equipped to educate their own communities about the dangers and prevention of HIV infection, several new prostitute-run organizations emerged towards that end while many existing prostitutes' rights groups took on the role of HIV education and prevention. Many received funding from prominent HIV/AIDS organizations. The AIDS epidemic has been the most successful catalyst for sex worker organizing.

In 1992, the Network of Sex Work Projects[3] was formed to provide a network for these various groups addressing sex worker rights and AIDS prevention, making connections with projects in the Asia Pacific region. Eventually they replaced the International Committee for Prostitutes' Rights as the global network for sex workers, gaining access, recognition, and consultative status in many high-level debates and conferences on HIV/AIDS. This period of time was important across the globe as groups of people, overwhelmingly women, who were involved in the sex industry, and their allies, made their informal networks formalized. Some examples of these grassroots organizations are:

- In 1992, the Venezuelan group Association of Women for Welfare and Support (AMBAR), and APRODEM in Chile were formed to establish a voice for sex workers in South America.
- In the early 1990s, Calcutta's Durbar Mahila Samanwaya Committee (Durbar), and South Africa's Sex Worker Education and Advocacy Taskforce (SWEAT).

Today, some of these early organizations are defunct due to funding issues, as are many projects providing harm reduction and support programmes for sex workers (Busza, 2006). Despite the political implications of the panics surrounding trafficking and migrancy and the links to the sex industry (Weitzer, 2007), sex worker organizations still survive in many parts of the world and lend their voices to international discourse on prostitution and prostitutes' rights. The Internet has successfully promoted a surge of further networking among the global groups and their supporters, and many listservs were created to facilitate communication. Sex workers have also made their voices heard in other venues, such as The Fourth World Conference on Women in Beijing, China, 1995, and world and regional UN meetings, AIDS conferences, and Harm Reduction conferences.

Labour rights

The various gatherings of sex workers reinforced what was detailed in the Second World Whores' Congress: the fact that many sex workers considered themselves deserving of having their human rights recognized. Beyond basic human rights, sex workers needed to demand that their profession be recognized as real work – an activity they participate in to earn their livelihoods – in order to be eligible for the labour rights and protection of any other citizen. Unfortunately, non-recognition of sex work as labour by many governments was problematic, as '[t]he argument that sex workers should be entitled to the free choice of work, or indeed any of the labour or human rights discussed here, is of course, void if the State does not choose to define prostitution as work, but simply as unlawful activity' (Bindman, 1997). Thus, many of the organizations that formed have for the most part made decriminalization of prostitution a priority with so far rare but valuable successes. One clear success is the New Zealand Prostitutes' Collective who, together with politicians, campaigners, researchers and concerned allies, victoriously campaigned for many years for decriminalization (see Gall, 2006: 151). This culminated in the New Zealand Prostitution Reform Act 2003 which decriminalized prostitution for those over the age of 18.[4]

However, Gall (2007) and Mathieu (2003) document why sex workers are typically reluctant to organize. Having been in the marginalized shadows of society due to stigmatization, social exclusion, and legal threats most of their lives, most sex workers have learned to navigate these shadows well in order to avoid problems. Obstacles preventing sex workers from collectively organizing have been mainly those of exposure and loss of anonymity, which could endanger them in situations such as keeping their children, harassment by authorities and the public, loss of housing opportunities, arrest and incarceration, threats to family life and family members, loss of 'day jobs' in other fields, loss of social status in their communities, and much more. Sex workers are, in effect, caught in a dichotomy: if they organize, they will be silenced by loss of freedoms; if they are silent, those freedoms will never be realized.

Nonetheless, activists continue to be persistent. In addition to the World Charter for Prostitutes' Rights, other documents have been created over the past decade. These include the Sex Workers' Manifesto from Calcutta, and the Sisonke Mission Statement from South Africa. In October 2005, in Brussels, Belgium, 120 sex workers and 80 allies from 30 countries across Europe gathered for The European Conference on Sex Work,

Human Rights, Labour and Migration. Over two years after the conference the Declaration of the Rights of Sex Workers in Europe was agreed and signed by all 120 sex workers and 80 allies in attendance. They also adopted the red umbrella as a symbol of sex workers' rights, and this is now used globally by sex worker movements (Figure 6.1).

Declaration of the Rights of Sex Workers in Europe[5]

All individuals within Europe, including sex workers, are entitled to the following rights under international human rights law. All European Governments are obliged to respect, protect and fulfil:

I. The right to life, liberty and security of person
II. The right to be free from arbitrary interference with one's private and family life, home or correspondence and from attacks on honour and reputation
III. The right to the highest attainable standard of physical and mental health
IV. The right to freedom of movement and residence
V. The right to be free from slavery, forced labour and servitude
VI. The right to equal protection of the law and protection against discrimination and any incitement to discrimination under any of the varied and intersecting status of gender, race, citizenship, sexual orientation, etc.
VII. The right to marry and found a family
VIII. The right to work, to free choice of employment and to just and favourable conditions of work
IX. The right to peaceful assembly and association
X. The right to leave any country, including one's own, and to return to one's own country
XI. The right to seek asylum and to non-refoulement
XII. The right to participate in the cultural and public life of society

Figure 6.1   The Red Umbrella symbol of the International Union of Sex Workers
Source: Designed by David Rumsey

Sadly, the issues raised by the European group are the very same issues brought up almost 20 years earlier during the Second World Whores' Congress. Decriminalization continues to be at the heart of many sex worker rights organizations. For instance, in 1997, *Anti-Slavery International* published a paper called 'Redefining Prostitution as Sex Work on the International Agenda' (Bindman, 1997). In 1998, the International Labour Organisation published a report on the economic sector of the sex industry, and included decriminalization in its policy recommendations (Lim, 1998). In 1999, the CEDAW Committee recommended decriminalization of prostitution in China, calling it sex work, and also recommended that governments make more lenient laws and recognize sex work as a choice of work (UNHCHR, 1999, 2000, 2001). This was widely criticized by conservative, feminist, and religious groups. Most recently, Jamaica's health ministry has come out in favour of decriminalization (Lewis, 2008), and Ban Ki Moon, the Secretary General of the United Nations, has urged governments to eliminate harsh laws against prostitution and cease persecution of sex workers (Ditmore, 2008).

Current Sex Worker Activism

In many countries, sex workers have been actively standing up for their rights by forming organizations or coming together under existing organizations. There are many different types of sex worker organizations in the majority and minority world that campaign for sex worker rights in different ways, depending on the pressing issues that members face. For instance, Canada has a long tradition of sex worker rights organizing (Gall, 2006: 144). Organizations there include Stella in Montreal, the Exotic Dancers' Association of Canada whose mission statement is: 'The Exotic Dancers' Association of Canada promotes setting standards in the exotic entertainment industry to ensure a better quality of life'.[6] In countries where basic human rights are questioned, such as living free from persecution and access to health care, these are the main issues for which groups campaign. In Cambodia, the Cambodian Prostitutes' Union (CPU) and Women's Network for Unity (WNU) successfully fought and stopped unethical tenofovir (a proposed HIV vaccine) trials on sex workers and are currently working with Cambodian Men, Women Network for Development (CMNWD) to get the government to repeal a law that was recently passed conflating trafficking with prostitution.

In order to highlight the flavour of the different movements that exist in various parts of the world, the next section gives some examples of organizations in Australia, the USA, India and Brazil.

Organization spotlight: Scarlet Alliance, Australia

Formed in Australia in 1989 in response to concerns by sex workers about unfair treatment and violations of rights as a result of the HIV/AIDS pandemic, the Scarlet

Alliance (SA) is a national umbrella organization for all sex workers' organizations in Australia. It is government funded and supported, working on issues of Australian sex worker rights throughout Australia and internationally.

Scarlet Alliance is currently involved in HIV/AIDS outreach and education among sex workers, and is a member of the Australian Federation of AIDS Organizations (AFAO). They advise the government and policy-makers on issues affecting sex workers, on current sex industry legislation and on other legislation that may affect sex workers. They also educate other organizations and governmental departments on sex work-related issues. Internationally and domestically, SA has been effective in promoting best models of minimizing the transmission of HIV and other sexually transmitted infections among sex workers and their clients, and participates in conferences and meetings on health, law, research, human rights, feminism, community education, immigration, and globalization by presenting on issues that affect sex workers. They promote the peer education model of service delivery, which has been shown to be one of the most effective methods of empowering education. The Scarlet Alliance have also produced two valuable publications: *A Guide to Best Practice: Occupational Health and Safety in the Australian Sex Industry* (2000), and *Principles for Model Sex Industry Legislation* (2000).

Organization spotlight: 'Sex Workers' Outreach Project and the Desiree Alliance, USA

In 2002, Robyn Few was arrested by federal agents and was eventually convicted on conspiracy to promote prostitution. In response, she formed SWOP-USA in October 2003 to promote the decriminalization of prostitution. SWOP-USA, whose founding members included Carol Leigh, Stacey Swimme, Avaren Ipsen, and Michael Foley, was inspired by and modelled for the most part on SWOP Australia. SWOP-USA's first action was the Green River Memorial, held on 17 December 2003, to memorialize the women who had been murdered by US serial killer Gary Leon Ridgeway, dubbed the 'Green River Killer' (Levi-Minzi and Shields, 2007). This became the International Day to End Violence Against Sex Workers, and is now observed by sex workers globally. In September 2004, a conference on prostitution was held at the University of Toledo, Ohio, by the Social Work Department at which several of the SWOP-members and other activists attended and presented. The morning after the last day of the conference, the group of allies gathered at a restaurant for breakfast and the idea to hold a sex worker-run – and focused – conference was born with Las Vegas, Nevada, as the proposed location.

That spring, organizational non-profit papers were filed and the Desiree Alliance was created as the organization that would present the conference. BAYSWAN, SWOP-USA, COYOTE, Best Practices Policy Project, in collaboration with the University of Nevada, Las Vegas, Departments of Sociology and Women's Studies and the Women's Research Institute of Nevada all pulled together to put on the first sex worker-led conference in the USA since 1997. The conference was named 'Re-visioning Prostitution

Policy: Creating Space for Sex Worker Rights and Challenging Criminalization', and was held in July 2006.

The advent of the conference, attended by almost 250 people including sex workers, academics, allies, and activists, spurred the rights movement further and several new SWOP chapters were born. There are now ten chapters across the USA. Desiree Alliance held another conference in San Francisco in July 2007, in conjunction with the Sex Worker Film and Arts Festival, Whore College, and SWOP's Sex Work Enthusiasts Education and Training (SWEET) 'School for Johns'. In October 2007, the Best Practices Policy Project and Different Avenues (sex worker outreach and service providers) held a Sex Worker Leadership Training Institute in Washington, DC. Desiree Alliance's 2008 conference was held in Chicago, and its allies and members plan to hold annual conferences, galvanizing the movement and encouraging leadership in activism. SWOP-USA is forming a legal non-profit to further their abilities as regional organizers, and at the time of writing have joined with the Erotic Service Providers' Union (ESPU) to place another initiative to decriminalize prostitution on the ballot, only this time in San Francisco.

Organization spotlight: Durbar Mahila Samanwaya Committee (DMSC, or Durbar), India

The Durbar Mahila Samanwaya Committee (or Unstoppable United Women's Committee) is an organization of 65,000 male, female, and transgender sex workers in West Bengal, India. Durbar started as a result of the STI/HIV Intervention Programme (the Sonagachi Project) in the Sonagachi Red Light district, run by Dr Smarajit Jana. Jana implemented the peer education model for educating sex workers and preventing the spread of HIV and STIs.

The participants in the project soon realized that to be effective in fighting HIV, there were many issues sex workers faced that had to be addressed: exploiters within the sex industry; stigmatization of sex work and workers which prevented access to services available to the rest of society; and laws which render many of their activities criminal. To change these issues, they officially formed the DMSC in 1995. They also formed the Usha Multipurpose Cooperative Society, a cooperative bank, to address their exclusion from mainstream banks and loans; a vocational training centre to train children of sex workers and retired sex workers in vocational skills; and started a child care crèche to allow sex workers secure supervision and care for their children during working hours.

In 1999, Durbar took control of the Sonagachi Project, and set about replicating the project across the state. Under the original project they had seen unusually encouraging results. Between 1992, when the project was started, and 1995 during assessment surveys, the percentage of people in the brothels using condoms rose from 2.7 to 81.7 per cent. Furthermore, HIV/AIDS infection rates only rose to 5 per cent during the same time, when other brothel districts in India were reporting a rate of 55 per cent (Nath, 2000). This success earned them grant money with which they were able to further their own programme while aiding others to start them in other areas. The project is still considered a model of best practice for HIV/AIDS outreach, education, and prevention for marginalized communities.

In 1997, Durbar organized the first National Conference of Sex Workers, which was attended by 6,000 sex workers and activists from across India and beyond. During that conference, they sought to set up 'Self-Regulatory Boards' (SRBs) which oversee the industry, preventing abuse of sex workers, entry of under-age sex workers and entry of coerced workers. In 1999, the boards were officially recognized, and set up in conjunction with authorities from the Department of Social Welfare and the Women's Commission. They comprise 60 per cent sex workers and 40 per cent other community members, including lawyers, counsellors, local officials, and doctors.

The SRBs work in conjunction with the other members of Durbar, as well as with the Sathi Sangaathan (an organization of the sex workers' regular clients, or *babus*) to monitor their areas for newcomers, particularly to pick up exploitation of under-age or trafficked people. If the newcomer is neither under-age nor trafficked, they are put in contact with their local Durbar branch leaders and peer educators. Since the SRBs have been in existence, the average age of sex workers in the area has risen from 22 in 1995 to 28 in 2006, and since 1996, they have rescued over 470 women and girls who were either under-age or there against their will. SRBs have also helped in addressing grievances sex workers have had with employers (UNDP, 2003).

Even with all of their success, Durbar must still be ever vigilant as constant challenges to their effectiveness and sustainability arise: most recently in the guise of the recently proposed legislative reform of the Immoral Traffic (Prevention) Act. The continued stigmatization of sex and sex work continues to threaten the rights of sex workers in India. Nonetheless, Durbar is the single largest sex worker organization in the world, and might be seen as a model of effective practice.

Organization spotlight: Davida (Of the Life) and Rede Prostitutas Nacional (the National Prostitutes' Network), Brazil

Gabriela Leite had been a leader in organizing prostitutes' rights since one of her friends was arrested and then tortured to death by police in 1978 (Hinchberger, 2005; *Marie Claire*, 2007). She helped organize a protest with other prostitutes in the streets, and they succeeded in getting the police chief removed. This bolstered their resolve to make changes to the way society saw them. After attending a women's rights event in Rio de Janeiro at the invitation of a city council woman, she received a grant from the Progressive Institute of Religious Studies to start Davida, which was officially inaugurated in 1992. Leite attended the Second World Whores' Congress in 1986. Upon her return to Brazil, she organized the first national meeting of sex workers in 1987, which led to the formation of the National Prostitutes' Network (NPN). Today

Figure 6.2   Demonstration about indiscriminate rescues and raids of sex workers. Organized by the voluntary organization Sangram, Maharashtra, India. www. sangram.org/

that network comprises over 30 organizations with 20,000 members throughout Brazil (*Marie Claire*, 2007).

Davida and the NPN originally found themselves most concerned with police violence against prostitutes, and only took a more activist approach to HIV/AIDS as an organizing priority after meeting with the government in 1989. Since that meeting, sex workers across the nation have been integral to Brazil's internationally-acclaimed HIV/AIDS prevention programme. The extent of their partnership became world-renowned when the government of Brazil consulted with them on whether or not to not accept a US$40 million grant from the USA to fight HIV/AIDS in 2004. The grant came with a catch: Brazil would have to sign the anti-prostitution oath and denounce prostitution as degrading to women. Together, the government and the sex workers agreed that the risks to HIV out-reach and the further marginalization and stigmatization of sex workers was too great a risk to their programme, which had been one of the most successful globally, and they turned down the US funding. HIV infection rates remain half of what they were predicted to be ten years ago by the World Bank (Hinchberger, 2005).

The refusal of the US money caused the NPN to suffer a deficit in funding which inspired them to think of new ways to garner money for their projects. The result was Davida's Daspu, a clothing line designed, made and modelled by the prostitutes. 'Daspu' is a play on 'Daslu', which is the name of one of the most upscale boutiques in Brazil, and is also short for 'Das Putas', or 'of the whores'. Their launch took place during Rio Fashion Week in 2005, but rather than an upmarket venue, they debuted in the less-glamorous shadows of the *favela* (shantytown). The newspaper the following day featured Jane Eloy's photo (a Daspu prostitute model) right next to that of Gisele Bündchen (a world-famous supermodel). That media coverage in conjunction with a lawsuit brought on them by Daslu's CEO thrust them into both the national and global spotlight. The lawsuit was eventually dropped, and Daspu now serves as a point of pride and unity for Brazilian sex workers.

Unionization

Official unionization has been a recent phenomenon (since the 1990s), particularly, but not exclusively, in localities where the rights of sex workers have been recognized. The idea that women and men, who are voluntarily engaged in selling sexual services (both direct and indirect), are selling sexual, emotional and erotic labour has been translated into a social movement that has found support through official unionization. One of the first examples comes from New South Wales in Australia in 1996. Prostitutes formed the first union for sex workers after the government decriminalized prostitution. The Australian Liquor, Hospitality, and Miscellaneous Workers' Union accepted them after much groundwork was laid by unionist Ruth Frenzel and prostitutes' rights activist Maryann Phoenix (Walsh, 1996).

Some of the most successful organizing of sex worker rights can be found amongst exotic dancers. Fischer (1996) documents how the struggle for dancers to have their rights recognized as workers found expression in the Exotic Dancers Alliance. Chun (1999) describes the tensions between the prohibitionist stance that sex workers are exploited through the commodification of their bodies with the increasing union activities of dancers who find access to empowerment and a collective voice (see Kempadoo, 1998). Sex workers who are engaged in the legal sex industry and the wider adult entertainment industry have found more success in campaigning for better working conditions and labour rights.

Gall (2007) documents how sex workers have achieved unionization in seven countries: the UK, Germany, the Netherlands, Australia, New Zealand, Canada and the USA. The formation of unions from the sex worker rights movement symbolized a shift from civil and political rights to more specific and pragmatic focus on economic and worker rights. Gall (2007: 78) charts how sex workers have become unionized through a series of six conceptual shifts:

1 A transition from 'self-help' to 'self-activity' in the workplace.
2 Sex workers are the source of change and not advocates or allies.

3   Recognition for the need to move beyond civil and human rights but to instead pursue worker and union rights.
4   Focus on improving terms and conditions at work.
5   Engaging in union activities and behaviours.
6   Utilizing the discourse from the sex workers' rights movements to campaign for dignity, justice and respect.

From surveying the many different types of unions that have developed in the seven countries, Gall (2007: 79) categorizes the different concerns and what he calls 'grievances' from sex workers regarding their working environments and types of sex work:

- *Brothel or parlour and escort agency workers*: Charges for working (fees); 'tools of the trade' such as linen, sexual aids, condoms and lubricants, food and drinks; mandatory tips to staff; determination of client charges; discipline and monitoring; personal safety; health and safety; working conditions; job insecurity victimization.
- *Independent prostitutes*: Personal safety; police harassment; the right to run an 'immoral business'; the use of business cards; compulsory health testing; availability of health services.
- *Exotic dancers*: Fees for working; fines and charges; pay rates; working conditions concerning dressing rooms; nature of interaction with customers.
- *Sex chatline workers*: Unilateral management setting and monitoring of performance targets; inability to refuse calls; lack of training and advice on how to handle customers; poor pay and benefits.
- *Porn actors and actresses*: HIV/AIDS and STI health testing and medical insurance issues; long working hours; low pay rates.

The International Union of Sex Workers

The global nature of the sex industry and the sex worker rights movement has lent itself to the internationalization of this early unionization process. This has been aided by global communications and the frequent use of the Internet and other computer-mediated communication that has enabled organizing to exist beyond country boundaries. The international flavour of the organizing also has a political motivation. The setting up of one union to represent sex workers under a global umbrella highlights, that despite country, legal and cultural differences and diversity, sex workers experience a common set of negative treatments and discriminations across the world. Internationalization of the unionization movement demonstrates the common features of stigma, marginalization, exclusion, violence and a lack of workers' rights.

These common experiences gave rise to the creation of the International Union of Sex Workers in 2000 as a grassroots organization formed in Soho, London (Clamen and Lopes, 2003). The main tenets of the campaign were for decriminalization, full labour rights and the ultimate aim to join a trade union (Lopes, 2001). Although the IUSW is based in London, Gall (2006: 156) notes how solidarity across borders is the essence of the union: 'The IUSW has sought not merely to reflect the international nature of the sex work and sex workers but also to become an agency for the protection and advancement of sex workers' collective interests on an international basis'.

Internationalization of a union is a tactical approach to campaigning for labour rights; human rights; gender-specific issues such as sexual harassment; as well as providing a platform to engage in, respond to and shape public, social and criminal justice policy.

In 2002, the IUSW formed a branch of the municipal workers' union, the GMB, in London and began to establish contractual rights for sex workers (particularly those who worked in lap dancing venues), and health and safety rights (Lopes, 2006). Lopes documents the successes such as a code of conduct in table dancing clubs for workers, managers and clients; greater contractual rights (women work as independent contractors); and disciplinary and grievance procedures. There are some very practical examples of the work that the IUSW has done to assist sex workers. For example the x:talk project offers free English language lessons to female, male and transgendered sex workers.[7] Under the slogan 'open, organise, empower', the project offers seven different languages and specifically aims to give language skills to sex workers so they can become empowered with clients and employers in the work setting. The IUSW are a key lobbying organization in the UK, and have also won the first ever 'unfair dismissal' case in the sex industry.

Barriers to effective unionization

The rise of a sex workers' rights movement and unionization in some countries is a significant step towards recognizing the rights of those involved in the sex industry. However, Gall (2007: 81) notes that of the seven countries where unionization exists, membership can be estimated at approximately 5,000 people. There are considerable barriers to effective organization and the influences of unions once they have formed (see West, 2000). If unions were to be judged on their outcomes such as radical law reform, public tolerance, de-stigmatization or improvements to working conditions, then several evaluations demonstrate their limited effects (Mathieu, 2003; Poel, 1995; Weitzer, 2000; West, 2000). Despite the significant milestone of becoming part of an official union, there is still progress to be made before distinguishing the IUSW and other unionization activities related to sex work as a strong and influential collective. One of the significant reasons for the limited effects is that the relationship between sex workers and those who manage establishments, which could be considered the employer–employee relationship, is different in nature and law from those relationships that are normally reflected in union organization. In this regard, unionization is more tenuous because the relationship is less defined. Given moves towards an increase in criminalization in the UK, and the refusal to acknowledge sex as work for some people involved in prostitution, the struggle to get workers' rights recognized continues to be a difficult and frustrating one.

Some of these barriers are for straightforward resource reasons. Local activists often become national leaders and the burden of organizing, raising funds and encouraging subscription can fall on a few. Gaining a critical mass of actual supporters through subscription membership may be more difficult amongst sex workers who are faced with concerns over secrecy and anonymity. Also, those who are able to join unions and become official members are not representative of the whole sex industry (West, 2000). Only certain markets are open to formal organization, reflecting the social hierarchy amongst sex markets. For instance, some who work on the street do not have access to the same resources, education levels and social skills that sex workers who come from more advantaged class, education and economic positions can draw upon. Also, Gall (2007: 81) points out that as independent contractors, individual rather than collective responsibility is emphasized and in a competitive market where colleagues are in direct financial rivalry, there is less incentive for collaboration. Hence, Gall (2007: 84) concludes that there are significant 'obstacles to collectivism and solidarity in terms of both consciousness raising and organising.'

The Struggle for Sex Workers' Rights

The weaknesses of sex workers' organizing stem from unrepresentative membership; the problematic relationship that a rights-based perspective has with branches of feminism which aim to eradicate prostitution because of a belief that it is violence against all women; and the practical resource demands such as time, facilities, and funds. There are more philosophical doubts regarding the scope and influence of sex worker rights movements and sex workers gaining legitimate recognition and rights by becoming unionized. While focusing on the relationship of female sex workers to their 'employment' status, O'Connell Davidson (1998) puts forward the argument that the prospects for collective action for sex workers are deeply problematic due to inherent contradictions in gendered power relationships between prostitutes, men who buy sex and the people who manage the sex industry. In addition, systematic inequalities based on gender, race and ethnicity which are at the centre of capitalism mean that sex workers will always be stigmatized. Nevertheless, evidence from the IUSW and other organizations, in both resource-rich countries and developing parts of the world, suggest that collectives can make local changes as well as gain solidarity at an international level to provide a strong voice to resist harms and injustices. Never before have there been as many rights-based sex worker groups and this suggests that a social movement has begun which may take time to grow but has powerful grassroots origins.

Notes

1 **Susan Lopez-Embury** is a sex workers' rights advocate and freelance researcher, currently in collaboration on a project with the Sociology Department at the University of Nevada, Las Vegas. She received her BA from UC Berkeley in Peace and Conflict Studies, and her MSc in Social Policy and Planning in Developing Countries from the London School of Economics, where she conducted extensive research into global groups of sex workers organizing for their rights. A former exotic dancer of 15 years, in 39 cities around the world, Susan co-founded the nonprofit organization Desiree Alliance and presently serves as its assistant director. In this capacity, she helps each year to organize the Alliance's national conference, which creates space for dialogue and knowledge-sharing between hundreds of sex workers, service providers, academics, and allies across the United States. She is also founder and director of the Sex Workers Outreach Project, Las Vegas, where she

works with local sex workers to address their needs in terms of safety and community. In her free time, Susan writes articles about and speaks publicly on sex work.

2 International Committee for Prostitutes' Rights (ICPR), Amsterdam 1985, quoted in Pheterson (1989: 40).
3 This is distinct from the UK Network of Sex Work Projects discussed in Chapter 8.
4 The Report of the Prostitution Law Review Committee in the Operation of the Prostitution Reform Act 2003 can be found at: www.justice.govt.nz/prostitution-law-review-committee/publications/plrc-report/index.html
5 www.sexworkeurope.org/site/index.php?option=com_content&task=view &id=35&Itemid=77
6 www.exoticdancerscanada.com/
7 www.xtalkproject.net/

Suggested Reading

Gall, G. (2007) 'Sex worker unionisation: an exploratory study of emerging collective organisation', *Industrial Relations Journal*, 38(1): 70–88.
Kempadoo, K. and Doezema, J. (1998) *Global Sex Workers*, London: Routledge.
Lopes, A. (2006) 'Sex workers and the labour movement in the UK', in R. Campbell and M. O'Neill (eds), *Sex Work Now*, Cullompton: Willan.
Nagel, J. (1997) *Whores and Other Feminists*, London: Routledge.
Pheterson, G. (ed.) (1989) *A Vindication of the Rights of Whores*, Seattle: Seal.

Weblinks

Beijo Da Rua (E-zine for Davida and Rede Prostitutas Nacional): www.beijodarua.com.br
Desiree Alliance: www.desireealliance.org
Durbar: www.durbar.org
Global Sex Worker Organizations: www.desireealliance.org/resources/regional_organizations.htm
International Union of Sex Workers: www.iusw.com
Scarlet Alliance: www.scarletalliance.org.au
SWOP-USA: www.swop-usa.org

Study Questions

Level one

- What are some of the challenges that all sex workers experience globally?

Level two

- Why has unionization happened and what are the benefits?

Level three

- Why are sex workers' rights human rights?

7

CRIME, JUSTICE AND THE
SEX INDUSTRY

This chapter examines the legal and socio-cultural dimensions of the sex industry within which the 'problem' of prostitution, as a crime against morality, is organized, perceived and regulated. The cultural context and social construction of 'the prostitute' form the backdrop for the legal models of control. It also examines the shift from enforcement to 'welfarist' models of social control and the current politics of prostitution reform. These key themes need to be contextualized within a broader understanding of globalization, the global sex trade, Europeanization and current social policy and prostitution reform, in order to analyse crime, justice and the sex industry in the twenty-first century. The final discussion focuses on the UK policy context where criminalization has become the method of regulation for female prostitution, whereas male sex work is largely ignored.

────────── **History Repeats Itself[1]: The Making of an Outcast Group** ──────────

As discussed in Chapter 1, the history of prostitution is framed by attempts to repress and make morally reprehensible the women and men involved in prostitution, while aestheticizing the desires and fantasies associated with the 'prostitute' woman. In ancient Greek society there were varying forms of prostitution, from temple prostitutes to brothel slaves. Temple prostitutes and courtesans achieved a certain level of autonomy, education and status (Henriques, 1962; Roberts, 1992), yet they were regulated by codes of dress that distinguished them from 'respectable' women. The medieval brothel was recognized as a 'necessary evil'. Quoting theologian Augustine, Mazo-Karras (1989: 399) stated 'remove prostitution from human affairs and you will destroy everything with lust'. Women's sexuality, immorality, love of ornament and shrewishness were common themes of medieval sermons. In iconography of sinfulness, lust is represented as a woman (Mazo-Karras, 1989: 400). In 1198, Pope Innocent III urged Christians to rescue whores and subsequently Magdalene homes sprung up across Europe which were monastic communities. Mazo-Karras writes that prostitution was one of a range of options available to women not able to marry for lack of dowries, sex ratios or because there were too few labour opportunities following a rise in the population after the Black Death in 1348. Prostitution in medieval times was tolerated, institutionalized and taxed.

The growth of Christianity and Protestantism contrasted the ideal of the good wife and mother with the bad girl and sinner and in Victorian times ideals of social purity and morality contrasted with dire economic poverty for working-class and lower-class women involved in growing sex for sale markets predominantly in the cities (Kishtainy, 1982; Walkowitz, 1989). The effects of Victorian morality and the social purity movement, together with the social organization of gender relations, have in Britain created a legacy, enshrined in law by the Wolfenden Report (see below) and subsequent sexual and street offences legislation. Indeed, the social attitudes and values established during the nineteenth-century Victorian period created the framework in which the problem of prostitution as a crime against morality is organized, perceived and regulated today.

The Victorian period led to a particular focus on regulating the bodies of working-class women and the spaces they worked – prostitution was perceived as 'The Great Social Evil' (Diduck and Wilson, 1997). Indeed, the problem of prostitution is understood by the state as a problem relating to the women involved and so prostitution is dealt with by regulating women and their bodies. In the *History of Sexuality* (1979), Foucault documents how the outlawing of male homosexual prostitution and increasing representation of prostitution as predominantly a relation between male purchasers and female providers led to a focus on prostitution as a problem of women.

Drawing upon Foucault, Alain Corbin's (1990) analysis of commercial sex in nineteenth-century France describes how the inter-related discourses of municipal authorities, hygienists (those who carried out medical examinations), the police and the judiciary combined to organize the regulation of prostitution and the objectification of the prostitute around three major social needs: to protect public morality; to protect male prosperity; and to protect the nation's health from sexually transmitted diseases, as the prostitute was perceived as an active agent for the transmission of disease. For Corbin, these three social needs are expressed in five key images of the prostitute:

1 The prostitute as *putain* (French for 'whore') 'whose body smells bad'.
2 The prostitute as the safety valve which 'enables the social body to excrete the seminal fluid that causes her stench and rots her'.
3 The body of the prostitute is symbolically associated with the corpse, with death and decay.
4 Associated with disease, particularly syphilis.
5 The prostitute as a submissive female body 'bound to the instinctive physical needs of upper class males'.

These images reinforce the ambiguous status of the female sex worker as 'at once menace and remedy, agent of putrefaction and drain ... at the beck and call of the bourgeois body' (1990: 212–13). Corbin goes on to show how these discourses and images led to a series of principles that structure the regulation of prostitution and the bodies of prostitutes up to the present day: the principle of tolerance; the principle of containment; and the principle of surveillance (contain, conceal and keep under continual surveillance).

The first task of regulation is to bring the prostitute out of the foul darkness and remove her from the clandestine swarming of vice, in order to drive her back into an enclosed space, under the purifying light of power. (Corbin, 1990: 215)

Consistently, street prostitution has been aligned with vice, crime and disorder, with images of moral and physical contagion prolific in the eighteenth and nineteenth centuries (Walkowitz, 1992). Although prostitution was not illegal in the 1800s, the Vagrancy Act 1824 was applied to arrest women from the street for disorderly conduct. These same discourses of 'unruly' and 'uncontrollable' dangerous women are echoed in the twenty-first century through the increasing use of anti-social behaviour legislation and mechanisms to control and contain sex workers (Sagar, 2007).

The Contagious Diseases Acts

One of the important milestones in the social construction of 'the prostitute body' occurred in the mid-nineteenth century. Three Contagious Diseases Acts were passed in the 1860s (1864, 1866, 1869) that enabled the police and the medical profession to force women to undergo a medical inspection and, if found positive, they could be detained against their will in a Lock hospital for up to three months (Self, 2003: 41). Judith Walkowitz (1980) writes that working-class prostitutes were subject to a police and medical registration system established under the Contagious Diseases Acts (passed to stem the spread of sexually transmitted diseases in garrison towns and ports). If the woman refused, then she could be imprisoned for three months with hard labour. There were military reasons for the urgency of this legislation that included concerns about the 'natural' use of prostitutes by soldiers abroad in the British Empire and the men contracting venereal diseases. These 'nation-state' concerns about the strength of the military were used to justify the criminalization of women through medical incarceration in Lock hospitals.

These Acts were, for Walkowitz (1977), linked to the regulation and surveillance of the urban poor and the regulation and ordering of public space. So the Acts were a sanitary measure, but their reach extended beyond this to the surveillance of the neighbourhoods in which women lived: 'The Contagious Diseases Acts were part of the institutional and legal efforts to contain ... occupational and geographical mobility [and] an attempt to clarify the relationship between the unrespectable and respectable poor' (1977: 72). The most common trope for prostitution at this time was via symbols of vagrancy, immorality and disease.

In her historical analysis, Walkowitz found that rural poverty, migration patterns, the growth of cities, urban areas and casual labour, low wages and 'lay-offs' combined to compel women to sell sex. Women perceived their prostitution activity as casual and temporary with the average age of registered women being 20–23 years; women moved on to marriage or common law relationships and domestic life. However, the Acts forced them to accept their status as public women, as 'just' prostitutes. For Walkowitz (1980), as long as selling sex is temporary or casual, the woman is not labelled nor are her future choices. The Acts served to fix her identity as a 'prostitute' and thus destroyed the chance to reintegrate with urban poor.

These Acts were repealed in 1886 after various groups campaigned about the unfair treatment of women and the forced medical examinations written into law. Josephine Butler was pivotal in leading these campaigns that spoke out against the condemnation of women and the lack of attention to men in the public health debate. Self writes:

> The eventual repeal of the Acts came about, not so much as a result of the campaign against the medical examination and registration of women, which dominated the initial debate, but in response to the investigative journalism of W. T. Stead, whose salacious articles in the *Pall Mall Gazette* were filled with lurid details of the violation and trafficking of children. Only the briefest glance at the original articles is needed to establish this fact, as they are scattered with emotive drawings of small children with adult men. Consequently, the public pressure which finally ensured the passage of the CLA Bill 1885 came about, not because the public cared about the fate of poor women, but because the middle classes feared for the safety of their respectable daughters. (2003: 4)

Laite (2008) notes how in the late nineteenth century and at the beginning of the twentieth century, medical discourses were the mechanism through which prostitution was criminalized. There were two dominant discourses prevalent that attempted to do something about prostitution: the social purity movement which attempted to 'rescue and reform' (Laite, 2008: 209); and then later the social hygiene movement at the time of the First World War. At this later time, concerns were that the promiscuity of prostitutes (note, not that of the soldiers) would spread venereal disease (namely syphilis). The desire for medical practicality as well moral standards was used as justification for using the law against women in the sex industry (Bartley, 2000). Although there were some welfare and religious-based groups who professed they were trying to assist women to a 'better' life, these campaigns kept up the momentum of the social construction of 'the prostitute body' as a contagious, immoral and deviant aversion to femaleness. This historical backdrop had a significant impact on what happened in the twentieth century regarding prostitution laws. Self (2003: 9) argues that the Wolfenden Report (1957) and its recommendations, which resulted in the Street Offences Act 1959, 'strengthened the impact of a law which incorporated the "common prostitute" as a member of a legally defined group of women and placed a judicial stamp of approval on [the type of] social stigmatisation'.

The legal regulation of prostitution (see Table 7.1) has therefore specifically targeted the women who sell sex and it was during the Victorian period in particular that we find the category 'prostitute' was attached to a woman's identity as a fixed (not temporal) category through the enforcement of legislation – what she did became who she was (O'Neill, 2001; Walkowitz, 1980).

Post-war Britain and prostitution reform

In the post-war period, a departmental committee chaired by John Wolfenden was set up to examine homosexuality and prostitution at the request of the Secretary of State for the Home Office, Sir David Maxwell Fyfe, who was 'concerned that London streets gave a

Table 7.1   The legal regulation of prostitution in Victorian England

Date	Regulation
1824	In the Vagrancy Act 1824, the term 'common prostitute' was first introduced into statutory law (Self, 2003). The Act made it an offence to sleep on the streets or beg. 'Powers to penalize anyone acting in a "riotous and indecent manner" were used by the police to watch, charge, and prosecute women on the streets' (Edwards, 1997: 58).
1839	The Metropolitan Police Act made loitering an offence in London. This was extended to towns/cities outside of London in the 1847 Town Police Clauses Act.
1864	Contagious Diseases Act introduced the compulsory medical examination of prostitute women in 11 naval ports and garrison towns.
1866	Contagious Diseases Act. Extended police powers and introduced (following French system) registration and fortnightly inspection.
1869	Contagious Diseases Act. Extended the number of towns where the Act was in force. Walkowitz states that this became a systematic measure for the surveillance of the working-class through the policing of working women in any place where 'public women' may congregate – pubs, beer shops, music halls, fairs, common lodging houses, residential areas.
1872	Parliament suspended the Acts and repealed them three years later.
1885	Criminal Law Amendment Act – the age of consent was raised from 13 to 16.

deplorable impression of British immorality to foreign visitors' (Self, 2004: 3). In 1957, an influential document was produced entitled *Report of the Committee on Homosexual Offences and Prostitution* but became commonly known as the Wolfenden Report. Maxwell Fyfe wanted women off the streets and into 'call girl flats'. The Wolfenden Report was (until the recent Home Office *Coordinated Prostitution Strategy)* 'the main reference point for post-war legislation on prostitution and related offences in Britain ... it attempted to bring the existing disparate body of legislation into a new synthesis' (Matthews, 2003: 491). The Wolfenden Report heralded the following changes:

- It applied a more rigid distinction between law and morality ... claiming that however 'immoral' prostitution was, it was not the law's business.
- It also rationalized resources directed towards the control of prostitution while increasing the certainty of convictions.
- It encouraged a more systematic policing of the public sphere in order to remove visible manifestations in London and other urban centres (Matthews, 2003: 492).

Thus, according to Wolfenden, the law was concerned only with 'the manner in which the activities of prostitutes and those associated with them offend against public order and decency, expose the ordinary citizen to what is offensive and injurious, or involve the exploitation of others' (Wolfenden, 1957: 80). The formal need to prove annoyance was removed and a cautioning system was introduced:

> Through this system the women entered the court as a 'common prostitute' whose guilt was assumed in advance and who could be safely convicted on police evidence alone. In this way the offender was never in a position to challenge the (double) moral standard on which the legislation was constructed, which in turn reinforced the claim that the law was not concerned with private morality. (Matthews, 2003: 492)

Given this historical context, criminological/sociological theories explain involvement in prostitution as being related to sub-culture (Phoenix, 1999); dislocation and drift (Wilkinson, 1955); economic need and poverty (McLeod, 1982); or feminist responses that argue sex is deeply implicated in structures of inequality through the class structure especially for working-class/underclass communities, the state and the regulation of the body and/or marked by violence and oppression (O'Connell Davidson, 1998; O'Neill, 2001). These theories are further discussed in Chapter 1.

Drawing on the historical literature, we can say that in current times prostitution is tied to the history and social organization of sexuality, gender relations, and capitalist exchange relations. It is, on the one hand, a taken-for-granted aspect of urban life, based on economic need and a desire for sexual pleasure and experimentation – albeit, for many, an unwelcome 'social problem'. On the other hand, it is seen as largely a problem of women and of women's immorality – thus until recently (with the introduction of kerb-crawling legislation in 1985 and the Sexual Offences Act 2003) it is women who are regulated and controlled. As Walkowitz identifies in her social history of prostitution in Victorian England, the police and medical registration system under the Contagious Diseases Acts combined to label poor women and facilitate 'their ultimate isolation from the community of the labouring poor marked an important formative stage in the making of an outcast group' (Walkowitz, 1977: 93).

This legacy of prosecuting the woman and not her client carved out by the Wolfenden Report (1957), the Sexual Offences Act 1956 and the Street Offences Act 1959 is shifting in the UK, especially as policy-makers and advisers look to the Swedish model that criminalizes the clients of sex workers for buying sex (see Chapter 5). Before examining the policing of prostitution, contrasting modes of regulation across Europe and current Home Office policy, a summary of the key legislation is provided.

A Summary of UK Legislation

Currently selling sex is not criminalized in Britain, and is regarded as a private transaction conducted between two consenting adults. However, there are many pieces of legislation that seek to regulate and 'limit certain undesirable effects of prostitution while maintaining low levels of criminalisation' (Matthews and O'Neill, 2003: xvii). In practice, this creates a paradoxical situation where, although prostitution may not be illegal, it is impossible for women or men to sell sex without breaking a number of laws in the performance of their work. For instance, street sex workers routinely commit the offence of soliciting in public or quasi-public spaces (under the terms of the Street Offences Act 1959 and Civic Government (Scotland) Act 1982) while their clients may be arrested for kerb-crawling (under the terms of the Sexual Offences Act 1985 and Criminal Justice and Police Act 2001). Placing advertisements for sexual services in a public place and conducting sexual practices in public view are also illegal. Yet these laws are enforced selectively and inconsistently by the police, who have favoured a form of regulation whereby sex work is spatially contained and informally tolerated so long as public complaints or political priorities do not demand a 'Zero Tolerance' crackdown (Matthews, 2005). However, in instances where the authorities are able to identify individual sex workers or their clients as causing persistent annoyance to communities, they may be served with Anti-Social Behaviour Orders (ASBOs), Criminal Anti-Social Behaviour Orders (CRASBOs)[2] or injunctions. It has been documented how these new civil orders which quickly turn to criminal sanctions where a breach of conditions occurs, are a quick route to criminalizing sex workers and not improving conditions for communities or individuals (Sagar, 2007). Such orders are becoming widespread, and make it impossible for some individuals to sell sex without breaching an order, and hence becoming liable for arrest and imprisonment. Table 7.2 outlines the main legislation currently relating specifically to street sex work in England, Wales and Scotland.[3]

Table 7.2   Key legislation pertaining to street sex work, England, Wales and Scotland

Offence	Act	Maximum penalty
England and Wales		
Soliciting or loitering for purposes of prostitution	Street Offences Act 1959	A fine
Causing or inciting prostitution for gain	Sexual Offences Act 1956; Sexual Offences Act 2003	Six months or fine (magistrates' court) to seven years (Crown Court)
Kerb-crawling (with persistence and in a manner likely to cause annoyance)	Sexual Offences Act 1985; Criminal Justice and Police Act 2001; Sexual Offences Act 2003	Arrestable offence; seizure of vehicle or driving ban
Anti-social behaviour	Crime and Disorder Act 1998	Serving of ASBO, with up to 6 months' imprisonment for breach
Scotland		
Any person loitering, soliciting or importuning in a public place for purposes of prostitution	Civic Government (Scotland) Act 1982 s.46	On summary conviction a fine not exceeding £50
Men soliciting or importuning for immoral purposes	Sexual Offences Act 1976 s.12(1)(b)	Summary conviction six months imprisonment or on indictment two years
Men persistently soliciting or importuning in a public place	Criminal Law Amendment (Scotland) Act 1995 s.11(1)(b)	As above
Anti-social behaviour	Antisocial Behaviour, etc. (Scotland) Act 2004 s.4 and s.7 (repeals section 19 of Crime and Disorder Act 1998)	Serving of ASBO (s.4) or Interim ASBO (s.7), breach of which results in on summary conviction 6 months' imprisonment or a fine not exceeding the statutory maximum or both and on indictment to 5 years imprisonment or a fine or both

This national regulatory framework is regarded as flawed by many commentators. One example of this is in the increasing use of Anti-Social Behaviour legislation (and ASBOs) to prevent kerb-crawling and soliciting, even though laws exist which are intended to deal with any nuisances caused by these activities. ASBOs may be served which prevent women from working in particular areas, or even selling sex anywhere in the UK. Breach of ASBO conditions may result in a prison sentence, despite the fact that selling sex is no longer an imprisonable offence and has not been so since 1983. In many instances, the conditions attached to ASBOs work against the aims of support groups (see Chapter 8) providing health and exiting advice to working women.

Acknowledging the outdated legislation and even the contradictory nature of the laws in relation to prostitution, both the Scottish Executive and the Home Office (governing England and Wales) began a legislative review in 2004. The aim was to prompt a public debate on how to deal with the issues raised and to develop a co-ordinated strategy. The Home Office published its response to the review of legislation and policy, *Paying the Price: A Consultation on Prostitution*, in 2004 along with an outline for a strategy 'aimed at reducing the harms associated with prostitution, experienced by those involved and by those communities in which it takes place'. This review considered the case for stricter enforcement of existing legislation as well as selective decriminalization of street sex work, keeping a wide range of options open. Concurrently, the Scottish Executive conducted a similar consultation and produced *Being Outside: Constructing a Response to Street Prostitution*, which 'reviews the legal, policing, health and social justice issues surrounding street prostitution in Scotland and to consider options for the future' (Scottish Executive, 2005). Additionally, two further pieces of government-funded research shaped government and policy responses to street sex work: *Tackling Street Prostitution: Towards an Holistic Approach* (Hester and Westmarland, 2004) and *Solutions and Strategies: Drug Problems and Street Sex Markets* (Hunter and May, 2004). Table 7.3 summarizes the key legislation and policy.

Policing: From Enforcement to Multi-agency Responses

From the Victorian era onwards the police have enforced the laws surrounding prostitution within a context of policing both public spaces and female sex workers. In the 1970s and 1980s, vice squads emerged that dealt with 'vice' related crimes – prostitution, sexual offences, and paedophilia. Benson and Matthews conducted a survey of vice squads in 1994 and again in 2004. They found that in 2004 many of the vice squads had been disbanded and that there had been a shift to more localized and generalized policing responses; and a shift from a police-centred approach (dealing with enforcing the law) to a broader welfarist strategy that included other agencies. Vice squads disbanded in Cardiff, Liverpool, Manchester, Luton, Leicester and other areas. In Liverpool, vice and drugs squads disbanded and a centralized incident unit was established. Responsibility for prostitution shifted to neighbourhoods – the aim being to link police responses to local

Table 7.3   Summary of contemporary key legislation and policy

Legislation

- Sexual Offences Acts 1956 – illegal to live off immoral earnings
- Street Offences Act 1959 – outlaws soliciting in public
- Sexual Offences Act 1985 – power of arrest for kerb-crawlers
- Section 1 of the Crime and Disorder Act 1998 – serving of ASBOs
- Police Reform Act 2002 – formalized use of ASBOs
- Sexual Offences Acts 2003 introduced new trafficking legislation and legislation relating to the sexual exploitation of children[i]

Policy review

- Home Office review of sexual offences legislation – *Setting the Boundaries* (2000)
- Home Office and Scottish Executive review of prostitution policy (2003–4)
- Home Office *Paying the Price: A Consultation on Prostitution* (2004)
- Home Office *Coordinated Prostitution Strategy* (2006)
- Home Office *Review of Tackling Demand* (2008)

Note: [i]The Sexual Offences Act 2003 introduced specific legislation for dealing with the commercial sexual exploitation of children. This covers children of both sexes aged under 18 years and includes:

- Paying for the sexual services of a child under 18 years: penalty 7 years' to life imprisonment depending on type of sexual act and age of the child.
- Causing or inciting a child to become a prostitute or to be used for pornography: up to 14 years' imprisonment and/or an unlimited fine.
- Controlling the activities of a child in prostitution or pornography: up to 14 years' imprisonment and/or an unlimited fine.
- Arranging or facilitating the prostitution of a child or the use of a child in pornography: up to 14 years' imprisonment and/or an unlimited fine.

concerns. In Manchester, police liaison officers worked with relevant agencies, street prostitutes, and local police. Thus there was a change in styles of policing that reflected changing priorities as well as the fact that the allocation of policing resources was tied to performance indicators and government targets. A decrease both in the public visibility of prostitution and in public complaints meant a shift in priorities.

However, this shift from enforcement to welfarist policing was also a response to campaigns and complaints by residents who wanted street sex work removed from their neighbourhoods and campaigns from researchers and law reformers calling for an end to the anomalies, contradictions and loopholes in the laws surrounding prostitution. Examples of these anomalies include the fact that a woman is labelled a 'common prostitute' after two cautions and a 'common prostitute' refers only to a woman. Three amendment bills failed to remove 'common prostitute' in 1967, 1969 and 1990 (Edwards, 1998: 61–2).

Prior to the Sexual Offences Act 2003, having sex with an under-age girl was illegal yet a girl of over 13 or a boy of over 10 could be prosecuted for soliciting (Diduck and Wilson, 1997). The maximum sentence was seven years' imprisonment for having sex with a girl under the age of 13 years, yet if the girl is over 13 but under 16 the maximum sentence was 2 years' imprisonment. This was totally at odds with the Children Act 1989 where a child is defined as anyone under 18 years, as well as relevant European and international instruments. So alongside a growth in multi-agency responses to street sex work, we also saw a growth in multi-agency policing, working in partnership with other agencies, including welfare agencies, to address the multi-faceted issues of street sex work. At this time policy-oriented research was also commissioned that supported multi-agency responses.[4]

Ideological Constructions of Sex as Crime

What is clear from criminological and sociological work in this area is that differing ideological constructions of prostitution will have an effect on shaping law and policy and thus justice. Enforcing the law has everything to do with the way that the law is interpreted by police officers, front-line workers and by the courts and Crown Prosecution Service. Whether the focus is upon women, men, children and young people, kerb-crawling or trafficking, the social meanings which underpin or can be 'read off' the written law need to be uncovered to understand the relationships between crime, justice and the sex industry and towards any attempt at law reform. As Edwards states, 'the current schism between prostitution as sex and a matter of privacy and prostitution as a crime marked by exploitation will shape the climate in which the reconstruction of legal prostitution will take shape in Europe' (1998: 67).

Indeed, Scoular and O'Neill (2007) argue that the move from enforcement towards multi-agency interventions can be explained by reference not only to shifting police imperatives and the opening up of welfarist responses, but also, crucially, to changes in governance that involve 'the move away from coordination through hierarchy or competition and towards network-based forms of coordination' (Newman, 2003: 16). Increasingly termed 'progressive governance', these new arrangements, while appearing to devolve power to partnerships (such as local area partnerships and multi-agency fora), upon closer examination reveal more expansive forms of control.

In *The Culture of Control* (2001), Garland identifies two dominant approaches to the way in which governments act on crime: a re-emphasis on punitive exclusionary forms of punishment (e.g. 'criminology of the other': a focus on exclusion through zero tolerance, punitive segregation and exclusion through anti-social behaviour orders) alongside what he describes as the development of 'adaptive responses' which feature a greater rationalization, commercialization and devolution of criminal justice functions. Such adaptive responses utilize 'local' resources in 'preventative partnerships' which feature a range of multi-agency and community actors including 'the criminal as rational actor' who is increasingly brought into programmes of self-governance via, for example, cognitive behavioural techniques, desistance programmes and, as Scoular and O'Neill (2007) outline, programmes of role exit such as those proposed in the Home Office strategy document.

Within a ten year period between their surveys (1994–2004), Benson and Matthews found that a shift had taken place from enforcement to welfarist policing responses and, in part, an acknowledgement of the contradictions in existing legislation. This changing legal context has seen the introduction of the Sexual Offences

Act 2003[5] as 'the first major reform for over a hundred years' (Self, 2004: 1) with a strong focus on preventing the sexual exploitation of young people involved or at risk of involvement in prostitution and upon trafficking for the purposes of prostitution (see Chapter 4). The Act also defines prostitution offences as gender-neutral although the policing of the laws is usually against women.

Informed by *Paying the Price*, the 2006 Home Office *Coordinated Prostitution Strategy* and key policy documents mentioned in Table 7.3, the New Labour government promoted a zero tolerance approach to street sex work with an emphasis upon responsibilizing and rehabilitating street sex workers away from a life of sex and sin. In 2003, David Blunkett called for a 'new' moral framework to protect communities and 'save' women and children from the evils of what is now to be termed 'commercial sexual exploitation':

> We now have practical experience of what works so we can reach out and protect those trapped on prostitution and offer them exit routes ... We in this century must do what Josephine Butler attempted over 100 years ago, in a very different era and in a very different way. (Home Secretary, Home Office Press Release, 27 June 2003)

We are reminded of Helen Self's notion of 'history repeating itself' with shades of the campaign for social purity and the rescuing of fallen women from the great social evil led by Josephine Butler and the social purity alliance. At the same time there has been a rise in discourses that focus upon trafficking as a problem of prostitution linking organized crime to the commercial sex industry (Kantola and Squires, 2004).

The Home Office strategy tells us that prostitution is 'commercial sexual exploitation' and the strategy seeks to address this issue by: tackling demand via 'disrupting the market' and 'deterring punters'; focusing on routes out and prevention of involvement; and ensuring justice, by strengthening and enforcing the law against those who exploit and abuse women, young people and children. Moreover the strategy suggests tolerating off-street prostitution where two or three women are working together in the interests of their safety, and targeting sexual exploitation of trafficking 'victims'. The UK Human Trafficking Centre opened in Sheffield and a UK action plan on trafficking was published in March 2007 (www.ukhtc.org).

In summary, the Home Office strategy focuses upon partnership approaches to dealing with prostitution as a social problem and a crime in order to protect communities where street sex work takes place through coordinated welfarist policing and the enforcement of the law to divert, deter and rehabilitate those women who do not choose to exit as the most 'responsible' option. Critics (see the collection edited by Pearce and Phoenix, 2009) from a range of disciplines have suggested that the potentially positive outcomes of the strategy include:

- strengthening approaches to child exploitation by ensuring a holistic approach that includes work with schools;
- including 'communities' through consultation processes such as community conferencing;
- expanding court diversion and reforming the soliciting law;
- expanding the Ugly Mugs scheme through Crimestoppers;
- recruiting police liaison officers and developing local action planning on trafficking.

The detrimental aspects of the strategy are that:

- The complexity of the issue has been missed in an attempt to remove the visible aspects of street sex work.
- There is a lack of detail in the strategy that leaves many unanswered questions, such as where are the resources to come from to responsibilize women to exit and refrain from selling sex? And what happens to women who cannot exit or for whom it will take a long period of yo-yoing in and out before they are able or ready to exit (Sanders, 2007)?
- The primary focus on routes out not only misses the complexity but will create more problems and risks for women who may be pushed underground and away from the help and support of sex worker organizations offering health and welfare support.
- The economic variety of off-street working practices is absent and because the primary concern is routes out, not health and human rights, the government 'will not, therefore, tackle genuine areas of vulnerability and exploitation' (Boynton and Cusick, 2006: 191).
- Multi-agency work by health care workers may be disrupted especially if funding regimes lead to focus on exit at the cost of the current balance of services (see Chapter 8).

The lessons from history show very clearly that now in the twenty-first century the identity of the 'prostitute' is still fixed along a victim trajectory supported by discourses of sex and sin linked to immorality and trafficking that ignore material on the subjecthood of women and intersections with poverty, transnational communities and migration, globalization and the opening-up of markets, including the adult entertainment industry. The social organization of the sex industry is therefore tied to history and the dynamics of the control of deviance and legal regimes linked to the hegemonic or ideological perspectives of governments (O'Neill 2007a, 2009; Phoenix, 2009).

The Social Organization of the Sex Industry

The key legal regimes used to manage and control/organise the sex industry internationally are shown in Table 7.4.

Europeanization and the Council of Europe

At a European level, a debate took place in the Parliamentary Assembly of the Council of Europe on 4 October 2007 following a report of the Committee on Equal Opportunities for Women and Men, by the rapporteur, Mr Platvoet. The text adopted by the Assembly includes the following: 'The Parliamentary Assembly unreservedly condemns forced prostitution and trafficking in human beings as modern-day slavery and one of the most serious violations of human rights in Europe today' The Assembly strongly condemns forced prostitution and trafficking in human beings and has called on all member states, which have not yet done so, to sign and ratify the Council of Europe

Table 7.4 Models of controlling prostitution

Model	System
Regulation	The system enforced by the police through the Contagious Diseases Acts and operating predominantly in Europe during the nineteenth century involving 'compulsory registration and regular medical checks of prostitutes working on the streets or in licensed brothels' (Self, 2003: 4).
Prohibition	The system most commonly used in the UK and other countries. Prostitution is not illegal but nor is it 'seen as an acceptable way of life either and the general intention is to discourage the practice' (Self, 2003: 4) by criminalizing a variety of 'objectionable' conduct.
Neo-abolition	The Swedish government have criminalized buying sex. It is no longer a crime to sell sex. However, as Self (2003) argues, women who do so are part of a criminalized world and are, drawing on Petra Ostergren's paper (2003) exposed to much danger including taking risks, denying they are paid for sex, paying exorbitant rents, 'feel hunted by the police and dare not report abusive customer' (Self, 2003: 4).
Legalization	Prostitution is legal under certain state- specified conditions. The licensing of legal brothels or spaces, zones by the state where selling sex can take place legally. For example, the brothels in Nevada, 'tippel zones' in the Netherlands and licensed brothels in Australia (see Harcourt et al., 2005).
Decriminalization	The removal of all laws that criminalize selling sex. New Zealand decriminalized prostitution in the Prostitution Reform Act 2003. The Act 'repealed the prostitution-related legislation on our statute books and created a new legal environment for the sex industry' (Jordan, 2005: 19).

Convention on Action to Combat Trafficking in Human Beings. With reference to voluntary prostitution, their position is that states should formulate an explicit policy on prostitution and avoid double standards – refrain from criminalizing and penalizing prostitutes, as double standards force prostitutes – underground or into the arms of pimps, and instead should seek to empower women sex workers.

> Regarding voluntary prostitution, defined as prostitution exercised by persons over the age of 18 having chosen prostitution as a means to make a living of their own accord, the Assembly notes that the approaches adopted in the 47 member states of the Council of Europe vary widely. (http://assembly.coe.int/Main.asp?link=/Documents/AdoptedText/ta07/EREC1815.htm)

The majority (20) of European states are identified as abolitionist (those who hold the perspective that prostitution should be eradicated):

> As an organisation based on human rights and respect for human dignity, the Council of Europe should take a stance on prostitution which reflects its core mission. Basing one's judgment on respect for human dignity does not mean taking a moralistic approach, however. It means respecting people's decisions and choices as long as they harm no-one else. … [States, they add, should] address 'the structural' (poverty, political instability/war, gender inequality, differential opportunity, lack of education and training), including in countries from which prostitutes originate, to prevent people being 'forced' into prostitution by circumstances

Importantly, the Council for Europe states that governments should refrain from criminalizing and penalizing prostitutes; develop programmes to assist prostitutes to leave the profession should they wish to do so while ensuring those who remain are not abused by police; ensure that prostitutes are given a say in policies regarding them; and ensure that they have enough independence to impose safe sexual practices on their clients. This very liberal approach to 'voluntary' prostitution or commercial sex is not being taken up in the UK.

UK Social Policy Developments

A review of the demand for prostitution has also taken place in 2007/8, led by Home Office Minister Vernon Coaker and early signs indicate that the UK may well be following Sweden's neo-abolitionist position by criminalizing the purchase of sex. The outcomes of the review of tackling demand were announced on 21 September 2008, with a strong motivation to make paying sex a crime, although the proposals still have to be approved by the Houses of Commons and Lords. The aims of the New Labour government are clear as the press release on the Home Office website notes:

> The Home Secretary has announced plans to shift legal responsibility to those who pay for sex when the prostitute involved has been forced into that role ... Home Secretary Jacqui Smith said the changes will make it illegal to pay for sex with someone 'controlled for another person's gain' ... Minister for Women and Equality, Harriet Harman, said, 'We must protect women from being victims of human trafficking – the modern slave trade'. The trade only exists because men buy sex, so to protect women we must stop men buying sex from the victims of human trafficking.[8]

The current approach conflates voluntary sex work with trafficking too easily and makes assumptions about the relationship between the demand and supply of sexual services as the only reason there are women involved in selling sex. Critics (such as Weitzer, 2007) are very concerned that the intentional law to protect those who are coerced against their will is a backdoor approach to control all prostitution and penalize men who are buying consensual commercial sex (see Chapter 5).

In Scotland, as reported by Gerry Braiden:

> Senior council officials and police chiefs in Glasgow are working with their counterparts in Sweden in an attempt to tackle prostitution within the city. Representatives of both the Swedish police and government have already visited the city this year and are scheduled to come again within the next few months as Glasgow prepares its case to lobby the Scottish Government for powers to adopt a zero tolerance approach to buying sex. Although kerb-crawling has been illegal since last year, Glasgow wants the law extended to people purchasing sex from private flats, saunas and brothels. The local authority would in tandem attempt to persuade sex workers to give up prostitution. (Braiden, 2008)

Sex worker rights organizations, researchers and support groups are vociferously opposed to this because of the negative outcomes for women. As discussed in Chapter 1, there is a bifurcation of feminist responses to sex work, with one camp arguing that prostitution is work and the other (backed by government policy and policy-makers) arguing that prostitution is violence and exploitation, and not something to be tolerated in the twenty-first century. A major problem identified by critics is that a focus on getting sex workers to exit leads to

> social inclusion to those who responsibly exit and 'resume' normal lifestyles and continued exclusion to those who remain involved in (street) sex work, and who are constructed and reproduced in law as anti-social and the outcome for those who do not responsibly exit involves further criminalization and marginalization. (Scoular and O'Neill, 2007: 765)

Research, especially feminist research, has persistently documented the fact that criminal justice responses to prostitution have historically focused on those who sell sex, while the men involved in buying and procuring/pimping are absent in the available literature (see O'Connell Davidson, 1998; O'Neill, 2001; Phoenix, 1999). Yet, Campbell (1998) argues that in terms of their socio-demographic characteristics, the existing research suggests that men who pay for sex are not necessarily 'socially inadequate or deviant' but merely 'ordinary'. In Campbell and O'Neill's (2004) summary of research conducted on clients[9] (see Section 7 of the full report *Working Together to Create Change*, at www.safetysoapbox.co.uk), it is evident that men who buy sex come from across social groups and divides: there is no one type of client. For more detail on the characteristics of men who buy sex, see Chapter 5.

Kinnell (2006a) argues that moral censure is heaped on women and policy should promote sex workers' safety. Moreover, that a substantial subsection of the general male population who buy sex do so for mundane reasons. Kinnell further suggests that if we take 80,000 as the estimated figure for the number of women selling sex in the UK with a client base of 800 per year, this averages out at about 20 clients per week. Clients represent the full range of occupations from managerial to unemployed and reports suggest between 44 and 54 per cent are married or co-habiting. Kinnell adds that they remain in the market for several years and that this calls into question 'efficacy of attempts to reduce the market for commercial sex activity by moral exhortation, education or police activity' (2006a: 220). Criminalizing clients serves merely to criminalize men who would not otherwise have contact with the criminal justice system, and this represents the other side of the coin relating to the historical focus on prosecuting women who sell sex (see Sanders and Campbell, 2008).

There are, however, alternative views regarding the root causes of prostitution. Radical feminist views locate the demand for sexual services only with men who buy sexual services. Hence, this argument follows that if the demand is removed, then prostitution would reduce, or better, would cease to exist, and women would not find prostitution a viable option. For instance, Coy et al. (2007) reduce the sex industry to the process of men choosing different women as if they were going to the supermarket. This view locates the power to choose, dictate and objectify women entirely with the male consumer. The demand for sexual services is considered to be part of a larger process of objectifying women and reducing their selves to body parts. Coy (2008: 193) refers to 'disembodiment' as the core of women's experiences in prostitution which is located in the power of command that men have over women during the commercial sex act.

Alternative views of the silenced male customers' perspective need to be part of the story of 'demand'. Sanders' (2008a) empirical work on clients (see Chapter 5) argues that much of the sex industry involves consensual interactions between clients and sex workers and that there is evidence that demonstrates that many male clients engage in the sex industry with a set of morals, etiquette and codes of conduct. In her study, most men demonstrated a clear sense of where exploitation happened, the coercion from boyfriends for some women and the danger associated with the street sex market. They actively took steps not to visit sex markets where there was possible overt exploitation.

On the other hand Coy, et al. (2007: 25) research argues that the decision-making processes of men who buy sex 'are located within dominant discourses of gendered sexual mores and local availability of women who sell sex'. That 'legality contributes to normalisation' and for 'the growing category of men who view buying sex as a form of mainstream consumerism, as leisure/entertainment, there is no shame'. To address gendered sexual mores and the purchasing of sex, Coy et al. (2007) recommend primary prevention through work in schools; secondary prevention through awareness-raising and access; and tertiary prevention through kerb-crawler interventions.

Male sex work: unregulated and invisible in law

Currently, men who sell sex are governed by the now gender-neutral laws on soliciting and loitering where any 'person' soliciting for the purposes of prostitution can be arrested, under the Sexual Offences Act 2003. Yet, the regulation of the sex industry is, historically and currently, discussed only in relation to female commercial sex and rarely does male sex work appear in either the statute books or any policy guidelines. One exception is the Sexual Offences Act 2003, which introduces an offence of 'sexual activity in a public lavatory'. Johnson (2007) analyses this law and notes that although the law is written as gender-neutral, there is a specific intention of the law to address gay sexual activity, known as 'cottaging'. These private sex acts that take place in public environments have also been used to target the gay community, including men who pay for sex with men.

Whowell (2008) maps the known areas of male sex work in the UK using data from the UKNSWP 'Directory of Services'. There are some 51 regions of Britain that have specific support services for male sex work, suggesting that the spread of male sex work is as wide (if not as prevalent) as female sex work. Despite the widespread nature of male sex work for men, which is both street- and indoor-based, the soliciting and loitering laws are rarely applied to male sex workers. There is also evidence of young boys, especially those with a specific vulnerability such as being part of the 'looked after' care system, or having a learning difficulty, being at risk of commercial sexual exploitation (Palmer, 2002). Yet despite the widespread commonality of male sex work, in the Home Office Coordinated Prostitution Strategy (2006), male sex work hardly featured (Gaffney, 2007). It has been argued by Gaffney and Whowell (2009) that there has been a blatant blindfold put over the concerns and issues regarding men involved in selling sex, as the sex industry extends beyond prostitution to pornographic artists, exotic dancers and specialist services (such as domination and asphyxiation). Such a denial of the existence of the varied nature of male sex means that there is a lack of services to deal specifically with these needs, which are often different from female sex work. At the time of writing, the current New Labour proposals to make it a crime to pay for sex from someone 'controlled for gain' could have serious implications for male sex work.

Alternative approaches for the UK

There is a plethora of responses to address the 'problem' of prostitution at the intersections of crime, justice and the sex industry. Some focus upon multi-agency approaches that are multi-stranded and based upon harm minimization directed at the most vulnerable women selling sex and offering options to those who want to move on or out of the industry (Melrose, 2009). Inter-related strategies include court diversion schemes that seek to divert women from the criminal justice system and generally work in partnership with services to support women and their needs, such as health, housing, welfare and counselling needs (Pitcher, 2009). Community mediation is another option to manage relationships between residents and sex workers in areas where street sex work takes place (Pitcher et al., 2006), where the focus is upon shared interests and degrees of tolerance, not zero tolerance. Safety zones and managed areas have also been discussed by local authorities, police force areas, some politicians and researchers. However, despite support for the range of alternative measures described here, including the New Zealand model of decriminalizing adult sex work, the approach which is the most dominant in 2008 in the UK is a focus upon responsibilizing women to exit through zero tolerance of street-based sex work; selective tolerance of off-street sex work; and a shift in focus to criminalizing the client for kerb-crawling and possibly those purchasing sex (the latter in keeping with the Swedish model). Other aspects of the sex industry, such as male sex work and legal implications, are not addressed in current policy (see Gaffney and Whowell, 2009).

Crime, Justice and the Sex Industry: Justice for Whom?

The concept of justice put forward in the Home Office Coordinated Strategy is not premised upon a rights-based framework or what we can call a holistic concept of social justice (O'Neill, 2007a), but rather a definition of justice promoted through prostitution control that equates to fulfilling or operationalizing the law in this area. In turn, this approach is based upon historical antecedents that frame prostitution as a crime against morality – prostitution is not illegal but associated activities that offend against public order and moral decency are.

Thus, the Home Office Coordinated Strategy under the section on 'Ensuring Justice' states: 'Enforcing the law against those who exploit and abuse individuals through prostitution was recognized by respondents as the best way to address commercial sexual exploitation and to send a clear message that it will not be tolerated' (Home Office, 2006: 10).

Scoular and O'Neill (2007) argue that the government have co-opted radical feminist concerns about violence and exploitation of women into techniques of governance and control. By prioritizing 'exiting' as a means of facilitating social inclusion, rather than offering recognition, rights or redistribution to sex workers, inclusion becomes a tool facilitating 'rehabilitation'. This approach cuts off possibilities for a broader understanding of social inclusion and social justice in relation to the complex experiences, structures, processes and practices of sex work for the women and men involved. The suggested reforms offer a genuine attempt to understand and suggest ways forward and look like they are helping women – but they do so by sustaining the binaries between good and bad, deserving and undeserving women, so that only those who 'responsibly exit' are socially included, leaving those outside increasingly marginalized. Although there is mention of poverty, homelessness, abuse, low self-esteem, poor educational achievement and other indicators of deprivation (Home Office, 2004: 21–3), these are not used to discuss social justice, especially in relation to the distributive and associational aspects of social justice but, rather to further criminal justice control over those individuals who are constructed as responsible for the harms in prostitution and to support the model of exit-focused intervention.

A more complex analysis and account of crime, justice and the sex industry should produce a more complex understanding of the lived experiences of those who sell sex and, together with the more holistic accounts of social justice, a better set of resources could be developed in collaboration with the women and young people involved. The latter might include legislative reform, welfare support, exiting; alongside rights, recognition and increased resources to target structural and social inequalities. Thus, an expanded understanding of social justice via social inclusion that could provide the leverage for a radical democratic approach to prostitution reform, that is also in keeping with the more expansive notion of social justice and arguably the model of decriminalization operationalized in the New Zealand model could be engaged.

Notes

1 We borrow this title from the excellent chapter by Helen Self (2004) *'History repeating itself: the regulation of prostitution and trafficking'*.
2 Anti-social behaviour orders (ASBOs) are civil orders made in court and can be applied for by the police, local authorities and registered landlords – but not the general public. Their aim is to protect the public/neighbourhoods from individuals who engage in anti-social behaviour that causes distress and harassment. Upon receiving an ASBO, a

sex worker is normally prevented from visiting a certain area/streets. If a breach of these conditions occurs, then the matter becomes a criminal offence. CRASBOs are added on to a criminal conviction and may be accompanied by restrictions, e.g. on loitering. See www.homeoffice.gov.uk/crime/antisocialbehaviour/orders

3 There is also other legislation that might be invoked, for example, in relation to procurement, buying sexual services from a minor and living off the earnings of prostitution, but these apply equally to indoor as well as street sex work.

4 For example, in 1990, O'Neill was commissioned by Nottingham Safer Cities (Home Office funding to address the problems of cities with high crime rates to help create 'safer cities') to conduct research on prostitution with a view to developing a multi-agency response. Using participatory methods, her report led to a multi-agency forum that served to facilitate multi-agency responses to addressing issues of street sex work that included magistrates, police, probation, public health and drug agencies and most importantly, sex workers as key participants.

5 From May 2004, when the new Sexual Offences Act 2003 came into force, the principal Act governing these offences was the Sexual Offence Act 1956. This consolidation Act brought together five previous statutes: the Criminal Law Amendment Act 1885, the Vagrants Act 1898, the Incest Act 1908, the Criminal Law Amendment (White Slavery) Act 1912 and the Criminal Law Amendment Act 1922. The advantage of a consolidation Act, from a government point of view, is that, as it does not make any substantial alteration to the law, there is no cause for debate during its brief passage through Parliament. This means that both Parliament and the public are denied the opportunity to consider its implications. Consequently, the legislation governing sexual offences at the beginning of the twenty-first century originated in the Victorian and Edwardian period, making the Sexual Offences Act 2003 the first major reform for over a hundred years (Self, 2004: 1).

6 (http://assembly.coe.int/Main.asp?link=/Documents/AdoptedText/ta07/EREC1815.htm).

7 (http://assembly.coe.int/Main.asp?link=/Documents/AdoptedText/ta07/EREC 1815.htm)

8 'New prostitution rules will protect trafficked women', press release, 22 September 2008. Available at: www.homeoffice.gov.uk/about-us/news/new-prostitution-rules

9 Based on research by: McKeganey and Barnard (1996) Glasgow (n = 143); Faugier, Hayes and Butterworth (1992) Manchester (n = 120); Ward and Day (1997) (n = 107: clients = 11 non-paying partners, = 96) Kinnell and Griffiths (1989) Birmingham client interview (n = 126); Campbell (2001) Liverpool (n = 154).

──────────── **Suggested Reading** ────────────

Diduck, A. and Wilson, W. (1997) 'Prostitutes and persons', *The Journal of Law and Society*, 24(4): 504–35.

Gaffney, J. and Whowell, M. (2009) 'What about men?', in J. Phoenix (ed.), *Sex for Sale*, Bristol: Polity Press.

Pearce, J. and Phoenix, J. (eds) (2007) Special Edition on the Home Office Prostitution Strategy, *Community Safety Journal*, 6(1).

Scoular, J. and O'Neill, M. (2007) 'Regulating prostitution: social inclusion, responsibilization and the politics of prostitution reform', *British Journal of Criminology*, 47(5): 764–78.

Self, H. (2003) *Prostitution, Women and Misuse of the Law: The Fallen Daughters of Eve*, London: Frank Cass.

Study Questions

Level one

- How are prostitution and the sex industry managed in the UK?

Level two

- To what extent have the social attitudes of the nineteenth century framed the 'problem' of prostitution and the making of an outcast group and how has this impacted upon current legal regimes?

Level three

- The UK Network of Sex Work Projects recognizes and supports the rights of individual sex workers to self-determination. This includes the right to remain in sex work or leave sex work (see www.uknswp.org). Critically discuss.

8

COMMUNITIES, SERVICES
AND WELFARE

This chapter picks up on themes discussed in Chapter 7 and continues to discuss the relationship between criminal justice policy and the management of prostitution. This is done in the context of community's demands, activism and vigilantism. A fresh perspective on the relationship between communities and sex workers is presented which discusses solutions through mediation and working in partnership. In addition, the balance between social policy and welfare provision, the emphasis on exiting programmes and the need for joined up services are explored.

Communities, Safety and Street Sex Work

Impact on communities

While not exclusively, street-based sex work has tended to be located in areas of comparative deprivation (Hubbard, 1999a). A number of reports document the negative impacts of street sex work and kerb-crawling on residents in local neighbourhoods. For example, Matthews (1993) notes the accompanying increase in noise and volume of traffic in neighbourhoods where street sex work takes place, the infringement of residents' private as well as public space and an increase in harassment of women living in the area. Campbell et al. (1996) found in their survey of residents in an area of sex work in Liverpool that many reported problems of litter, increased traffic and noise. Pitcher et al. (2006) document a range of concerns about the environmental impact of street-based sex work, including nuisance and incivilities, certain public spaces becoming 'no-go' areas due to fears about safety and litter associated with sex work, particularly discarded condoms, drug paraphernalia and sometimes human waste. Some residents also report encountering abuse or harassment from sex workers and their clients.

> Nuisance and related issues included 'banging doors, punters, men trying to pick other people up in the street'. Nuisance and lack of tolerance was for some directly related to numbers and the concentrated presence of street sex workers in residential areas. (Pitcher et al., 2006: 19)

Local businesses in areas of street sex work may also complain about the use of loading areas or alleys for sexual transactions, particularly with the resulting debris that they are forced to deal with (Edwards, 1991).

Residents may often associate street sex work with drug markets and this may add to their fear and anxiety (Bourne, nd; Pitcher et al. 2006). While the two markets may often coexist and many street-based sex workers have been drug market customers at some time, the relationship is complex and varies significantly from area to area (May et al., 1999). It has also been suggested, although with little evidence to support this, that the presence of sex markets contributes to a general degeneration of an area and attracts criminal elements, creating an intimidating atmosphere and negatively impacting on house prices, the viability of local businesses and insurance premiums (Home Office, 2004). This perspective may be associated with the 'broken windows' hypothesis propounded by Wilson and Kelling (1982) which identifies a potential causal path from disorder to criminal behaviour in a neighbourhood.

Nonetheless, the visible presence of street sex markets in areas which are already experiencing social and economic deprivation can be seen by residents as adding to an overall ambience of criminality, which can contribute to fear of crime (Hubbard et al., 2007). The resulting impact for some residents may be that they feel anxious about leaving their homes or walking about at night unaccompanied.

Although the main objections of residents to street sex work appear to be based on concerns about environmental nuisance and potential increase in criminality, some people may simply be uncomfortable with the idea that sex is being exchanged for money. Others may be less concerned about sex markets that are not as clearly visible, particularly indoor locations, but express discomfort with street-based sex work and the perceived impact it has on the general propriety and morality of their neighbourhood. Pitcher et al. (2006) found that such concerns often focused specifically on the potential effect on children living in the area, who might witness sexual transactions or come across used condoms or needles. O'Neill and Campbell (2006) note concerns about soliciting near places of worship which were seen as having a substantial effect on the quality of life of parents and children. It is this corruption of 'family' space that prompts much opposition to street sex work and other visible manifestations of sex markets, such as advertising in telephone boxes (Hubbard, 2002). These concerns are echoed in the report of the Wolfenden Committee (Home Office, 1957: 82), which sees the control of prostitution as being justified by its visibility, which represents 'an affront to public order and decency' for the ordinary citizen. As argued in Chapter 7, this construction of prostitution as 'public nuisance' serves to legitimate actions to remove street sex work from residential streets and excludes sex workers from consultations on local strategies (Kantola and Squires, 2004; Phoenix and Oerton, 2005).

While many complaints to authorities about street sex work are based on people's lived experiences or tangible fears of the side effects of sex markets in their area, it is also notable that some object to street sex work even when it has little immediate impact on them. For example, Walker et al. (1994) suggest from the evidence of their research in one city that many sexual transactions and much kerb-crawling takes place relatively unobtrusively. This is confirmed by Pitcher et al. (2006: 18), who found in a study of five neighbourhoods that many residents did not feel that sex work impinged significantly on their quality of life, as 'most of it is during the night time when it can't be seen'. The study also found that many sex workers endeavoured to reduce levels of nuisance to residents and tried to avoid situations of conflict. Sex workers often felt safer working in or close to residential areas, where there were people around to call upon if they were threatened. In a study in New York, Thukral and Ditmore (2003) also found that sex workers they interviewed attempted to work in a less visible way.

Nonetheless, not all sex workers or their clients are as considerate and there are some very real concerns that have been documented. It is generally when residents feel reduced to a state of powerlessness by the inaction of local statutory agencies that they are themselves more likely to respond to what they see as an infringement of their rights to access, and feeling secure in public and private space. Other factors that may trigger community reactions include the influx of new populations or 'gentrification' of an area, media campaigns, or the emergence of local activists with a personal or political stake in 'cleaning up' the neighbourhood. Community responses may also relate to a tacit acceptance of what is perceived to be a 'tolerable' level of sex work in an area (Hancock and Matthews, 2001). These responses tend to focus on street-based work, with indoor work rarely being seen as a public nuisance in the same way, because of its relative invisibility. For example, Perkins and Lovejoy (2007: 121) comment that 'residents quite often don't even know that they have a brothel in their suburb until focus is placed on it by the media or by police harassment'. Sanders (2005a) notes that the majority of the community are accepting of women who work from their own homes, or who rent out 'working flats' where a couple of women may work or share the shifts. These arrangements are often discreet and sensitive to the local area, amenities and community. For instance, sex workers in a study by Sanders (2005a) spoke of how they would never set up a business near a school, or church. Where residents and neighbours had found out about sex work taking place in a private residence, some women reported aggressive confrontations, flyers sent through letterboxes, hate mail and threatening behaviour. This often had consequences for the individual's private life when family members came to know, and the process of humiliation from being 'outed' meant marriage break-ups and having to move home for some women.

Community responses to street-based sex work

The range of community responses to street-based sex work varies considerably across areas, although research and media reports have tended to concentrate on those neighbourhoods where there has been significant opposition to sex workers and kerb-crawlers, particularly those which involve active protest. The focus on these vociferous campaigns, however, masks the complexity of views and reactions by residents to sex markets and sex workers in particular. It also ignores the fact that, while many sex workers may be geographically mobile (Sanders, 2004), in some areas women working on the street also reside in the same neighbourhood and contribute to local economic and social life (Pitcher et al., 2006).

Many campaigns against sex work in residential neighbourhoods may be seen as relatively moderate. These include, for example, utilizing traditional political channels, such as writing to, petitioning or lobbying MPs or local councillors, or writing to the local press. In certain areas, however, more active protest has been evident. This can include picketing, routine patrols or surveillance of street sex work areas or more organized 'Street Watch' campaigns. In some publicized instances, street patrols have led to harassment and vigilantism against sex workers and their clients, for instance, in Balsall Health in the UK in the mid-1990s. Similar high-profile campaigns have been reported in other countries, for example, in the Sydney suburb of Canterbury, also in the mid-1990s (Perkins and Lovejoy, 2007). Quassoli (2004) notes political and media campaigns in parts of Central and Northern Italy throughout the 1990s against a range of issues in local neighbourhoods, including street prostitution. In some cases, media reporting of these campaigns has appeared to condone violence against sex workers. Although the Balsall Heath action was hailed by some press reports as a triumph of community activism, the tactics of some residents raised serious concerns of safety for sex workers and outreach workers providing services to them (Hubbard and Sanders, 2003). While local police initially had reservations about this form of protest, they later co-opted patrollers into a 'Street Watch' group (Sagar, 2005).

Street Watch evolved from Neighbourhood Watch in the UK in the early 1990s and was initially conceived as a vehicle for relatively unobtrusive patrolling by residents in order to provide intelligence to the police on suspected criminal activity. The Street Watch movement has been sanctioned by the Labour government and is often held up as an exemplar of citizen participation which helps to enhance community safety (Sagar, 2005). While its original focus was on more general crime, its centre of attention has increasingly become street sex work, with female sex workers and their clients being targeted by its members (Pitcher et al., 2006). Street Watch has been legitimated by police forces in some areas, although there have been serious questions about the extent to which some groups have overstepped their original monitoring role and tipped into more aggressive forms of action against sex workers and kerb-crawlers. Kinnell (2008) notes, for instance, that a proportion of violence against sex workers comes in the form of hate crime from residents, street walkers, opportunist youths and more organized groups who are 'protecting the neighbourhood'. Concerns have been expressed that such campaigns are unrepresentative, divisive and unaccountable and some residents have reported feeling intimidated by members of these campaigns (Pitcher et al., 2006; Sagar, 2005). Evidence suggests that local patrols fail to separate sex workers' personal lives from their working role and thus women have reported being harassed by residents when they have been out with their children, visiting family members or even attending events such as a family funeral (Hubbard and Sanders, 2003; Pitcher et al., 2006). Sanders interviewed a 22-year-old street sex worker who lived and worked in the same area, who was continually harassed by vigilantes:

I will be walking up the road with my daughter and they will stop me. I say to them at night when I am on my own and I am dressed in mini skirts then they have got a right to stop me but not at 3 o'clock in the afternoon, with my baby in the push chair with about six carrier bags. I mean, am I really doing business in that state? They still stop me. (2004: 1712)

In certain areas, residents' groups have also actively campaigned against projects supporting sex workers, with the result being in some instances that projects have been prevented from undertaking outreach work and delivering harm reduction services in those neighbourhoods (Hubbard and Sanders, 2003; Pitcher et al., 2006).

While much of the research and media focus has given prominence to community intolerance, there is evidence from some studies of sympathetic views towards sex workers, with specific examples of compromise and co-existence (O'Neill and Campbell, 2001; Pitcher et al., 2006; Thukral and Ditmore, 2003). These studies suggest that residential responses to street-based sex work are more complex and nuanced than is generally assumed in the development of national and local policy.

Welfare, Criminal Justice Policy and Regulation

Police responses to street sex work

Although in some areas the local police force has sanctioned initiatives such as Street Watch, generally the police are keen to discourage residents from taking individual action and have preferred to use existing police powers to protect communities and improve community safety. Historically, police forces in many areas have tended to maintain relatively low-level tactics of surveillance and order control, with attempts to contain street sex work within geographical areas where nuisance to residents is limited (Hubbard, 2006; McKeganey and Barnard, 1996). Where the volume of community complaints has risen, enforcement strategies have traditionally involved periodic 'crackdowns', focusing on the more visible aspects of street sex markets, particularly sex workers and kerb-crawlers, resulting in arrests and penalties for soliciting and related offences. Perkins and Lovejoy (2007: 124) report a similar police response to community action in the Canterbury area of Sydney, even though 'neither the clients nor many of the street workers were actually doing anything illegal'. Such actions fulfil a variety of short-term functions, particularly acting as a deterrent for sex workers and their clients and appeasing residents' concerns that the police are unresponsive to their complaints. Whether such responses have a lasting impact, however, is highly questionable and it has been argued that they can be counterproductive. Where the penalty for a sex worker is a fine, for example, there is often no option but to go back onto the street to earn the money to pay this, resulting in a cycle of re-offending and re-arrest (Edwards, 1993; Self, 2003).

With the introduction of the UK Sexual Offences Act in 1985 and subsequent pieces of legislation which gave the police greater powers to target kerb-crawlers, the focus turned towards the clients of sex workers (see Chapter 7 for further discussion). More recently in the UK, police have utilized Anti-Social Behaviour Orders (ASBOs) or civil injunctions, mainly against sex workers but also sometimes against kerb-crawlers, to 'protect communities from the harassment, alarm and distress caused by kerb crawlers and those involved in prostitution' (Home Office, 2004: 70). Criminal Anti-Social Behaviour Orders (CRASBOs) are also available as an 'add-on' to a conviction for offences not necessarily related to sex work and, as Sagar (2007: 157) notes, 'It is a procedure growing in popularity and one that eliminates the pre-consultation requirement of the ASBO'.

Breaching an order can result in up to five years' imprisonment rather than a fine and thus critics of ASBOs and other disposals increasingly applied to sex workers in the UK in recent years have referred to the 'net-widening' effects of these measures, which have 'expanded the punitive reach of the state' (Phoenix and Oerton, 2005: 101). Thus while on the one hand there has been a move away from the imprisonment of women for offences related directly to the sale of sex, the increase in civil measures, with the inevitability that they will be breached by many, has led in the UK to an increasing criminalization of female sex workers in particular. The consequence of serving a relatively short-term prison sentence, with little support, is that women emerge facing debt, may often have lost their accommodation and are forced back on the streets to earn money. The resultant stigma also makes it even more difficult for women to move into other areas of work.

There may be short-term gains for residents in neighbourhoods where ASBOs have been used extensively, as they report significant decreases in the numbers of sex workers and kerb-crawlers as a result of the measures discussed above. A frequent impact of campaigns by residents and policing strategies to clear an area of sex work, however, is to disperse workers and their clients to other areas, resulting in displacement of the problems (Pitcher et al., 2006; Sagar, 2007). The issuing of civil injunctions in one part of Vancouver led to a shift of sex work activity to neighbouring areas (Lowman, 1992). Furthermore, studies in the UK and other countries have shown that the impact of an increasingly punitive environment on sex workers is an increase in their vulnerability, causing them to work less safely through their own or their clients' fear of being arrested or harassed (Kulick, 2003; Sanders, 2004; Scoular et al., 2007). The conditions of some ASBOs, or the threat of enforcement, can also distance sex workers from crucial health, drug prevention and other services (Harcourt and Donovan, 2005a; Pitcher et al., 2006; Shannon et al., 2008).

While support mechanisms are supposed to be in place for sex workers when they are served with an ASBO, in reality, this support rarely exists, or is provided in an *ad hoc* manner which does not help those referred to address their complex needs. An interview with an agency representative in one city where ASBOs were applied consistently against sex workers Pitcher et al. noted:

> When an ASBO is served, before it's served, girls should be referred to support agencies and one of the weak areas ... is that women are not always referred before they get an ASBO, so the doors for support and exiting are not open to them. (2006: 26)

Similarly, services for sex workers on arrest for prostitution-related offences can be variable. For example, a study in New York (Thukral and Ditmore, 2003) found that out of a sample of 30 street-based workers, half had never been offered any services as a result of an arrest.

Partnerships and multi-agency responses

Since the late 1980s in the UK, multi-agency partnerships have been formed in many cities as a response to the conflicting interests of residents and sex workers and projects supporting them. With concerns about the public health impact of sex work (as discussed in Chapter 3), the emphasis has been on sexual health promotion and health-based interventions, as well as mechanisms to address community concerns about the other impacts of sex work on their neighbourhoods. The multi-agency prostitution forums that have developed generally aim to address a range of issues rather than just focusing on local enforcement (Matthews, 2005). They are often, but not exclusively, linked to Crime and Disorder Reduction Partnerships and usually have representation from the local authority, police, health authority and often agencies working with sex workers. Sometimes community representatives sit on these forums. Some forums do not include representation from sex workers or projects supporting them and in these cases their 'multi-agency' status may be brought into question (O'Neill, 1997). Depending on the political and policy context, these forums may oversee different forms of intervention according to local priorities, with varying levels of effectiveness.

Many multi-agency approaches include situational or environmental interventions intended to 'design out' or reduce the impact of street sex work, such as road closure, the introduction of speed bumps, CCTV or gating off alleys. These can have the effect of steering sex workers and their clients away from particular streets and denying access to areas commonly used for sexual transactions or other activities such as drug-taking. Such interventions have been deemed effective in removing sex markets from an area, or reducing the numbers involved, as well as the volume of traffic, although as Matthews (2005) notes, this has in part been dependent on the active participation of local residents. Certain interventions can be disruptive for some local residents and businesses, however, and can also lead to displacement of sex workers and their clients to adjacent neighbourhoods (Hubbard et al., 2007).

While some partnerships have adopted a 'zero tolerance' approach to street-based sex work, some have taken a more pragmatic stance towards related problems in residential neighbourhoods. For example, some police forces in the UK have in the past moved towards relocating sex workers in informal 'zones' away from residential areas, often working in conjunction with projects and other agencies providing support services to sex workers. There has, to date, been relatively little formal research into the feasibility and effectiveness of managed spaces for street-based sex work. There is some evidence from Germany and the Netherlands that zoning, if managed properly, can have a beneficial effect on both public order and the health and safety of sex workers (Van Doorninck and Campbell, 2006). Nonetheless, recent UK government policy has come out strongly against this option and it is unlikely that managed zones will be considered in the UK in the near future.

In response to the 'arrest–fine–arrest' cycle touched upon earlier, in some cities the health and crime agendas have come together with the provision of arrest referral or court diversion schemes. These steer sex workers towards support services after arrest, usually as an alternative to receiving a fine or other penalty. The availability and accessibility of specialist support services are essential in order for such schemes to be effective (Hunter and May, 2004).

Some partnerships have sought to reduce neighbourhood conflict over sex work through community mediation. Such interventions can fulfil a number of functions: they relay information about community concerns to sex workers and encourage them to adopt less disruptive working practices; they provide a response to community complaints and give residents the assurance that their concerns are being heard and acted upon; and they also help to raise awareness about the issues confronting sex workers. Community mediation has been found to be effective in reducing some of the tensions between local residents and sex workers and promoting greater understanding on both sides (Hester and Westmarland, 2004; Pitcher et al., 2006). A greater sense of cohesion has also been developed where support services for sex workers have worked closely with the local community, for example, in attending community or multi-agency meetings or participating in community environmental 'clean-up' events. Mediation may be problematic, however, where antipathy towards sex workers is entrenched and where vigilantism is common, and attention needs to be given to the balance of power between different negotiating groups. Pitcher et al. note that:

> Mediation or a similar process might be useful in identifying the more complex needs of residents and sex workers and points of commonality that could be fed into a multi-agency approach. It could also build capacity among sex workers, residents and agencies, offering a more democratic alternative to the notion that state alone can deliver change, although it should not be seen as a replacement for statutory responsibility. The situation in local areas may also be fragile, with ongoing changes to neighbourhoods and thus a sustained approach is required for interventions to be fruitful. (2006: 34)

The wider context in which multi-agency or partnership approaches to street sex work take place is also important: for example, media representations of sex workers inform the reactions of residents to street sex work in such communities. Thus, dominant media representation of female sex workers can help to justify law and order strategies designed to exclude them from particular spaces. The current tendency to depict sex work as anti-social and so out of place in 'communities' can fuel exclusionary actions. Pitcher et al.'s research (2006) showed that there are in fact different degrees of tolerance in neighbourhoods, suggesting that the co-existence of sex work and residential living is by no means impossible. In this study, being part of the community for sex workers – as was the case for other residents – was described in terms of 'living in the area, being part of the networks of schools and shops, taking part in community activities and community living and having friends locally' (Pitcher et al., 2006: 17). For example, some women interviewed talked about their relationships with other residents and participation in local activities:

I used to do a lot ... I used to help with the kids in the youth clubs and things like that. (Eastside sex worker)

I have friends here, I think I am part of the community. (Southside sex worker) (O'Neill et al., 2008: 81)

Some of the women Pitcher et al. (2006) interviewed felt alienated from the 'community': 'I didn't feel part of anything, I was just there' (O'Neill et al., 2008: 81).

Current Home Office policies prioritize the disruption of street sex work by tackling supply and demand and accelerating routes out. The Home Office (2006) suggests this can be achieved via local strategic partnerships, especially crime and disorder reduction partnerships which address community concerns. Community mediation and community conferences are mentioned in the strategy document as one possible tool to address these concerns (Home Office 2006: 17). There is limited data on the effectiveness of these models. O'Neill et al. (2008) argue that the approach to community conferencing could be widened beyond the quite narrow basis of crime and disorder (where there is a clear focus upon restoring justice after a crime or injury has occurred). O'Neill and Campbell (2004) come close to the model of a community conference in their research in Walsall using participatory action research methods (PAR, see Chapter 10 for further discussion). The approach taken here was research-driven, however, rather than led by the principles of restorative justice. O'Neill and Campbell (2006: 59) suggest that PAR develops social knowledge that is interventionist in partnership with communities and, moreover, because it seeks to promote social change, it provides 'a testimony to the possibilities for participation in local governance that can shed light on broader structures, practises and processes'.

In the case of communities affected by street sex work, there is a need to develop a better understanding of the issues at stake before looking at possible outcomes to address the issues – and the very people selling sex should also be included as part of the 'community'.

UK government policy on arrest referral and rehabilitation

UK policy concerning prostitution, particularly street-based work, is currently under review. Proposals were put forward[1] in the Criminal Justice and Immigration Bill in 2007–8 to redefine the notion of 'persistent' in relation to loitering and soliciting. While a welcome move was to remove the term 'common prostitute', further clauses proposed diversion of street sex workers to rehabilitation schemes on arrest. This appears to be very much in line with criminal justice interventions directed more broadly at those who use drugs. Up to the early 1990s in the UK, drug services tended to focus on a 'harm reduction' approach based on voluntary entry into treatment, with a range of interventions potentially available. With the increasing association of problematic drug use with crime, however, certain criminal justice interventions were introduced aimed at addressing perceived drug misuse through mandatory or quasi-compulsory drug testing and treatment (Hunt and Stevens, 2004). These include Drug Treatment and Testing Orders (DTTOs) and the Drug Intervention Programme (DIP). It has been argued that approaches based on state coercion run the risk of reducing the effectiveness of treatment and that evidence of success of these approaches is unclear (Hunt and Stevens, 2004). While short-term reductions in re-offending were apparent following contact with the DIP, the lack of a comparison group means that changes in behaviour cannot be attributed to one particular pro-gramme (Skodbo et al., 2007). Edmunds et al. (1999: 4) conclude that while there may be a role for coercive or incentive-based schemes that involve diversion from prosecution into treatment programmes, 'coercive schemes are poorly suited to reach offenders arrested for serious offences'. Sondhi et al. (2002), in their evaluation of arrest referral schemes, found that female crack-using sex workers were one of the groups least likely to engage in drug treatment, which they ascribe to the fact that they are not being referred to specialist services. May et al. (2001) also note that drug treatment services often may not be tailored towards the needs of sex workers.

Many drug-using sex workers face significant barriers to remaining in treatment and are likely to struggle to comply with the conditions (Hunter and May, 2004; Melrose, 2007b; Thukral and Ditmore, 2003). Others will need substantial support such as that provided by specialist projects, many of which face challenges to main-taining services due to lack of funding. While the evidence is thus equivocal on com-pulsory referral *per se*, it appears that coercive rehabilitation schemes on arrest, rather than helping to address the complex and diverse needs of sex workers, may often serve to further penalize them. There will also be substantial financial implications for providing the necessary support.

Linking service provision for sex workers with the criminal justice system is also likely to have a negative impact on relationships of trust between project staff and service users. It has been argued that to be at all workable, provision to support sex workers in making lifestyle changes should be part of an holistic approach, based on voluntary participation and linked to training and welfare programmes (Pitcher, 2006a). As discussed in Chapter 3, research on exiting shows that 'yo-yoing' is a key feature of the process of change for those who wish to move on and that for some people this may take many years (Sanders, 2007a). Desistance is linked crucially to individual motivation, structural and cultural factors and having necessary support. There appears currently in the UK to be an inherent tension between the welfare and criminal justice agendas in relation to street-based (female) sex workers, with little attention paid to the diversity of the sex industry or the experiences of those work-ing within it (Scoular and O'Neill, 2007).

Services for Sex Workers

The number of services available to support sex workers in the UK and Europe has grown considerably since the 1980s. There are also support projects available to sex workers in many other parts of the world. The focus of such services may vary according to funding sources, as well as the diversity of the industry. For example, Thukral and Ditmore (2003) found that services for street-based workers in New York were relatively limited. In the UK, whilst early support projects were funded largely by health authorities, with a general focus on sexual health, prevention of HIV and other sexually transmitted diseases and aimed at reducing harm, in recent years funding has often been linked to drug prevention and thus been primarily aimed at street-based workers. There is a broad consensus that to be effective, services should encompass a range of provision in order to take into account the diverse experiences and needs of sex workers.

Chapter 3 identified a range of support needs encountered by both street-based and indoor sex workers. While many projects aim to address a multiplicity of needs, either through their own services or in partnership with other agencies, the type of provision is influenced not only by conditions of funding but also by the perspectives of providers.

Perspectives on service provision

The theoretical and/or policy positions on sex work, discussed in Chapter 1 of this book, may influence the extent to which support is given, or what form that support takes. For example, we saw earlier that the dominant discourse in the UK and parts of Europe tends to present sex workers as victims. This has certainly framed UK national policy since the mid-1990s and is reflected in the focus of many multi-agency partnerships which direct policy at a local level.

Much of the recent policy debate in the UK has focused on the perceived 'needs' of the most vulnerable groups of sex workers, particularly women working on the street and girls and younger women who are sexually exploited. The needs of male sex workers and women working indoors, unless they are seen as being trafficked, have largely been ignored in this debate (Gaffney, 2007; Soothill and Sanders, 2005).

Currently in the UK, policy perspectives have been taking an increasingly prohibitionist stance, particularly in relation to considering criminalization of the clients of sex workers, but also, while making mention of the welfare needs of sex workers (women in particular), considering a move towards more regulated approaches designed to steer sex workers into services and out of sex work. There have been various critiques of this approach, particularly in terms of the detrimental impact it is likely to have on sex workers' safety and health. For example, Harcourt and Donovan (2005b: 126) note in their review of three different approaches to prostitution (prohibition, licensing and decriminalization) that: 'health promotion for the sex industry is much easier when the target group is not covert and is working without the daily fear of a criminal prosecution'. They found that most 'prohibitionist' regimes do little to reduce sex work or 'its related social ills' and have adverse consequences for public health. Elder (2008) comments on how the 'anti-prostitution pledge' policy in Nigeria has resulted in a reduction in funding for sex worker-specific health services which undertake work to address sex workers' HIV needs.

The philosophy of harm minimization, for example, promoting safer sex or methods of drug use in order to protect the health of sex workers, has tended to inform the culture of many support projects (O'Neill and Campbell, 2004). Accompanying this has been a user-focused approach to service provision, to ensure that services are tailored to workers' aspirations as well as needs. Increasingly in the UK and some other countries, provision is linked to 'exiting' as the main focus, with support being directed towards this aim. While some sex workers may wish to change their lifestyle, however, there may also be many who do not want or are not ready to move on, although they may often be in need of other crucial support to address immediate needs. If projects limit their services only to those who wish to leave the sex industry, the social and health needs of those who do not want to move on are neglected (Sloan and Wahab, 2000). In current UK government policy, it appears that responsibility to change is seen to lie with the individual sex worker, rather than their situation being seen as a result of structural factors and this also influences service provision (Harding and Hamilton, 2008; Phoenix and Oerton, 2005).

Sex workers' experience of services

Many sex workers have encountered barriers to accessing health, drugs and social care services, for example because of judgemental attitudes of some staff, inconvenient opening times or location of services (Bright and Shannon, 2008; Connell and Hart, 2003; Pitcher, 2006a). Stigma both because of being a sex worker and also because of sexuality can present a barrier to accessing services for many male as well as female sex workers (Gaffney, 2007). Fear of criminalization can make sex workers reluctant to make use of services and undermine sexual health promotion and harm reduction activities. Indoor workers may require fewer public services than street-based workers, yet they can face similar stigmatization to that experienced by street-based workers if they disclose their occupation.

Migrant workers may find it particularly difficult to access health and other services, because of fear of authorities and concerns that contact with services may result in deportation, as well as language barriers (UKNSWP, 2004). Harcourt and Donovan (2005b) found that where sex work is regulated in some form or another, for example, in Australia, the Philippines, Uruguay and some European countries, those who operate illegally ('clandestinas') are often excluded from mainstream services, are reluctant to approach other services for support or advice and thus are often missed by health promotion programmes.

Few sex workers have received adequate support for mental health problems, either through GPs or specialist counsellors. As Connell and Hart note of their male cohort:

> When discussing the impact that sex work had had on their mental health, the majority of men emphasised the pressing need for appropriate formal help, support, advice and service provision in this area. Current methods of support included the use of drugs, glue, gas, alcohol and cigarette smoking. At time of contact many men felt isolated, alone and vulnerable, unable to access appropriate support services to address and discuss their past and present experiences in and outside sex work and their impact, emotionally and psychologically. (2003: 92)

Jeal and Salisbury (2004) conducted a cross-sectional survey amongst street workers in an inner city area to find out about their experiences of health care. The findings demonstrated that whilst 83 per cent (n = 59) were registered with a GP, non-disclosure of sex work behaviour due to fear of judgemental attitudes and low numbers of follow-up consultations contributed to general poor health in this marginalized group. A comparative survey was administered amongst indoor sex workers by Jeal and Salisbury (2007) who concluded that street and indoor workers have very different health needs and experiences of health care. Indoor workers were much less likely to report chronic or acute illness, and more likely to have had sexual health screenings. The various surveys discussed here identify that different groups of sex workers need targeted health care and other services delivered in appropriate and sensitive ways to meet varied needs. Outreach services may be particularly important to reach certain groups.

Services provided to sex workers

Although many of the projects set up to work with and support sex workers in the UK in the 1980s had a main focus on sexual health and HIV prevention, many have expanded their services to accommodate the diverse needs of project users. Projects working with sex workers are run by a variety of organizations, including voluntary sector groups, local authorities, health authorities, drug services and youth services. Support and advice are offered not only in relation to sexual health but also violence and safety, housing, the law, education and training. While some projects work with a range of groups, some are aimed at specific client groups, including male sex workers, female workers, young people, street-based workers, indoor workers and migrant or 'trafficked' workers. Certain projects have a particular focus on exiting. Some support services are managed by or employ staff who have worked in the sex industry. Many of these projects have arisen as a response to perceived under-use of mainstream services by sex workers, linked to the barriers to accessing services identified earlier in this chapter. In the UK, there is also the UK Network of Sex Work Projects (UKNSWP), an umbrella organization to support sex work projects through providing information, guidance, networking opportunities and links to statutory agencies and international bodies supporting sex workers. The UKNSWP, which was established in 2002, has published a set of good practice guidance on services to sex workers in a number of different areas of provision. Chapter 6 discussed international examples of sex worker-led services which specifically design good practice guidelines. This section outlines the different types of service to sex workers, mainly in the UK but also in other countries.

Health, safety and welfare

While the majority of studies suggest relatively low rates of sexually transmitted infections (STIs) among sex working populations in the UK compared with other groups, there is seen to be a need to provide continuing support in a range of areas, including condom distribution, facilitating health checks, advice on safer sex and drug use and needle exchange services. Some projects provide targeted clinical sexual health services for sex workers, such as contraceptive clinics or hospital-based clinics, or mobile services with sex work project drop-in facilities (Ward and Day, 1997).

Some undertake community-based peer research (Shannon et al., 2008). Studies in Melbourne and New South Wales, Australia (Harcourt et al., 2001) show that street-based female sex workers have more general health problems than those working indoors and are less likely to use condoms than brothel-based workers. Transgender sex workers also reported a range of health issues that need a sensitive and tailor-made approach. The authors conclude that, while some street workers tend to have good potential access to health services through outreach, public and private services, targeted health services for sex workers are also required in many areas. In a study in New York, Thukral and Ditmore also noted that:

> Most health services for sex workers focus exclusively on gynaecological health and blood tests for sexually-transmitted infections. Services addressing drug users also focus on blood tests as well as needle exchange. These services are valuable but leave many health issues unaddressed. (2003: 72)

Sex worker support projects may also give advice or support on a range of general health issues, such as advice on nutrition or basic first aid. Many will make referrals to mainstream health services for pregnancy advice and other medical support and some provide health outreach staffed by nursing professionals (Hester and Westmarland, 2004; Pitcher, 2006a). In some countries or states where sex work establishments or sex workers are licensed, sexual health screening is enforced. This has been criticized for being a costly and invasive process which stigmatizes sex workers (Harcourt and Donovan, 2005b; Perkins and Lovejoy, 2007; UKNSWP, 2004).

Greater access to drug treatment, on a voluntary basis, is seen as essential to stabilization of drug use and to help sex workers who are dependent on drugs change their lifestyle and/or move on. Services need to be responsive to drug-using sex workers and available when they need them, otherwise they are likely to become difficult to contact (Hester and Westmarland, 2004; Hunter and May, 2004). Shannon et al. (2008) note the need to facilitate safer sex work environments in cities where there are overlapping sex and drug markets, such as Vancouver. Harm reduction and HIV prevention there have tended to focus mainly on injecting drug use, whereas there is seen to be a need for a range of interventions, including peer-based prevention, outreach and mobile services and settings for safer drug use. Aftercare and follow-up for service users who do not complete their intervention is also important. Many support projects working with sex workers provide information and advice on safer drug and alcohol use, referral to services and sometimes needle exchange (Pitcher, 2006a). Some projects offer their own community-based drug treatment service, with professionals on the premises to provide prescription and harm reduction services (Hunter and May, 2004).

Many sex workers are reluctant to approach the police to report violence because of prior experience of their case not being taken seriously, or because they fear they will be penalized (Campbell and Kinnell, 2001; Thukral and Ditmore, 2003). In response to concerns about safety and violence, many projects have developed 'Dodgy Punters' systems that enable them to collect information about violent assaults, distribute them to sex workers and sometimes share intelligence with the police

(Kinnell, 2008; Penfold et al., 2004). Through the UKNSWP, a national 'Dodgy Punters' scheme has been established in the UK that promotes good practice on reporting violent clients, sharing intelligence with the police and gathering evidence to enable the police to prosecute offenders.

Advice and practical services

Many sex workers are likely to need a range of different welfare and legal services. Street-based sex workers in particular, as was shown in Chapter 3, encounter various problems as a result of their work, including rent arrears, debt and child-care issues. As they have tended to be more vulnerable to arrest than indoor workers, they are more likely to require legal advice and services, although sex workers in indoor locations may also need specific advice, for example, on tax issues and more recently in countries such as the UK have been exposed to police raids, sometimes linked in with trafficking operations. In countries or states which take a prohibitive stance on sex work, individual workers have no security of employment and thus their ability to seek legal advice is severely constrained, as are the abilities of outreach services to provide support (Harcourt and Donovan, 2005b).

Access to suitable accommodation is a crucial need for many street-based sex workers and lack of housing, particularly on leaving prison, can force women back onto the streets and into the same situation they were in before arrest (Thukral and Ditmore, 2003). Lack of a stable address can also prevent sex workers accessing health and other services. Provision of long-term accommodation, accompanied by intensive support to help sex workers address their drug use and other problems is vital to overcome the cycle of re-offending. Some projects have responded to this problem by working with housing providers and developing agreements to provide accommodation for sex workers, linked in with support (Shelter, 2004).

Criminal justice advice and support

While generic arrest referral schemes have been found to be less appropriate for drug-using sex workers and there are serious questions about compulsory referral to drug treatment on arrest, there are examples in some cities of court diversion schemes which aim to steer street-based sex workers towards services rather than facing a fine or other penalty (Pitcher, 2006a). Recognizing that engagement with services is a long-term and often disrupted process, these schemes are more realistic in their conditions, with the expectation that sex workers will attend a minimum number of sessions with the support service in place of a penalty. While the conditions are minimal, projects have found that this process helps to start linking in sex workers with services and continuing with support after they have fulfilled the minimum requirement for attendance.

Although imprisonment directly related to street prostitution in the UK was discontinued in the early 1980s, sex workers, particularly women working on the street, can face a prison sentence for a number of reasons, including breaching an ASBO, non-payment of fines and prosecution for drug-related offences. Because of changes to the law and the introduction of new penalties, the likelihood of imprisonment for street-based sex workers has increased in recent years (Clark, 2006; Phoenix, 1999). As was noted in Chapter 3 and earlier in this chapter, street-based sex workers in particular encounter a range of problems and barriers to resettlement, including homelessness, drug dependency and experience of violent relationships. Sex workers thus require specialized services to address the diversity of need while in prison and on release. Many specialist projects in the UK provide support and advice for female sex workers, in areas such as mental and physical health, substance misuse, accommodation, legal support, family work and other practical assistance. Nonetheless, there is considerable scope for further awareness-training amongst prison staff, a more integrated approach to support and equality of access to aftercare (Clark, 2006).

Provision for migrant workers

Labour migration to more affluent countries as a result of economic need includes movement into informal and unregulated sectors such as sex work. Because the financial rewards of working in the commercial sex industry are comparatively high, increasing numbers of migrant women work in this industry in the UK and other European states (Agustin, 2006). Many male sex workers in cities such as London are also now from outside the UK (Gaffney, 2007). Many projects in parts of the UK and elsewhere work with migrant sex workers. This may require specific language skills and additional service provision (Ayres, 2005). Some provide services targeted only at 'victims of trafficking', which may include safe houses. These latter services are focused primarily on exiting support specifically for women, however, whereas more generic services for migrant workers may acknowledge the diversity of migrant sex workers and the agency of many workers and provide health, language and other support to enable them to work more safely (UKNSWP, 2008). The conflict between a focus on the criminality of illegal migration and the need for a more humanitarian approach to trafficked persons has also been noted (Goodey, 2003). Ditmore and Wijers (2003: 87) comment that divergent perspectives within the UN on sex work and its relationship to trafficking *per se* have resulted in 'a lost opportunity to strengthen migrants' human rights' (see Chapter 9).

Exiting support and strategies

Chapter 3 outlined some of the complex processes involved in leaving sex work and the 'trapping' factors that keep people in the industry, particularly street-based sex work. Economic need, drug dependency, and lack of alternative employment options, particularly for those with a criminal conviction but also because of the stigmatization attached to having been a sex worker, are all reasons for remaining in or returning to sex work. Services for sex workers can help them to develop additional skills and address other factors in their lives, to present a wider range of options. Many projects offer a holistic service, with support for making lifestyle changes being one of several interventions available depending on what sex workers see themselves as needing at particular times (Pitcher, 2006a). Sanders describes the role of specialist projects in providing the holistic support required by many:

> The gradual planned exit for street workers was often encouraged by specialist services working intensely to get women back into training, education, part-time employment, and

other vocational skills training or voluntary work. Suitable housing and accommodation was central to starting a new life and removing oneself from the temptations of the street culture, life, and networks. (2007: 84)

While many projects may not describe themselves as 'exiting' services, because their focus is more on the priorities that sex workers identify for themselves, nonetheless many service users are helped by these projects to make lifestyle changes that put them in a better position to move out of sex work, if that is their chosen option. Certain projects may have a specific focus on 'exiting' and there is an increasing emphasis on this as a primary aim by some funders of services to sex workers in the UK. This 'singular' model of exiting has been criticized for failing to recognize the complexity of the industry, sex workers' lived experiences and their social exclusion (Scoular and O'Neill, 2007). Entering and leaving sex work may not be a single, consistent process and, as we discussed in Chapter 3, many sex workers will move in and out of sex work at different stages in their lives because of particular circumstances (Hunter and May, 2004; Pitcher, 2006a; Sanders, 2007). Some may continue to see clients while working in other sectors, for financial reasons (Thukral and Ditmore, 2003). While some sex workers, particularly those working on the street, would like to move out of the industry if they were given realistic alternative options, for others, the motivation to leave may not be because of a negative attitude to the work, but because of concerns about long-term financial stability and other issues. While some workers may take a planned approach to leaving and require minimal support, others may require more sustained and focused assistance to make changes to their working situation. Some may wish to remain in sex work, yet still require a range of support services. To have a primary focus on exiting, premised on the assumption that selling sex is 'wrong', can also be counter-productive, as it can drive sex workers away from services (Gaffney, 2007; Harding and Hamilton, 2008).

It has been argued that a non-judgemental approach to provision can be more conducive to engagement. To take into account the diversity of those working in the sex industry and their different needs, it might be more productive for agencies working with sex workers to identify different lifestyle phases in order to target interventions appropriately (Harding and Hamilton, 2008; Williamson and Folaron, 2003). In a context of zero tolerance, however, the focus becomes one of 'exiting' as an end-result of all provision, rather than it being seen as one of many possible stages in the life of a sex worker. Arguably, the construction of sex workers as passive 'victims' in need of professional help, which serves to deny the agency of the individual, can further limit the options available to them and make moving on a more difficult process.

Note

1 But subsequently withdrawn pending further consideration but these rehabilitation orders are set to be re-introduced as proposed legislation in 2008–9.

Suggested Reading

Melrose, M. (2007) 'The government's new prostitution strategy: a cheap fix for drug-using sex workers?', *Community Safety Journal*, 6(1): 18–26.

O'Neill, M., Campbell, R., Hubbard, P., Pitcher, J. and Scoular, J. (2008) 'Living with the other: street sex work, contingent communities and degrees of tolerance', *Crime, Media and Culture*, 4(1): 73–93.

Pitcher, J. (2006) 'Support services for women working in the sex industry', in R. Campbell, and M. O'Neill (eds), *Sex Work Now*, Cullompton: Willan.

Pitcher, J., Campbell, R., Hubbard, P., O'Neill, M. and Scoular, J. (2006) *Living and Working in Areas of Street Sex Work: From Conflict to Coexistence*, Bristol: Policy Press (also available on the Joseph Rowntree Foundation website: www.jrf.org.uk).

Sagar, T. (2007) 'Tackling on-street sex work: Anti Social Behaviour Orders, sex workers and inclusive inter-agency initiatives', *Criminology and Criminal Justice*, 7(2): 153–68.

Sanders, T. (2007) 'Becoming an ex-sex worker: making transitions out of a deviant career', *Feminist Criminology*, 2(1): 1–22.

Study Questions

Level one

- What are the main problems experienced by residents in areas where street sex work takes place? What do you consider to be the most effective responses by local agencies to address these problems?

Level two

- It has been argued that there may be a role for more coercive schemes which divert drug users into treatment programmes through the criminal justice system. Do you think these schemes are appropriate for street-based sex workers who are drug users?

Level three

- The 'exiting' versus 'harm minimization' debate presents a false dichotomy. Discuss.

9

GLOBALIZATION AND THE
SEX TRADE

This chapter explores the global relationships between sex markets, people who travel to work in the sex industry voluntarily alongside the more complex notion of trafficking. We will focus briefly upon sex tourism and outline the international and European instruments used to tackle trafficking and prostitution.

────────────────── **Moving Across Borders** ──────────────────

In previous chapters we found that historically, selling sex is a deeply embedded cultural practice that has through time been coded and classified as prostitution, and more recently as sex work. We have also seen a shift in discourses from sin and morality to labour law and human rights that acknowledge the issue of violence and exploitation for women, men and young people working in the sex industry, largely as a result of the social stigma attached to the role 'prostitute' and the risks associated with 'moral revulsion' (Agustin, 2005: 618) assigned to selling sex. The term 'globalization' refers to the increased mobility, or connectivity, of labour, capital, goods and services, technology and communications and flows of people throughout the world. It is a relevant sociological concept through which prostitution can be understood.

As the eminent sociologist Zygmunt Bauman says, 'Mobility has become the most powerful and the most coveted stratifying factor ... the riches are global the misery local' (2001). Globalization and North–South relations as well as the 'internationalization' and 'mainstreaming' of sex work impact upon push/pull factors associated with routes into sex work. People will pay (agents) to travel for work in the informal economy of the sex industry. Forced migration is not a modern phenomenon and exists within the context of globalization and North–South relationships. There are complex factors that link the local with the global. Castles states:

> The growth in people trafficking is a result of restrictive immigration policies of rich countries. The high demand for labour in the North, combined with strong barriers to entry, have

created business opportunities for a new 'migration' industry. This includes 'legal' participants, such as travel agents, shipping companies and banks, as well as illegal operators. (2003: 15)

The globalization of the sex industry is linked to consumer capitalism and the opening up of adult entertainment markets. The sex industry makes huge revenue for nation-states. In 2008, the industry's annual revenue was around $2,111.1 million, up 6.8 per cent on the previous financial year. In 2009, IBISWorld expects revenue to grow by a healthy 4.4 per cent, contributing an estimated $1,545.3 million in value added to the economy from 13,131 establishments.[1] In the UK, in 2006, $1.2 billion were spent on sexual services, more than on cinemas or other forms of entertainment.

A number of theorists (Doezema, 1998; Kempadoo, 1998; Walkowitz, 1980) have written about transnational sex work (sex work across national boundaries). This has included British women working in Belgium and Europe in the 1800s; European women working in India in the latter part of the nineteenth century; and Korean and Thai women working as 'comfort' women for the Japanese military. Women have historically moved around the globe to join the informal sex economy: 'Specific political, economic and social events shaped the women's involvement in the sex trade at different times, in different places, within the context of globalizing capitalist system, colonialism and masculinist hegemony' (Kempadoo, 1998: 14).

The global sex industry inevitably involves the movement of people and capital. There is, however, currently a conflation with trafficking and prostitution that obscures the relationships between migration and trafficking. There is uncertainty about the numbers of women and men who migrate voluntarily and those who are forced. The focus at national, European Union and United Nations levels is upon the criminality of illegal migration and the victimhood of those 'coerced' or 'trafficked' into selling sex. Agustin (2005) writes that women are seen as victims, passive recipients and mute sufferers to be saved. Immigration policies protect the borders of nation-states yet the state is also instrumental in constructing markets for commercial sex.[2] Anderson writes:

The state directly generates demand for domestic workers through its policies on provision of care in private households for example, but also, the fact that it does not treat either domestic work or commercial sex as employment like any other has great significance for the markets for sex and domestic workers. It means that the (implicit) contracts forged with workers in these sectors are treated as a private matter, and the state thus creates what is effectively a radically free 'free market'. However, 'sellers' and 'buyers' of services are not equal, and certain immigration statuses create marginalized groups who are vastly unequal to buyers. (2006: 2)

Conflating voluntary sex work with trafficking

The broader social, political and economic context of the sex industry involves globalization and migration and the conflation of migration with trafficking.

Major drivers of change in the sex industry are economic, demographic, ideological, and technological. Globalisation is the umbrella term used to express many of these changes, which include increased economic interdependence of different countries through trade, the extension of the world market to areas of the world previously isolated, increased movement of people and of capital, and the rapid spread of new technologies and media across wide sections of the globe. (Ward and Aral, 2006: 345)

Ward and Aral argue that economic transitions and instabilities (such as changes in the economic and social structures of the former Soviet Union) have led to an increase in unemployment and more people looking for employment in informal sectors, such as case work, domestic service, agricultural work (such as fruit picking) as well as the sex industry. Economic desperation (i.e. poverty) can lead some women and men to migrate for work in the sex industry, sometimes people are coerced into sex work. Moreover, they argue that these economic dynamics combined with poverty and demographic issues can explain the increase in people working in the commercial sex industry. And that an increased supply of sex workers is more than matched by an increase in demand for sexual services:

In the United Kingdom, for example, the proportion of men who reported paying for sex doubled in the decade from 1990 to 2000. Global estimates again are difficult to provide but one review [Carael et al., 2006] found that in half of the countries studied at least 9% of men reported paying for sex in the previous 12 months. Opportunities and demand for commercial sex are likely to expand as divorce rates rise, people travel more, and in many countries adults spend a greater proportion of their lives living alone. (Ward and Aral, 2006: 345)

Agustin offers a note of caution and argues that whilst 'the gaze of researchers as well as government and non-governmental actors remains fixed on individual women who sell sex ... a range of other issues is neglected' (2005: 618). Indeed 'considerable social conflict is associated with the perception that commercial sex is taking over large sections of the world's major urban spaces and is related to international organized crime and illegal immigration' (Agustin, 2005: 620). It is a major concern to many theorists that migrating to sell sex is conflated with trafficking (Agustin, 2005; Butcher, 2003 Weitzer, 2007). There has to be space in policy debates to acknowledge both voluntary migrant sex work and voluntary sex work without dismissing the existence or seriousness of trafficking, or conflating the two separate phenomena (see Outshoorn, 2005).

Brents and Hausbeck (2007: 425) argue that it is useful to study local markets in order to 'examine how late capitalist forms of consumption might have an impact on the sale of sex, especially in comparison with expanding global touristic services'. Focusing upon legal businesses in Nevada, the authors map the 'mainstreaming' of the sex industry and the links with tourism and emotional labour, and examine 'Las Vegas as a global tourist resort'. Indeed, the authors state that shifts in the social organization of the sex industry are taking place: 'They are up-scaling, expanding services, clientele and markets and using business forms similar to mainstream businesses, including corporate forms and diversification, as they try to integrate into the tourist economy' (2007: 435). Thus, for these authors 'It is no longer useful to posit the sex industries as an "other" to late capitalist industry' (2007: 435).

At international and European levels of governance, the European Union and United Nations take a victim-centred approach to prostitution and, generally speaking, an abolitionist stance to the commercial sex industry. Yet the paradox is that the commercial sex industry makes huge revenue for nation-states and remittances home from migrant workers can keep their families from experiencing absolute poverty.

Key themes in the literature include: a focus on 'trafficking' and the exploitation of women predominantly from developing or poverty-stricken countries; and the public health issue, including the health needs of trafficked women such as risks related to violence, drug and alcohol addiction, or sexually transmitted diseases. On the other hand, the feminization of poverty, globalization, the growth of sex tourism, the growth of 'informal sector' work and migration 'to break away from oppressive local conditions caused by globalization' (Kempadoo, 1998: 17) lead many into the sex industry. As Bindman identifies, sex work is defined as a special human rights issue which separates it from other female (and male) low status informal labour, such as domestic or agricultural employment and service work. This separation:

> hides the commonality, the shared experience of exploitation, which links people in all such work. The distinction between 'the prostitute' and everyone else helps to perpetuate her exclusion from the ordinary rights which society offers to others, such as rights to freedom from violation at work, to a fair share of what she earns, or to leave her employer. (1998: 65)

Yet in Las Vegas, Victoria in Australia and in New Zealand, the mainstreaming of the sex industry is taking place and it is becoming integrated into the structures of labour law, unionization and the economy. Linked to all of these themes is a particular focus on violence against women and indeed a radical feminist approach to prostitution as violence/exploitation. What is clear is that in most parts of the world, the lack of international and national protection for sex industry workers makes them vulnerable to exploitation and violence.

International and European Legislation and Protocols

Historically, Bindman tells us, the international legislative process began with a conference in 1895 in Paris prompted by reports of 'white slavery':[3]

> European women being tricked, with offers of other employment or marriage, into brothels far from home. Women from western Europe were going to other parts of Europe, British women to the United States, and eastern European women to Latin America. (1997: 4)

Barry writes

> The campaign against the traffic became international with the first congress on the white slave trade held in London in 1899. The 'shocking' revelations at the congress were that women for the most part under aged were engaged for lucrative posts and then … transported to foreign countries and finally flung penniless into houses of debauchery. (1997: 11)

Between 1904 and 1949 there was a series of international agreements on the issue of 'trafficking' that involved forced or coerced recruitment, lack of consent 'and movement across frontiers' (Bindman, 1997: 2). 'Trafficking' made a distinction between forced involvement and 'legal' prostitution, for the latter was allowed under certain conditions. Subsequent instruments have focused upon trafficking in persons for the purposes of prostitution and provide a victim-based approach to human rights and protection (see Table 9.1).

Table 9.1   Relevant international and European instruments

Date	Instrument
1904	The first international agreement on white slavery
1948	Universal Declaration of Human Rights
1949	The Convention for the Suppression of the Traffic in Persons and of the Exploitation of the Prostitution of Others of 2 December 1949
1957	The Supplementary Convention on the Abolition of Slavery, the Slave Trade, and Institutions and Practices Similar to Slavery of 30 April 1957
1979	The UN Convention against the Elimination of All Forms of Discrimination against Women (CEDAW)
1999	Convention on the Elimination of All Forms of Discrimination against Women: Optional Protocol of 6 October. 1999
2000	The UN Convention on the Rights of the Child and its Optional Protocol on the Sale of Children, Child Prostitution and Child Pornography of 25 May 2000
2000	United Nations Convention against Transnational Organized Crime: Protocol to Prevent, Suppress and Punish Trafficking in Persons, Especially Women and Children 15 November 2000.[i] The purposes of this Protocol are: (a) To prevent and combat trafficking in persons, paying particular attention to women and children; (b) To protect and assist the victims of such trafficking, with full respect for their human rights; and (c) To promote cooperation among States Parties in order to meet those objectives
2002	The European Conference and Brussels Declaration on 'Preventing and Combating Trafficking in Human Beings'
2007	Council of Europe in resolution 1579

Note: [i]Article 3: Use of terms: For the purposes of this Protocol: 'Trafficking in persons' shall mean the recruitment, transportation, transfer, harbouring or receipt of persons, by means of the threat or use of force or other forms of coercion, of abduction, of fraud, of deception, of the abuse of power or of a position of vulnerability or of the giving or receiving of payments or benefits to achieve the consent of a person having control over another person, for the purpose of exploitation. Exploitation shall include, at a minimum, the exploitation of the prostitution of others or other forms of sexual exploitation, forced labour or services, slavery or practices similar to slavery, servitude or the removal of organs.

Recent research by Hubbard et al. (2007) found that Prostitution laws in the Netherlands, Sweden, England/Wales and Scotland are underpinned by shared assumptions about the gendered nature of sex work which dismiss ideas that sex work might be voluntary. Yet, against this dominant hegemony in Europe, the parliamentary assembly of the Council of Europe in Resolution 1579 (2007) take a rights-based approach to adult prostitution, but also distinguish between voluntary or forced prostitution. A summary of the resolution follows:

11.3. *Concerning voluntary adult prostitution,* Council of Europe member states should formulate an explicit policy on prostitution; they must avoid double standards and policies which force prostitutes underground or into the arms of pimps, which only make prostitutes more vulnerable, instead they should seek to empower them, in particular by:

11.3.1. refraining from criminalising and penalising prostitutes and developing programmes to assist prostitutes to leave the profession should they wish to do so;

11.3.2. addressing personal vulnerabilities of prostitutes, such as mental health problems, low self-esteem and childhood neglect or abuse, as well as drug abuse;

11.3.3. addressing structural problems (poverty, political instability/war, gender inequality, differential opportunity, lack of education and training), including in countries from which prostitutes originate, to prevent people being 'forced' into prostitution by circumstances;

11.3.4. ensuring prostitutes have access to and enough independence to impose safe sexual practices on their clients;

11.3.5. respecting the right of prostitutes who freely choose to work as a prostitute to have a say in any policies on the national, regional and local level concerning them;

11.3.6. ending the abuse of power by the police and other public authorities towards prostitutes by developing special training programmes for them.

As with the feminist and theoretical approaches to prostitution (see Chapter 1), a bifurcation has emerged around the issue of trafficking and prostitution linked to understandings of (1) prostitution as trafficking violence and sexual exploitation; and (2) prostitution as service work that any adult can offer or seek, inevitably linked to migration.

Sex Work and Migration

Let us look first of all at prostitution and migration. In April 2008, a seminar took place on sex work and migration in Hamburg, Germany. Participants were sex workers, sex work organizations, supporters and experts from Germany and Austria. Acknowledging the internationalization of sex work and highlighting the increase in migrant sex workers in Germany, the focus of the two-day event was:

- to discuss and exchange information and experiences regarding the similarities and differences of working conditions of national and migrant sex workers, their access to social and health care, their rights, and living conditions;
- to confront the participants with the themes of racism and discrimination;
- to come up with a document undersigned by all participants and others, that could and should be used as a political instrument to demand more rights for sex workers, especially for migrant sex workers. This was achieved through the creation of the St. Pauli Protocol.[4]

The St. Pauli Protocol reinforces the messages of the Sex Workers' Manifesto[5] including the declaration that:

- sex worker rights are human rights;
- sex workers should be included in debate, dialogue, guidance, legislation and the development of policies;
- sex workers/migrants should have access to health care and prevention;
- sex workers/migrants should have access to 'culturally and linguistically adequate information';
- sex workers should have equal labour rights and working conditions.

These principles are also operationalized by TAMPEP, an international organization founded in 1993 to support the needs of migrant sex workers across Europe: 'Our focus is on assessing the situation and needs of female and transgender sex workers of Central and Eastern Europe, Asia, Africa and Latin America, and developing appropriate responses'.[6]

The key aims of TAMPEP are:

- to promote a holistic strategy underpinned by the principles of respect and inclusion of sex workers;
- to advocate for the human and civil rights of female and transgender migrant sex workers;
- to facilitate the sharing of knowledge, experience and good practice across Europe, ensuring the needs and issues of sex workers from countries of origin, transition and destination;
- to further develop and implement effective and innovative health promotion and HIV prevention strategies and intervention models amongst migrant sex workers in Europe;
- to consolidate and further develop the TAMPEP network to coordinate efforts across Europe in ensuring appropriate responses to the legal, health and social care needs of migrant sex workers;
- to further develop and disseminate TAMPEP resources, including multilingual health promotion materials and guidelines for outreach work, peer education and cultural mediation;
- to gather quantitative and qualitative data concerning sex work in Europe, monitor and report on the changing patterns of migration, and the living and working conditions of female and transgender sex workers within Europe (www.tampep.eu/).

TAMPEP provides a very clear framework for the activities of the organization in differentiating between trafficking and voluntary sex work. TAMPEP recognizes the phenomenon of trafficking as a form of violence against women – as already established at the 1993 UN Human Rights Conference in Vienna – and as a denial of basic human rights to the women affected:

- TAMPEP agrees (along with other NGOs) that *women's migration* cannot be identified with *trafficking in women*, but that trafficking in women IS embedded in an international migratory process.
- TAMPEP distinguishes between prostitution and trafficking in women through recognising:
  - o Trafficking is an international crime and fundamental breach of human rights that occurs in other work areas other than prostitution.
  - o Trafficking in women is a blatant violation of women's human rights.
  - o Prostitution without violence, coercion or deceit is not a violation of human rights.
  - o An individual's right to choose prostitution and the selling of sexual services as work.[7]

TAMPEP argues that the European and international instruments provide an insufficient basis upon which to address the gender-based inequalities experienced by women migrating for work. First of all, a human rights framework should constitute a strategy for combating the trafficking of women. Currently the majority of the 'documents/ instruments refers to the area of crime prevention and combat of organized crime, or to the harmonization of Penal Codes and the cooperation in this field': the focus is upon organized crime and crime prevention. 'Recommendations and resolutions are not legally binding. Trafficking in women is reduced to the area of prostitution. The documents incorrectly combine trafficking in women and smuggling' (TAMPEP, 2005: 4). Moreover, in relation to permits to stay (in the country of destination), regulations are not clear and access to 'protection, care and stay permit are connected to the victim's willingness to cooperate with police and legal authorities' (TAMPEP, 2005: 5).

The International Union of Sex Workers (IUSW, affiliated to the GMB workers' union) argues that there are many people working by choice in the sex industry, yet the law endangers them. Ultimately sex between consenting adults is not violence but sex workers face disproportionate levels of violence because of the stigma attached to them and what they do.

Sex Work as Violence and Exploitation

The International Committee on the Rights of Sex Workers in Europe (ICRSE) (founded in 2004 and registered in the Netherlands) seeks to bring sex workers and their allies together on an European and international level:

- to further the social acceptance and respect for sex workers;
- to promote their civil and human rights;
- to organize the support of allies.

The foundation also works on ending the sexual stigma of women, gay men and lesbians and transgender people and in general to promote the self-determination of women. The foundation tries to reach these goals by:

- supporting networking amongst sex workers and their allies to advocate for legislative change;
- promoting communication and information sharing through the Internet and on paper;
- organizing conferences, study groups and meetings.

ICRSE operate from a rights-based approach to support women, men and transgender people working in the sex industry.

Anti-trafficking agenda

Trafficking is a serious crime and a violation of human rights. Organized crime networks aim to make illegal profits through crime, and hide their activities through

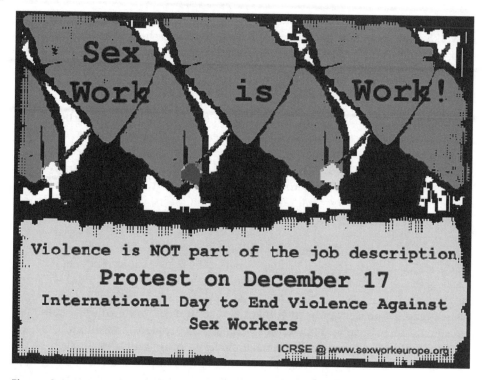

Figure 9.1 International day to end violence against sex workers
Source: Artist Petra Timmermans, www.sexworkeurope.org

physical violence, intimidation and sometimes terrorization. Ruggerio (1997) describes how the smuggling of people – contemporary slavery – creates profits for official and semi-official agencies, organized criminal gangs and the hidden economies the trafficked work in. Equally, he argues that the sectors (such as servants, domestic labour, mail-order brides) are not sharply distinguished from mainstream industries and institutions and at the same time are facilitated by entrepreneurs from conventional, official and criminal fraternities. Schloenhardt (1999) provides a network model of the complex and dynamic illegal markets that include amateur traffickers; small groups of organized criminals; international trafficking networks; corrupt public officials; informers; and recruitment specialists.

The criminal relationships between those who are considered to be involved in 'trafficking' are not always connected to sophisticated criminal groups. Bruinsma and Meershoek (1999) note from the police files of trafficking operations in the Netherlands that traffickers range from loosely organized professionals to organized criminal networks that link together the recruiter, the trafficker and the recipient in the host country. These authors highlight two main categories of criminal groups. First, the 'cliques of professionals' consist of two or three working together, forging traditional sexual relationships with women, and then using their international acquaintances to introduce women to other countries. Second, the organized crime groups are larger (up to 12 people) whom all have definite roles and tasks in the 'trafficking' process. Members of these groups own or work in brothels, clubs, bars and use violence to control the workers. The criminals work with travel and mediation agencies for false passports and documents for trafficking women. What is known of the trafficking rings suggests that they do not specialize in finding women just for prostitution. Of 161 people suspected of trafficking women in 1997 in the Netherlands, the majority were Dutch and also involved in other criminal activities such as smuggling arms, drugs or stolen cars, money laundering schemes and racketeering. Diversification has long been a trademark of organized crime as crime syndicates look for illegal profit-making activities within their transnational networks.

The kind of criminal groups that are involved in trafficking of women from places such as Eastern Europe to Western European countries is still not understood. Using police files and police organizations, Bruinsma and Meershoek (1999) set out three phases of the trafficking process:

(1) the recruitment of women from home countries;
(2) the trafficking of the women from their home country to the new country; and
(3) social control of employment in the sex industry.

These organized phases can be interlinked and controlled by one group of criminals, but equally, these organized phases can be separate, unrelated and within the control of individual women who want to make moves to other countries. In each of the recruitment, moving and working phases the complexities of the relationships and processes between the women and the 'traffickers' are simplified, diluted and wrongly merged by discourses, promoted by the media and some radical charities, that conflate voluntary migrancy with forced trafficking. The media simplify the discourse on trafficking by rendering all immigrant women working in the sex trade as trafficked victims.

The movement of female labour from one country to another does not necessarily equate with trafficking. Busza (2006) highlights the example of Vietnamese sex workers who paid recruiters to introduce them to brothels in neighbouring Cambodia where they knowingly and voluntarily came to work as sex workers. The women paid off their debt to the recruiters and mediators over a period of up to two years and either chose to continue working in the sex industry or took up other opportunities. Although there are international organized crime issues where women are kidnapped, sold by families and given false promises of work in the trafficking process (Busza, 2006), women who voluntarily migrate and find themselves in the sex industry can be wrongly categorized as victims of trafficking. Labelling all women who work in the sex industry who are not nationals of the host country as simply 'trafficked' is misleading. Most women do not work under duress but make economic decisions about how to earn money within their own set of circumstances, in order to support themselves, their immediate and distant family. For example, in China, the majority (90 per cent) of 4,235 women arrested (a mix of both nationals and non-nationals) for prostitution worked alone without any connection to organized crime (see Ren, 1999: 1415).

Trafficking in the UK

Little is really known about trafficked women in the UK. In 2000, Kelly and Regan published *Stopping Traffic: Exploring the Extent of, and Responses to, Trafficking in Women for Sexual Exploitation in UK*. The paper provides baseline data for women trafficked in the year 1998 and takes a human rights approach to the trafficking of women in prostitution.

> The research identified 71 women known to have been trafficked into prostitution in the UK in 1998. It is also argued that there is a hidden trafficking problem several times greater than we can currently document with certainty. Using various data it is estimated that there may have been between 142 and 1420 women trafficked into the UK during the same period. (Kelly and Regan, 2000: v)

The potential number trafficked is, of course, a statistical 'guestimate' and must be treated with caution. The authors recommend that a coordinated partnership response would be the most effective way forward to in reduce trafficking in prostitution. The key recommendations are based on obtaining better research and knowledge about trafficked women's experiences; challenges for the police to investigate trafficking; and greater central government input for long-term anti-trafficking campaigns. Some of these recommendations have been actioned and have led to the development of the Poppy Project.

The Poppy Project was set up in 2003 and is funded by the Office for Criminal Justice Reform (reporting to the Ministry of Justice) to provide accommodation and support to women who have been trafficked into prostitution. It has 35 bed spaces in houses throughout London. The Poppy Project outreach service works to improve the safety and well-being of women from all over the UK who have been trafficked and who are in need of short-term support and advocacy.[8] The Poppy Project is directly linked to the government's response to trafficking for the purposes of sexual exploitation/ prostitution. The UK Human Trafficking Centre has been established and is based in Sheffield (www.ukhtc.org/) and collaborates with the Poppy Project and the Home Office. Operation Pentameter 1 and 2 are police-led, multi-agency campaigns against trafficking for sexual exploitation that went 'live' in 2006 and involve police and partners across the United Kingdom. The aims of Pentameter 1 and 2 are to rescue and protect victims of trafficking for sexual exploitation and to identify, disrupt, arrest and bring to justice those involved in criminal activity' (see www.pentameter. police.uk).

STOP the TRAFFIK is a (London-based) global movement working to combat people trafficking, described as the fastest growing global crime: 'Around the world men, women and children are being treated as commodities – something to be bought, sold, and enslaved'. The NGO has more than 1,000 member organizations in 50 countries (www.stopthetraffik.org/what/). STOP the TRAFFIK case studies demonstrate the types of human rights abuses that the charity regularly works with.[9]

Case Study 1

In September 2006, Carol, a Zimbabwean girl aged 18, escaped from captivity of traffickers whilst in Tanzania. Carol was trafficked from Zimbabwe two years earlier when she was 16. Carol was orphaned and staying with her grandparents when this happened. One day on her way to school she was approached by two men who offered her a job. Carol was enticed by the job prospect as this would give her the opportunity to help out her grandparents, support her siblings and other relations. Carol left with the men and they took to a place where they raped her and then they transported her out of Zimbabwe to South Africa. She was drugged and placed in a coffin and crossed the Zimbabwean border. When she was in South Africa she was forced into prostitution. She was not allowed to go anywhere and was under lock and key.

Case Study 2

Prjua, aged 9 and her brother Ajay, a boy aged 7, lived on Thane train station in Mumbai, India, with their parents who were both alcoholics. Prjua and Ajay were regular attendees of the Asha Deep Day Centre, run by Oasis India, where they learnt to read and write and were given the opportunity to play. After attending daily for three months they disappeared. The project staff went to look for them. Prjua and Ajay's father told how a man had come and offered money for them and that he had sold them for the equivalent of $30. That was the last the father and the staff of Asha Deep Day Centre heard of them. In that area of Mumbai every 2–3 months, children disappeared, were kidnapped or sold into prostitution, forced labour, adoption or child sacrifice.

What is clear from the case studies above and the available literature is that forced or coerced prostitution and the trafficking in women and children for the purposes of prostitution are unacceptable and contravene the basic human rights of the person. So, everyone is in agreement that the cases presented above are unacceptable and the work of NGOs like STOP the TRAFFIK is necessary and should be supported through national, European and international legislation and instruments.

Where the issue becomes blurred, however, is over the bifurcation between prostitution as acceptable between consenting adults and prostitution as inherently exploitative and an expression of violence against women. There are concerns that anti-trafficking measures are not appropriately separated from immigration service actions with implications for trafficked and non-trafficked migrant women (Taylor, 2006). The UK, until 2007, resisted becoming a signatory to the Council of Europe Convention on action against trafficking in human beings, under which trafficked women are automatically granted residency in the country they have been trafficked into. In the UK there is a slow recognition that the human rights of women who are involved in sex work, for whatever reason, involves a complex interplay between immigration status, global poverty and the feminization of labour movement across the world.

For some radical feminists, as described in Chapter 1, prostitution is considered only violence against women. O'Neill (2001) argues that this approach treats prostitution in a reductionist way as a deviant activity, and as sexual slavery, which misses the complexity that is inevitably tied to economic, political and migratory dynamics. For radical feminists, prostitution and the wider sex industry serve to underpin and reinforce prostitution as a patriarchal institution that affects all women and gendered relations. Boutellier (1991: 207) suggests this particular approach views prostitutes as victims of male sexuality 'and thus male sexuality should be the main subject of concern'.

Yet as we discussed above, sexual labour is defined as a primary source of profit and wealth and is a 'constituent part of national economies and transnational industries within the global capitalist economy' (Kempadoo and Doezema, 1998: 8). These authors seek to uncover and present the complex relationships between personal agency, resistance to oppressive and exploitative situations and structures 'within the context of both structural constraints and dominant relations of power in the global sex industry' (1998: 8–9).

These authors constantly remind us that one cannot examine prostitution in isolation from economic, political, and social factors, for example, in relation to migrant sex workers to Japan from Thailand; Ghanian women emigrants in Côte d'Ivoire; migrant experiences from the Caribbean; child prostitution and identity in Thailand.

The major themes discussed in Kempadoo and Doezema's (1998) collection include:

- the specificity of racism;
- the existence of a 'canon' in prostitution studies;
- the impact of globalization;
- the impact of sexually transmitted diseases;
- the impact of the global prostitutes' rights movement.

Racism is examined particularly in relation to Third World sex workers, and includes two major dimensions: (1) racisms embedded in the structures of local industries; and (2) racisms involved in the cultural imperialism and international discourses on prostitution. The 'canon' in prostitution studies is premised upon constructions of prostitution and the prostitute/sex worker found in the literature of the 'First World': the USA and Western Europe. The canon serves to privilege Western categories, subjects and experiences in the internationalist discourses on prostitution.

Sex Work, Consumption and Tourism

Kempadoo and Doezema (1998) and O'Connell Davidson and Sanchez Taylor (1999) discuss the impact of globalization on sex industries and sex work internationally by focusing upon the development of sex tourism as a major industry. Using Cuba as an example, Kempadoo and Doezema (1998: 16) state that sex work 'fills the coffers of countries whose economic survival is increasingly dependent on global corporate capitalist interests'. Migration is another impact of globalization that is explored alongside the feminization of international labour migration; dislocation; involvement in oppressive and complex situations for some women and children against a backdrop of laws prohibiting or regulating prostitution; and migration and trafficking. In some cases it is the laws prohibiting legal sex work and immigration that can form the major obstacles (Kempadoo and Doezema, 1998: 14–19).

O'Connell Davidson and Sanchez Taylor explore the demand for sex tourism through research with male and female Western heterosexual tourists in the Caribbean and argue that the desire for 'others' can only be explained by reference to power relations, control and popular discourses that are gendered, racialized and economic (1999: 37).

> They are not like prostitutes ... They stay with you all day ... They rub in the sun tan oil, bring us the towel, she even washes your feet. What English tart would do that? The problem is getting rid of them. Once you've bought them, they stick to you. They even fight with each other over you. It's wicked [English sex tourist in the Dominican Republic]. (O'Connell Davidson and Sanchez Taylor, 1999: 39)

How does this impact upon social policy in the UK?

We know that in the UK street sex work is less visible than it was a decade ago and that, although for centuries women were the sole focus of regulation, the current policy focus is upon the regulation of men through criminalizing the demand for sexual services. For some theorists and activists, this is an inadequate policy response for many reasons, for it puts the safety of street sex workers at risk by pushing them underground and thus compromises a harm minimization approach. It criminalizes 'ordinary men' who would otherwise have no contact with the law, and buying and selling sex is not a crime when it is a consensual activity (see Chapter 5). Moreover, given the relative success of the New Zealand model where sex work is decriminalized, there is a significant groundswell of support for a harm minimization approach that includes the decriminalization of adult sex work (see Chapter 7). In the UK, there is also a strong focus on a particular discourse of 'trafficking' that does not acknowledge the complexities involved in what we might call the migration–trafficking nexus.

For instance, in a news article in 2007 Harriet Harman claimed there were 25,000 sex slaves in the UK, yet Pentameter 1 raided 515 indoor establishments and 'rescued' only 8 women[10]. There is something of a moral panic emerging over discourses of trafficking for the purposes of exploitation/selling sex. The United Kingdom Human Trafficking Centre was developed from the work of Pentameter 1, alongside national concerns over trafficking.[11]

The Migration–Trafficking Nexus

Agustin is not alone in arguing that there is an urgent need to disentangle trafficking (forced labour in the sex industry or other informal employment) from migration into the informal economy of sex work/domestic labour/agriculture/caring services. The UK appears to have minimized concern for the human rights of migrant workers to an almost singular focus on trafficking into the sex industry (defined as sexual exploitation). Whilst the 'blue blindfold' campaign[12] (a UK Human Trafficking Centre (UKHTC) campaign) identifies trafficking in agriculture/domestic labour and prostitution, it individualizes the issue as a problem of the victim or the evil trafficker (who puts their own economic needs above the welfare of their victim); or the ordinary UK citizen who can stem the 'tide' of trafficking by phoning Crime stoppers with information. It can be argued that this individualizing of the problem prevents a fuller understanding of the complex lives, journeys, and choices of migrants.

Defining 'forced labour'

How do we define 'forced labour' and 'victims of trafficking' for often, as we have discussed above, these are not always clear-cut? The International Labour Organization report of 2005 on

> forced labour in the global economy acknowledges, 'the line dividing forced labour in the strict legal sense of the term from extremely poor working conditions can at times be very difficult to distinguish'. And even if such definitional problems could be resolved, the Trafficking Protocol would remain a highly selective instrument with which to address the general problem of forced labour because, framed as it is within a Convention on transnational organised crime, the interventions that flow from the Protocol are necessarily only triggered by immigration offences and/or organised criminal activity. As argued below, this means they inevitably focus on an extremely limited and narrow part of the problem. (O'Connell Davidson, 2006: 5)

Definitional problems create tensions in government rhetoric between, on the one hand, protecting human rights *and* controlling UK border/immigration that are also linked to discourses of national safety/security; and, on the other, a singular focus on trafficked people as victims of agents/criminal gangs/evil employers without any recognition of the structural issues of immigration and informal employment. This is not a sound basis for policy-making.

What constitutes the trafficking process? Issues to consider

What is clear from research that spans politics, economics, and other branches of the social sciences is that the migration–trafficking nexus is the result of powerful market forces inextricably tied to globalization, capitalism-market forces and the mainstreaming of the sex industry. Should we then understand sex work as a form of 'informal employment'?
 Key issues to think about include:

- Women, men and young people working in informal sectors are vulnerable to human rights abuses – criminalizing demand will not stop the abuses. It will merely serve to make it riskier and harder to detect, pushing criminality further from view and reach.
- There is an urgent need to address how government policies contribute to informal employment, both in terms of the intended and unintended consequences of government policy.
- What are the push factors in countries of origin? Looking at the home countries of women situated in the migration–trafficking nexus, these are marked by economic and political problems, poverty being a major motivating factor.
- What is the role of global networks – not just those defined as organized crime/ criminal networks?
- Remittances migrants send home are incredibly important for local and national economies of poor countries/areas.

In summary, it could be argued based on the evidence that policy measures should focus not on individualizing victims of traffickers and traffickers/smugglers/networks but rather:

- should emerge from quality research that takes more than just a snapshot to inform policy making;
- should take a human rights approach to the issues, taking into account the welfare and human dignity of those working in the sex industry, as well as the rights of people who migrate. A human rights approach will be much more effective than one based solely or primarily on criminal justice.

Finally, we suggest that research undertaken in this area should be done so independently with the participation of the key parties utilizing participatory action research methods in order to avoid reproducing binaries (see Chapter 10) that ultimately help to reinforce the 'Othering' of women and men who sell sex. Thus, the knowledge produced is based on the inclusion, participation and evidence of key stakeholders, including the women and men who are situated in the migration–trafficking nexus that also maps mobility in the national/European and international contexts. This will lead to effective policy-making in this complex and emotive area. This could form one strand of a more constructive policy agenda.

Notes

1 www.ibisworld.com.au/pressrelease/pressrelease.aspx?prid=96
2 According to a report published by the TUC, 'Migrant workers in the UK, including those with the right to work here, are subject to such levels of exploitation and control that they meet the international legal definition of "forced labour"' (2005: 1). Migrant workers should benefit from the same rights that apply to every other worker in the UK, and the TUC is calling on the government to put much more emphasis on cracking down on employers who break employment law in its 'managed migration' policies.
3 See Self (2003) for more information on the 'white slavery' phenomenon.
4 no-racism.net/article/2583/ (accessed 28 September. 2008).
5 www.sexworkeurope.org/site/index.php?option=com_content&task=view&id=24&Itemid=201 (accessed 28 September. 2008).
6 www.tampep.eu/ (accessed 28 September 2008)
7 www.tampep.eu/documents/positionpaper_traffickinginwomen.pdf (accessed 28 September. 2008).
8 See www.eaves4women.co.uk/POPPY_Project/POPPY-Project.php (accessed 7 October 2008).
9 www.stopthetraffik.org/what/casestudies.aspx
10 www.pentameter.police.uk/docs/pentameter.pdf (accessed 9 November)
11 www.ukhtc.org/
12 www.blueblindfold.co.uk/poster_campaign_may2008.htm

Suggested Reading

Agustin, L. (2007) *Sex at the Margins: Migration, Labour Markets and the Rescue Industry*, London: Zed Books.

Goodey, J. (2004) 'Sex trafficking in women from Central and East European countries: promoting a "victim-centred" and "woman-centred" approach to criminal justice intervention', *Feminist Review*, 76(2): 26–47.
Gulcur, L. and Ilkkaracan, P. (2002) 'The "Natasha" experience: migrant sex workers from the former Soviet Union and Eastern Europe in Turkey', *Women's Studies International Forum*, 25(4): 411–21.
O'Connell Davidson, J. (2006) 'Will the real sex slave please stand up?', *Feminist Review*, 83(1): 4–23.

Study Questions

Level one

• What do you understand by the term 'migration–trafficking nexus?'

Level two

• What are the links between the sex industry and tourism?

Level three

• Sexual labour is defined as a primary source of profit and wealth and is a 'constituent part of national economies and transnational industries within the global capitalist economy' (Kempadoo and Doezema, 1998: 8). Discuss.

10

RESEARCHING THE SEX INDUSTRY

This final chapter will explore a range of methodological issues relating to researching the sex industry. Starting off with feminist epistemologies and models of research, the chapter will then lead on to look at key ethical issues when researching a sensitive topic and a hidden population. As the sex industry is increasingly popular as a dissertation topic for level three undergraduates, this chapter will include a section specifically focused on what is feasible, useful and appropriate research at this level.

─────────── **Feminist Epistemologies and Researching the Sex Industry** ───────────

While there is an extensive literature on social science research methodology and practice, only since the 1970s have feminist critiques of the construction of knowledge and research within the academic mainstream emerged (Reinharz, 1992). Feminist theorists within disciplines such as sociology and criminology have argued that, contrary to assumptions that research can be objective and detached, the researcher's choice of study topic, method and population to be studied is influenced by his or her positioning in relation to wider philosophical stances on sex work and prostitution. Factors such as gender, ethnicity and other personal characteristics inform the researcher's perception of the issues to be investigated, the theory behind that investigation and the approach to the research. As Letherby (2003: 5) comments: 'All research is ideological because no one can separate themselves from the world – from their values and opinions, from books they read, from the people they have spoken to and so on'.

Feminist critiques of traditional 'malestream' approaches to theory and research in the social sciences highlight that these have tended to be built upon the perspective of the male inquirer and his relationship to the social world. Thus the 'norm' in much social theory is premised on the 'typical' male and his concerns, which tend to relate primarily to the public sphere, whereas issues that are more likely to concern women within the private sphere, such as the home and personal relationships, are seen as peripheral and irrelevant to theory. Maynard (1998: 121) notes: 'In short, the male perspective has been afforded a privileged epistemological stance'. This has led to women being constructed as 'other' in relation to the male norm (Wilkinson and

Kitzinger, 1996). In turn, this perspective has permeated traditional social research, with the optimum standard seen as being a 'scientific' approach which is characterized in terms of the value-neutrality not only of the method but also of the investigator, with the goal being to uncover and explain the 'facts'. This perspective has been described as 'foundationalist' (Stanley, 1996) or 'positivist' (Denzin and Lincoln, 1998; May, 1997). It is often associated with quantitative research methods, particularly surveys, although as Fine (1998: 139) points out, this is not an exclusive relationship and 'qualitative researchers need to recognize that our work stands in some relation to Othering'. There are also aspects of quantitative research that 'are not directly attributable to either positivism or the practices of the natural sciences' (Letherby, 2003: 65). Maintaining a 'gendered' divide between quantitative and qualitative methods, with the former being seen as a male preserve and the latter as 'women's research' is also seen to be unhelpful, as it serves to reinforce a false hierarchy in which women researchers and their chosen methods are seen as subordinate to the more 'rigorous' numerical approach (Letherby, 2003). In fact, as Bryman (1998: 140) has pointed out, in some debates about quantitative and qualitative research, while research methods may be selected to fit a particular view of social reality, 'this does not tie them exclusively and ineluctably to particular epistemological viewpoints'. If one takes a 'technical' rather than a specific theoretical approach to the choice of method, therefore, it is possible to integrate qualitative and quantitative research according to their perceived appropriateness to the subject of study.

Nonetheless, although the qualitative/quantitative divide may not always be as clear-cut as sometimes suggested, these do constitute different ways of exploring and 'knowing' the social world, each with a distinct ideological basis (Oakley, 2000). Perhaps what is more important is not which methods are selected, but the need for the researcher to be explicit about the reasons for their selection. Equally relevant is consideration of how the research will be analysed and used and here there tends to be a distinction between mainstream and feminist research, with the latter being more concerned with reflexivity, the positioning of the researcher within the process and the production of knowledge derived from people's lived experiences, than arriving at generalizations.

Feminist Models of Research

As there is no single model of feminism, similarly there are different feminist views on styles of research. Nonetheless, these feminisms have certain commonalities, particularly in acknowledging the importance of positioning at the centre of the investigation 'women's diverse situations and the institutions and frames that influence those situations, and then to refer the examination of that problematic to theoretical, policy, or action frameworks in the interests of realizing social justice for women' (Olesen, 1998: 300). Where some feminisms diverge, however, as we saw in Chapter 1, is in the interpretation of 'social justice'. A priority to ground research and analysis in women's experience and knowledge is also characteristic of most feminist approaches, although when considering research into sex work it is notable that some researchers who would consider themselves as coming from a feminist standpoint do not recognize the agency and experiential knowledge of sex workers who do not conform to the 'victim' stereotype. As noted in Chapter 1, Bell (1994) argues that some theoreticians who firmly locate themselves as feminist fighting oppressive patriarchal regimes actually perpetuate the victimhood status of women by making generalizations and assumptions about experiences in sex work which deny agency.

Central to much feminist research methodology is an acknowledgement of the location of the researcher as part of and influencing the research process. From this, it follows that feminist researchers are concerned with the extent to which unequal power relations between the researcher and the researched might be minimized (Maynard, 1998; Oakley, 2002). Some earlier feminist theorists emphasized the importance of women's shared experiences and it has sometimes been argued that a woman investigator is more likely have greater understanding of issues affecting women than a male researcher would although the research process may still involve certain ethical and methodological dilemmas (Finch, 1984; Oakley, 1981). While the researcher and the researched may share the same gender, however, there are nevertheless other factors to be taken into account, including race, class, sexuality and personal background, which help to shape the research process (Harding, 1990; Kitzinger and Wilkinson, 1996). It is therefore equally important to explore and acknowledge difference as well as commonalities (Bola, 1996). The researcher is also inevitably in a position of privilege in relation to the individual(s) being researched and has control over the interpretation and presentation of data (Letherby, 2003; Oakley, 2002). What differentiates feminist methodologies from other mainstream research, however, is that 'feminism forces the researcher to confront such issues, rather than ignore them' (Maynard, 1998: 132).

Feminist epistemologies

So far, we have considered feminist critiques of mainstream research paradigms and alternative methodologies and approaches to research methods arising from feminist perspectives. This section explores some of the main epistemologies or theories of knowledge that provide the background to much feminist research.

Feminist empiricism

Feminist empiricists do not contest the appropriateness of a scientific approach to research, but argue that much scientific inquiry is distorted through sexist and androcentric bias. Thus what is seen as objectivity is in fact the world represented from the perspective of men, with women's experiences being marginalized. This bias informs the research process, from the stage of defining problems to be investigated and the formulation of hypotheses, through the research design to the interpretation of data. The problem is not with traditional methods of research themselves, therefore, but with the way in which they are practised and also by the characteristics of the researcher. Women and feminist researchers (male or female), are more attuned to these androcentric biases and thus are in a better position to produce more objective accounts of the world that include women's experiences as central. Thus, 'good science' does not challenge the validity of empiricism and its goals, but does reject the notion that scientific inquiry is value-free. As Harding notes:

> Feminist empiricism holds on to the idea that a goal of science is to produce less biased, more objective claims, but it also insists on what is overtly forbidden in empiricism – the importance of analyzing and assigning different epistemological values to the social identities of enquirers. (1990: 93)

Feminist standpoint epistemology

Other critiques of positivist approaches to research, most notably constructivism and interpretivism, have developed concurrently with feminist epistemologies.[1] These perspectives hold that inquiry into the human world is fundamentally different from scientific inquiry and thus requires a different methodology. They also reject the notion of value-neutral inquiry, but they argue that empiricist approaches omit the possibility of explaining common understandings and meanings grounded in experience and practice. 'Accordingly, constructivists and interpretivists in general focus on the processes by which these meanings are created, negotiated, sustained and modified within a specific context of human action' (Schwant, 1998: 225). Arguably, feminist standpoint epistemologies can be seen as sharing some features with constructivism.

Feminist standpoint theory or epistemology argues that 'masculine' scientific approaches to understanding the world have little relevance for women and that theories and investigations of the social world should be grounded in women's experiences. Standpoint theorists share with feminist empiricists the view that knowledge is grounded in experience and yet traditionally in Western research that experience has excluded the perspectives of women. Unlike feminist empiricism, however, they do not accept the primacy of scientific method, but rather conclude that all methods of inquiry are innately biased and that only inquiry from the standpoint of women, or a feminist standpoint, is able to overcome that bias. Women and other oppressed groups are not only in a better position to understand their own marginalization, but, it is argued, because of their knowledge of their oppressors, are able to develop a clearer understanding of the world in general (Harding, 1987, 1990; Hartsock, 1983). Letherby (2003: 45) notes that feminist standpoint epistemology shares with feminist empiricism a belief 'that "truth" exists independently of the knower'. Certain problems with this theory have been raised: for example, that feminist standpoint epistemology gives a limited definition of power and oppression focusing exclusively on male domination and ignoring differential power relations between women; and the implication that the perspective of one group is more 'real' than others. Other writers have noted that there are differing feminist standpoint perspectives in existence, with some theorists taking a more realist stance that draws attention to the effect on people's lives of power relations and the potential for different standpoints in relation to different forms of power; whereas others stress the importance of experiential knowledge in the conceptualization of social relations (Ramazanoglu and Holland, 2002).

Although feminist standpoint epistemology has been seen to be relevant not only for white heterosexual women, but also black women, lesbians and other marginalized groups, its many critics have raised questions about potential hierarchies of disadvantage and it is unclear how it is able to deal with fragmented identities (Letherby, 2003; Olesen, 1998). Nonetheless, this approach represents an important development in challenging traditional perspectives on truth and methods of inquiry and raising the importance of taking into account the experience of marginalized groups when theorizing and researching social relations. In relation to research on sex work, for example, O'Neill (2001: 30) points to the need 'to examine prostitution from a critical feminist "woman-centred" position (a version/development of standpoint(s) feminism) that acknowledges the lived experiences of women working as "prostitutes" within the context of sexual and social inequalities'.

Postmodernism and feminism

During the 1980s and 1990s, postmodernist theorists introduced a sceptical perspective on claims to objectivity and universality in scientific inquiry, arguing that the criteria which demarcated 'true' and 'false' were a function of the traditions of modernity and the Enlightenment and thus could not be separated from that tradition. Critics of some forms of postmodernism have argued that it leads to relativism or, alternatively, that it again can privilege one discourse or theory over others (Benhabib, 1990). There have also been concerns that feminist theories which had previously been developed would be abandoned along with other theories of modernism. Some feminist writers, however, saw an opportunity for feminism to draw on postmodernist theories in rejecting the universalism rooted in modernity, to produce a new feminist postmodernism that recognized the diversity of women's needs and experiences as well as their commonalities. 'Thus, the underlying premise of this practice is that, while some women share some common interests and face some common enemies, such commonalities are by no means universal; rather, they are interlaced with differences, even with conflicts' (Fraser and Nicholson, 1990: 35). Further, the concept of deconstruction arising from postmodernist theory raises questions about binary oppositions characterizing Enlightenment ways of thinking (Ramazanoglu and Holland, 2002). Concerns remain about whose voices are heard and how women's experiences are recorded in postmodernist and other feminist theories (Olesen, 1998).

Implications of feminist perspectives for research

Despite some questions about internal consistency and their practical applications, feminist epistemologies have presented major challenges to traditional perspectives on social inquiry that have direct relevance for research into sex work. Not least of these are the introduction of a critical reflexivity, a rejection of traditional claims to objectivity and binary ways of thinking and an acknowledgement of difference and the importance of context. At the heart of feminist approaches to research are the lived experiences of research participants, positioning the researcher in the process and a concern that research should not exploit or harm participants. These also raise some methodological, practical and ethical considerations for researchers, discussed later in this chapter. First, we consider participatory approaches to research, relating to the principles of feminist theories discussed earlier, and their application in research into sex work.

Participatory and Visual Methodologies

Participatory action research (PAR) is a methodology encompassing social research, the production and exchange of knowledge and actions or interventions (O'Neill, 2001, 2007b). Typically, it enables the participation in the research process of those individuals or groups who are normally the subjects of traditional methods of research. Its focus is on the process as much as the outcomes of research and because it involves the very people who have a stake in the issue or problem being researched, has a greater chance of developing purposeful knowledge leading to social change and solutions to community problems. In some forms of participatory research, the style of interview attempts to break down traditional hierarchies between the researcher and the researched, through developing a reciprocity whereby the researcher invests his or her personal identity in the research relationship and turns the 'interview' into an interactive process (discussed in Letherby, 2003). In others, members of the community to be studied are trained as co-researchers and involved in the entire research process, including presentation of the findings and recommendations. The advantages of a participatory approach include the insight that can be provided by community members and peers, which may be lacking from the researcher perspective, an increased feeling of ownership of the research and, where co-researchers are trained and supported, development of additional skills (Clark et al., 2001; Patton, 1997).

Some participatory processes also involve 'creative consultation', a process that involves a combination of PAR and participatory arts (PA). 'Creative Consultation is an approach to research and consultation that aims to incorporate the voices and views of communities directly into the process of policymaking and service delivery' (O'Neill and Webster, 2005: 2). Visual and other arts-based methodologies can help to create safe spaces for consultation which enable research participants to tell their stories in their own way. In one local study into sex work, O'Neill and Campbell (2001) trained a group of community co-researchers who participated in a study to develop partnership responses to street-based sex work. As part of the PAR methods an arts worker was commissioned to conduct creative consultation workshops, supported by the researchers, thus combining traditional research methods of interviews, observation and focus groups with creative arts workshops.[2] O'Neill et al. describe the benefits of this process:

One outcome of the consultation research was to show that collaboration (with local committees, agencies, residents, as well as sex workers) produces rich understanding as well as 'social texts' useful to the wider community (including local and national policy makers). Together, the research team were able to document the complexity of the issues and developed a multi-layered package of responses (some of which were actioned). (2008: 83)

The images that emerged from the creative consultation: 'Safety SoapBox: Sharing our true colours' are documented at www.safetysoapbox.co.uk (Figure 10.1). A chapter written jointly by O'Neill and Campbell and the community co-researchers was also published in an academic book (see O'Neill et al., 2004). This chapter enabled the community representatives to present their personal experiences and concerns, and discuss how some people's views had changed as a result of the research process.

Figure 10.1 Image created by a resident whose views on sex workers changed during the course of the project

There are also other models of inclusive research methodology in the sex industry (see Boynton, 2002; Pyett, 1998). Women who work in the sex industry were trained as interviewers in peer-led research by Pyett and Warr (1997: 540). Using 'indigenous' interviewers, a 'critical reference group' from the Prostitutes Collective of Victoria in Australia was recruited. Training sessions including interview techniques, research process, ethical issues, designing the interview schedule and sampling criteria formed part of the empowerment and education process.

Participatory action research is not without its critics. Some have argued that it can lead to considerable bias, which challenges the validity of the data. Researchers working so closely with participants can risk becoming involved in intra-community politics or become so emotionally involved that it compromises the research (O'Neill, 2001). More traditional research and evaluation methodologies, however, have sometimes been criticized for their irrelevance to policy and practice. There are also ways in which the researcher can check back with colleagues to ensure research rigour, for example, through having an advisory group overseeing the research or evaluation process and thus, as Pitcher (2006b: 73) notes: 'Participatory methods, if carefully scrutinized, do not have to lead to sacrifice of the evaluator's capacity for independent judgement and balance'.

Methodological and Practical Considerations for Researching the Sex Industry

The starting point of a research study is the research question, situated within the researcher's choice of theory and epistemology. Before beginning a study with any group, consideration needs to be given to the research design, including the choice of method, how to define and access the group, the size of the sample and the end product of the research. Anticipating practical and methodological issues in advance of undertaking any research study can help to ensure that the research is kept on track and that the methods employed are defensible.

Choice of method

While it has been argued that feminist research does not need to embrace purely qualitative methods, and some have pointed to the dangers of maintaining a paradigm divide, it remains the case that qualitative methods are more popular amongst feminist researchers. Nonetheless, there are many approaches to qualitative research, with a range of methods to choose from, including life history, in-depth interviews, oral narrative, case studies and participatory action research, as discussed earlier. Certain methods may be more relevant for particular research projects: for example, ethnographic approaches such as participant observation, while having the potential to generate rich data, may be more appropriate for a longer-term study. Factors such as cost may also influence the research design. The use of multiple methods can enable researchers to triangulate the data and also situate individual responses and actions within their social context, which helps to 'secure an in-depth understanding of the phenomenon in question' (Denzin and Lincoln, 1998: 4).

While police statistics or other quantitative secondary data may be useful to contextualize a study into aspects of the sex industry, it is clear from reports analysing these that they are likely to undercount the numbers of people involved in the industry (see Chapter 3 for further discussion on statistical evidence). Qualitative studies are likely to generate more in-depth data on the characteristics and experiences of people working in the industry. Whichever method or combination of methods is chosen, it is important to consider their appropriateness for addressing the research question; the extent to which they are feasible in the circumstances; and to present a rationale for their selection.

As well as theoretical, ethical and methodological issues relating to research design, there are also practical considerations regarding health and safety and the viability of certain research methods when designing a study relating to sex work. For example, research with street-based sex workers may often take place within the context of their working lives and hours of work and thus contact may sometimes be fleeting or interrupted. Traditional interview techniques may not always be the most appropriate if this is likely to be the main form of contact. Pitcher et al. (2008: 164) describe the complications of access and research continuity in their research with street-based sex workers, which involved not only formal interviews with sex workers but 'adopting a mixed methods approach which included interviews and observation, spending some time on the beat during typical working times (generally at night), having informal conversations and observing the working environment'. O'Neill (2001: 74) documents the challenges encountered in her research with women involved in sex work and the need to spend considerable time developing relationships of trust: 'Initially, women were not happy about meeting and talking to me off street. As trust developed, women were more willing to meet and talk but not to be taped; later still women agreed to talk to me about their life-histories and that these narratives be taped'.

Similar issues of trust and access arise when undertaking research with managers of establishments. For example, Sanders makes the point that:

> Although not usually characterized by the violence and vulnerabilities of the street scene, the premises of illegal brothels may be well known but getting a foot in the door is a difficult prospect – especially if the researcher is a woman. Owners, managers and workers are suspicious of unknown inquirers, and women who enter the building are normally looking for work (i.e. competition) or are spying for the opposition. Rarely has it been reported that a researcher has introduced herself or himself to sex workers without a third party mediating the initial introductions. (2006b: 476)

Once the researcher becomes known and trusted within the network of business owners, she or he can make fieldwork visits without needing to be accompanied.

Other practical issues may arise around the identification of the function of some players in the sex industry. For example, we discussed earlier in this book the blurring between the role of pimps and partners of sex workers. In their study of pimps, partners and managers in four different geographical areas, rather than pre-defining roles, May et al. (2000) allowed respondents to choose for themselves which category they felt best reflected their status. This avoids the privileged 'outsider' researcher falsely categorizing people's experiences based on what they think rather than allowing people to define their own experiences.

In the non-contact sexual services industry, observations and interviews may operate side by side. There has been a long-established tradition of mainly women who are already involved in the sex industry becoming researchers and taking on a participant observation role. For instance, much of the excellent rich ethnographic research on lap dancing has sprung from researchers who have this insider status. Scholars such as Ronai and Ellis (1989), Frank (2006, 2007) and Egan (2003) demonstrate the pros and cons of having insider knowledge, whilst at the same time juggling the dual role of researching oneself and the processes of work, commodification, sexual labour, etc. that form part of one's life as a dancer. Egan and Frank (2005) note that the importance of the participant observer role is that the reflexive process of doing the research when involved in some way in the commercial sex industry is pivotal for making clear the standpoint and position of the researcher.

The gender of the researcher is an interesting and important dynamic in the context of sex work research. The social identity of the researcher affects the data collection and possibilities. O'Connell Davidson (O'Connell Davidson and Layder, 1994: 219) reflects on her own gender identity as an essential characteristic for her to gain access to the indoor sex markets: it is 'only because I am a woman that I am able to participate as a receptionist' and maintains that a male researcher would not be able to assume such a position because, for instance, they could not legitimately answer the phone or welcome clients in the expected way. Hence, the sex industry is one of those unique settings that reveals the gendered stratification of 'parts of the social world which are invisible to men simply because they are men' (1994: 219). However, this is not to say that male researchers cannot investigate aspects of the sex industry. Hubbard (1999b) notes that as a male researcher using a sexual health project as the main point of access, there were certain requirements and difficulties to overcome, but that perhaps these are generic to any researcher irrespective of gender. Hubbard (1999b: 233) states that the researcher endeavouring to find out more about the sex industry needs to fulfil four main criteria if gatekeepers are to comply:

(1) that the knowledge produced will work towards reducing the stigma surrounding prostitution;
(2) that the researcher has some insight into the reality of the sex industry;
(3) a recognition that prostitution is not always about victimhood but that it can be a form of work;
(4) a belief that health and safety risks should be minimized. These criteria are a useful guide in the research design stage for those wishing to investigate any aspect of the sex industry.

Researching men who buy sex

Although there has been much less research and attention on those who buy sex than on those who sell sex – reflecting a significant gender bias in women who sell sex being over-researched compared to the male purchasers – there is still a significant body of international research on men who buy sex. This research is conducted using a whole range of qualitative and quantitative methods, but primarily interviews. Accessing clients has been done in various ways: rehabilitation programmes and prisons (Monto, 2000); street and indoor sex market venues (Campbell, 1998); advertisements in the media (Barnard et al., 1993); sexual health clinics (Groom and Nandwini, 2006); and the Internet (Peng, 2007). It is often the case that the researcher is a female in this type of research which can introduce gender-based dynamics that have to be managed effectively by the researcher. O'Connell Davidson and Layder (1994) and Grentz (2005) note that the sexualized nature of this research was problematic and emotionally difficult to handle. However, the context in which the research is conducted is important in managing how the participant engages with the research process. There are also important issues of trust and confidentiality that need to be considered in the research design stage. Men who buy sex are as concerned about their privacy and remaining anonymous as those who sell or manage sex work. In addition, as many men engage in the sex industry in secret, without people in their private lives knowing, there is a therapeutic nature to the interview process.

Internet-based research

The Internet has become a significant methodological tool in the study of the sex industry, both in terms of accessing individuals and observing sex markets and behaviours amongst those who are involved in selling and buying. Durkin and Bryant (1995: 197) note that the prognosis for computer sex research brings an opportunity for systematic data gathering using computer-mediated communication to understand electronic erotica and sexual behaviour. Sharp and Earle (2003) describe how the Internet reveals the secret world of what they term 'cyberpunting' and 'cyberwhoring', yet these suggestions are made with little acknowledgement of the ethical, methodological and epistemological complications of this form of research. The place of the researcher in Internet-based sex research is central to the relationship between the researcher and the researched, the quality of information shared and the ethical responsibility of the researcher. Establishing research relationships online or observing interactions in the virtual arena takes on a range of issues regarding the identity of the researcher and how they manage the disclosure of their status and purpose (see Sanders, 2005c). The ambiguity of the public virtual domain of bulletin boards and chat rooms poses a set of ethical dilemmas for the researcher who 'lurks' in virtual spaces to find out about behaviour, and possibly use the verbatim text that is exchanged in this platform. Sanders found that the sex work community is incredibly suspicious of engaging in online relationships with others who do not appear to be legitimate members of their self-defined community (Sanders, 2005c). When using the Internet to contact men who buy sex, Peng (2007) was met with various sexual remarks and inappropriate suggestions which became a source of distress and anxiety.

Sampling issues

Due to the challenges of access to sex workers and others working in the sex industry, the sample of interviewees may often be opportunistic rather than representative. For example, access may often be through 'gatekeepers', such as agencies working with sex workers. Using this method alone, however, will generate a limited sample of individuals in contact with those agencies and thus will not be representative of all sex workers (Garland et al., 2006; Shaver, 2005). The implications of this for policy development are discussed below. While snowballing methods may help to expand the sample beyond people accessing specific services, there is still likely to be bias towards those who are interested in participating or those within a specific social circle. Shaver (2005: 296) points to the implications of obtaining a skewed sample, which can result in the replication of stereotypes: 'the stories of those less interested in participating and those not in crisis are rarely reported. Targeted sampling, although widely used, is only as good as one's ability to penetrate the local networks of the stigmatized population'.

In certain situations, sample bias is inevitable. This can, to some extent, be corrected through the use of multiple methods which enable the researcher to verify different accounts of the same or similar situations or actions. Nonetheless, given the diversity within the sex industry, as with other groups, it is unlikely that one research study will represent the population as a whole and thus it is important to be explicit about the limitations of methods used. As Muir (2008: 126) observes from undertaking case study research in urban environments: 'the general lessons that can be drawn ... in relation to bias are to assume that it will occur, to be alert for it, and to use it as data'.

Researcher health and safety

Although research into sex work is by no means unique in presenting safety challenges to researchers, given the nature and working hours of the sex industry, there are important considerations to take into account when sending researchers into the field (see Boynton, 2002). Ideally, where researchers are interviewing late at night or in isolated venues, they should pair up. This is not always feasible, however, particularly where research budgets are stretched. Pitcher et al. (2008) document various mechanisms to ensure researcher safety, including interviewing where possible in public or semi-public spaces such as cafés; on the premises of support projects or in outreach vans where confidentiality can be maintained; and logging in and out with other researchers when entering and leaving the field. Sanders (2006b) also discusses various safety procedures that researchers can adopt, including finding gatekeepers who are able to act in a protective role.

Personal safety is thus a major issue to consider when designing a research study in the sex industry. The potential emotional impacts of undertaking research with individuals who have experienced violent, traumatic or distressing events in their lives, such as sex workers, have also been noted by researchers (e.g. O'Neill, 2001; Pearce et al., 2002; Sanders, 2005a). Research into a subject where there are strong views can also lead to feelings of anger and discomfort which need to be handled. For example, Sanders (2008a) describes feelings of anger and despair when interviewing men who buy sex from female sex workers. Letherby (2003) discusses the need for researchers to manage emotions, but also the complexities of this for feminist researchers who may feel the need to challenge discriminatory views. Pitcher et al. (2008), in their research with residents in areas of street sex work, found it particularly difficult to deal with hostile views from some residents who were highly antagonistic towards sex workers and described them in offensive language. They conclude that researchers need 'to maintain a professional distance from these views', a perspective with which Letherby (2003) concurs, noting that if researchers refrain from challenging the views of interviewees, they may produce further insights into the nature and extent of prejudice. If the views of interviewees are challenged, this can also affect the research. While professionals in other fields such as social work or counselling tend to have their own formal support mechanisms, no such system exists as a matter of course for academic researchers. Where researchers work in a team, they can devise methods for supporting one another emotionally. The situation is more complicated for lone researchers, who often have to find their own means of managing their emotional responses to fieldwork.

What Is Appropriate and Ethical Research?

While not exclusive to feminist methodologies, feminist research, alongside questioning arising from other qualitative approaches, has contributed to the development of a body of literature on what constitutes ethical research practice. Some of the issues have been discussed earlier, particularly in relation to the need for reflexivity and acknowledgement of power differentials between the researcher and the researched. Bodies such as the British Sociological Association and Social Research Association produce guidance on ethical protocols covering issues such as informed consent and preserving confidentiality of research participants. Individual institutions also have their own ethical protocols and committees to oversee these, as outlined later in this chapter. In addition, organizations such as the UK Network of Sex Work Projects (www.uknswp.org) give guidance on research ethics pertaining specifically to sex workers and support projects. In this section, we consider some of the main ethical considerations to take into account when undertaking research with sex workers. These include negotiating access; confidentiality and informed consent; transparency of process and roles; and sensitivity to the needs of research participants. Academic researchers also need to gain approval from their institution's ethics committee, which can raise problems in relation to choice of subject, methodology and safety issues (Sanders, 2006b).

Negotiating access and clarifying processes

Sex workers are often perceived to be a 'hard-to-reach' group and thus initial access may often be through gatekeepers such as support projects, which may help to introduce researchers to the local situation and enable them to become known to service users in a relatively informal and relaxed setting (Sanders, 2006b; Shaver, 2005). As was noted earlier, however, this method alone may give access to a limited sample of interviewees who may not reflect the diversity in the industry, which has the potential to lead to policy formation based on inaccurate portrayals of the local sex worker population (see Agustin, 2007b). Pitcher et al. note:

> This is particularly pertinent when considering that policies tend to draw on studies based on relatively limited samples of sex workers, sometimes presenting a particular moral or political stance, which may go some way towards explaining the association of street sex work with victimisation and abuse in recent UK policy documents. (2008: 165)

It is thus important to consider additional mechanisms for reaching and recruiting research participants. Negotiating access through gatekeepers is also not without its challenges. For example, the researcher needs to demonstrate the validity and viability of the research; persuade the agency that their intervention will not compromise relationships of trust between agency staff and service users; and that the research will not harm respondents (Sanders, 2006b).

Positioning the researcher

An additional consideration when gaining access through services working with sex workers is that the researcher may not be seen as independent from that service, which may influence individuals' responses. This is particularly pertinent when, as sometimes happens, researchers observe or participate in outreach sessions run by services, which can lead to some confusion of roles (Pitcher et al., 2008; Sanders, 2006b; Wahab, 2003). Thus clarity about the research process, the end product(s) and the role of the researcher is particularly important throughout, to assure respondents about how their contribution will be used and presented. Distribution of a participant information leaflet or flyer which explains the aims and intended outcomes of the research, the anticipated audiences and issues such as confidentiality, as well as contact details for further queries, is also considered good practice.

Researchers have often documented their experience of shifting identities in ethnographic research and the 'insider–outsider' dilemma. For example, Wahab (2003: 628) talks about her complex identity when involved in a research study with sex workers in Seattle, where she was both a member of the academic community and working with a project providing support and advocacy to sex workers: 'social worker, voyeur, wanna-be-sex-worker, advocate, friend, goodie-two-shoes.' Sanders (2006b) discusses the ethical dilemmas involved in becoming a 'complete observationalist' when doing research with indoor sex workers and the advantages and disadvantages in blurring roles to gain insider status, which can lead to a loss of distance. Wahab (2003) also describes how through working and undertaking research with sex workers, her perspective on and approach to the issues changed dramatically as a result, from viewing sex work as exploitative to developing a greater understanding of the diversity of the women's personal and working lives, leading her to become a member of a prostitutes' rights organization.

Confidentiality and informed consent

The researcher has a responsibility to protect the interests of interviewees, which includes preserving the anonymity of participants. This means not only using pseudonyms when quoting from individuals, but also being sensitive to the way in which data are used in public documents, as in some instances it may be possible to infer people's identities from quotes or descriptions. When undertaking research with sex workers, given their precarious legal and social situation, it is particularly important that no information is given out that may compromise their privacy. Preservation of confidentiality is not only applicable to public documents but also to the way in which data are stored.

Prior to involving individuals in a research study, it is important that their cooperation is based as far as practicable on their freely given consent, which should be based on full information about the process and end results of the research, their entitlement to refuse or withdraw at any stage, how the interview or focus group will be conducted, how the data will be used and their confidentiality assured. Sometimes a consent form may be used, which is signed by the interviewee and sometimes also the interviewer, although this also raises issues of confidential storage of information. It is recognized that there are limitations to the notion of informed consent, particularly with groups of individuals who might be seen as vulnerable. Guidance from the Social Research Association (SRA, 2003: 31) states that 'in conducting research with vulnerable populations, extra care must be taken to protect their rights and ensure that their compliance is freely entered into'. Gaining 'informed consent' for informal methods of data collection such as participant and non-participant observation, however, can be problematic in some instances (Punch, 1998; Shaver, 2005). As Muir (2008: 126) notes: 'The experience of trying to obtain informed consent, especially to observation, was that it is almost impossible to be sure that it has taken place'. Sanders (2006b: 480), in her research in indoor establishments, obtained prior consent from sex workers and managers in the venues, but at their request, did not disclose her researcher status to clients, a situation she describes as a delicate 'research bargain'.

The situation described by Sanders is an example where there is a need to balance the interests of different parties involved in transactions and to consider where disclosure to one party might adversely affect one or more of the others involved (so in the case of the managers and sex workers, disclosure to clients would be detrimental to their business and interfere with the client–worker relationship). As it was the workers themselves, within their work setting, who were the primary focus of the research, non-disclosure to clients who were not the focus of study can be seen as defensible. The use of covert methods more generally, however, is strongly discouraged by research bodies such as the Social Research Association and British Sociological Association. The ethical guidelines produced by the SRA (2003: 34), for example, state that 'Covert observation and any other forms of research which use deception can only be justified where there is no other ethically sound way of collecting accurate and appropriate data'. In the case of studies focusing on sex workers, their managers, partners or clients, it is clear from examples given earlier that it is quite feasible to undertake ethical and safe research which ensures methodological transparency and participant consent, which suggests that covert methods are generally to be considered inappropriate and unethical in these circumstances. As Punch notes:

In general, serious academics in a sound academic community will espouse trust, reject deception and abhor harm. They will be wary of spoiling the field, of closing doors to research, and of damaging the reputation to their profession – both as a matter of principle and out of self-interest. In practice, however, professional codes and sound advice may not be all that clear and unambiguous in the field setting, in all its complexity and fluidity. (1998: 180)

Thus, setting out to deliberately deceive research participants is generally considered to be poor research practice, but within methods such as participant observation, concealment and 'economy with the truth' may sometimes be unavoidable.

Participant-focused approaches

Research guidelines often specify the importance of taking a 'participant-focused' approach to a research study. This includes respecting the rights and dignity of interviewees, taking care to be aware of and respond to their safety needs, preserving confidentiality and being clear that they have a choice about participating in the interview. Social researchers should also avoid being unnecessarily intrusive into people's personal lives and be aware that some questioning may cause stress, which requires sensitivity to their emotional responses during the course of the interview. Consideration may be given to preparing a handout of relevant sources of advice, support and guidance, to which the interviewee may turn if required. In the case of research with sex workers, the researcher also needs to respect their personal space, particularly if they are working, so that they are not prevented from interactions with clients and the clients are not deterred from approaching them. Similar guidelines have been documented by many researchers working in the field (e.g. Pearce et al., 2002; Sanders, 2006b; Shaver, 2005; Wahab, 2003) and are also similar to those often issued by projects to outreach staff working with sex workers.

We noted earlier that the social researcher is inevitably in a position of power over the research participant, no matter to what extent she or he is involved in the design of the study. It is possible to minimize disparities in power, however, through some of the processes described above, but also in ensuring that the voices of participants are heard and in the case of vulnerable groups, given equal weight to those in a more privileged position (O'Neill, 1996; Pearce et al., 2002). For example, Pitcher et al., (2008) note the importance of balancing the views of sex workers against the perspectives of community representatives, to present an alternative to common preconceptions about street sex workers and demonstrate that many sex workers also have concerns about the neighbourhood in which they work and a sense of responsibility towards local residents.

Other mechanisms for counterbalancing power differentials in research include checking back on the content of interviews with participants, discussing with them how these will be presented and involving participants more closely in the research process, as discussed earlier.

Analysing and presenting research findings

Responsibility towards research participants does not end when the researcher leaves the field. The nature of the ongoing research relationship is partly determined by the methodology, but at the very least it is suggested that the qualitative researcher check the validity of their data with respondents. These 'member checks' may, of course, lead to some respondents exercising their right to veto the use of certain parts of their interviews, resulting in a somewhat 'sanitized' version of the material, as documented by Oakley (2000). When undertaking research with marginalized groups such as street-based sex workers, there may also be difficulties in verifying the content of interviews if participants are transient and thus the researcher has to use their judgement on how far to pursue this. Sometimes researchers will also negotiate interpretations of the data with participants, particularly in participatory approaches. This also raises the question of how the researcher will deal with conflicting understandings (Ramazanoglu and Holland, 2002). If the researcher takes the final decision in interpreting the data, reflexivity on the process and methodological transparency is important: 'At best you can be as aware as possible that interpretation is your exercise of power, that your decisions have consequences, and that you are accountable for your conclusions' (Ramazanoglu and Holland, 2002: 161). The participatory action research study described by O'Neill et al. earlier gives an example of how involvement of community co-researchers can produce insights through a process of collaboration. Not all research participants will want this level of involvement, however, and it is then up to the researcher to decide how the analysis proceeds and how the voices of subjects are represented (Letherby, 2003).

Where research participants are not centrally involved in reporting the findings of research studies, the researcher needs to consider how to share these with people who have taken part in the research. A lengthy research report or academic paper may be of interest to other members of the academic community, but they are unlikely to be read by most research participants or local community representatives. There are other ways of presenting findings that enable the researcher to give something back to the community of study, however. These can include the production of short summaries of key findings, visual representations and discussing the findings with different audiences (such as projects which have facilitated the research process, at drop-ins with sex workers and at community meetings). While it may sometimes be difficult to see how research will lead to a change in policy, it is important to consider mechanisms to bring the findings to the attention of those responsible for developing policy locally and nationally.

Making Research Policy Relevant

Involvement in policy development is a relatively new venture for researchers and academics. If researchers are concerned about influencing policy, however, it is important that they work more collaboratively with local and national stakeholders and partnerships to disseminate the recommendations arising from the research and take them forward. In a more collaborative or participatory approach to research, involvement in the process goes beyond the production of the final report and ensures that the messages are understood and, it is hoped, acted upon. Too often, however, as was noted earlier, policy is based upon limited or skewed investigations. As Bamberger and Podems (2002: 93) comment: 'While participatory consultations with all stakeholder groups are recommended, time and resource constraints – and the concern of governments to keep control of the evaluation process – have often meant that only a limited number of voices are reflected in the planning and evaluation reports'. The lessons from feminist methodologies are that research should reflect the voices of participants, value different experiences and not arrive at sweeping generalizations, but rather lead to action that has the potential to improve the lives of participants.

Although much qualitative research, particularly that with a primary focus on ethnographic methods, has often been regarded as lacking relevance to policy development, Pitcher et al. (2008) note the importance of presenting findings accessible to a range of audiences and taking additional steps to share the findings with national policy-makers and local partnerships. Truman (2002) discusses how feminist evaluation and active dissemination strategies can help to influence planning and service provision. Involving local agencies in the research process itself, for example, ensuring they are represented on the research advisory group, or through participatory methods, can also promote greater ownership of the findings and recommendations amongst the policy community.

Studying the Sex Industry as an Undergraduate

It is encouraging to note that more students are becoming interested in researching the sex industry at undergraduate level. Typically, there is interest in pursuing this subject for an extended project such as a dissertation where there are opportunities and expectations of empirical data collection. However, it is rarely appropriate for undergraduates to take on original empirical work within such a sensitive area and with potentially vulnerable, hard to research groups. This section looks at the reasons why researching the sex industry first hand is not appropriate at undergraduate level, but also suggests ways that the sex industry can be studied through secondary sources.

What is appropriate investigation?

There are three main reasons why designing and conducting 'new' empirical work with sex workers or those who work directly in the sex industry is particularly problematic and difficult at undergraduate levels: ethical, methodological and practical difficulties.

Ethical

1   Any empirical work now needs to pass through a series of ethical review processes to ensure that the project is appropriately designed, in accordance with institutional and professional codes of conduct and ultimately reaches the benchmarks of ensuring no harm is done to research participants or the researcher. These processes are formal, lengthy, bureaucratic and involve detailed work to get a project up to the required standard. In addition, there can also be a similar process required by the gatekeeper (such as a charity, official agency or the health service for instance). These review processes are above and beyond the expectation of undergraduate research and also the objectives of the project.
2   Social scientists have obligations to ensure that research is carried out that can be useful and that the findings can be fed into processes of change and development. This means that the project needs to consider the implications of the findings, and work out how the findings can be disseminated to make the most of them. Again, this is beyond the scope of the undergraduate project.

3   There are ethical responsibilities for not researching a particular group unless necessary, otherwise this leads to over-researching. In the past decade there has been a tremendous amount of research on the sex industry, and often this has been with the same groups of people (e.g. street sex workers, drug users, those in the criminal justice system). Given that street prostitution is the smallest section of the wider industry and that outreach groups are traditionally approached as gatekeepers (Agustin, 2007b) there is a real risk of over-researching these groups. Also, the research inquiry must be genuine rather than stemming from some voyeuristic interests in marginal or 'deviant' groups.

Methodological

1   An undergraduate dissertation is the first place that a student learns about methods. This is only the beginning of a longer apprenticeship to becoming a skilled researcher. The next logical step is postgraduate study which is often the breeding ground for competent and professional researchers who can springboard into empirical work as part of a Masters course, for instance. However, at undergraduate level, students rarely have the nuanced skills, or experience needed to apply qualitative research techniques to a group of people who are often entirely marginalized from society.
2   Designing ethical research means that the correct systems of support are in place for the respondents, in case there are after affects from the research. This would be difficult for an undergraduate to provide effectively.

Practical

1   *Time:* Setting up an empirical project requires a considerable amount of time. There are several distinct stages to go through which are often dependent on third parties and time delays are usual. For instance, gaining access to gatekeepers, going through complex ethical review procedures, piloting the data collection tools, continuing to ensure access, and then doing the data collection takes considerable time. Afterwards, the transcription (or other forms of analysis) and the analysis phase can take longer than expected. This is all before the writing up phase.
2   *Resources/Money:* It is good practice that participants are paid for their time and this is usually not possible with undergraduate projects. In addition, if lengthy interviews are carried out, transcription services will be required as the time it takes to transcribe can also put pressure on any undergraduate project (note that it normally takes approximately 7 hours to transcribe a one-hour interview).
3   *Access:* Undergraduates may well have interesting ideas and even be connected to parts of the sex industry, but ultimately, gaining access and working through the informed consent process does not always produce effective relationships and the project must begin again or adapt in order to be successful. An undergraduate who is working in tight and set timeframes does not have this flexibility.

The uses of secondary sources

There are other ways in which undergraduates can successfully and ethically research the sex industry using secondary sources. There are many documents that can be the subject of analysis:

- 'grey material' such as reports, accounts from individuals, NGO leaflets and publications;
- government documents: consultation papers, legislation, website content, press releases, strategy documents, amendments and guidelines;
- debates in Parliament which can all be accessed via Hansard;
- testimonies of sex workers published as novels and autobiographies;
- media sources: newspapers and magazines;
- films, documentaries and other television programmes;
- the Internet: websites that relate to the sex industry (which do not show illegal activities) such as individual advertisements, support organization websites, social movements, message boards, chat rooms, blogs and other individualized information.

Options for empirical work

Although the implications of conducting empirical work at undergraduate level are complex, there are certain topics and questions which target other groups of people which are more appropriate. Given the attention that has been given to prostitution management and policy in recent years in the UK, there are several organizations in most towns and cities that are involved in the design and delivery of services (see Chapter 8). It is these groups that could be appropriately targeted for research purposes. For instance, it could be possible to design and conduct qualitative research with professionals who work with the sex industry, policy-makers and local authority officials who are engaged with policy design, implementation and delivery. In addition, religious groups are often involved in delivering grassroots services and could also be an area of investigation.

Resources and Archives

UK Network of Sex Work Projects' specialist collection on sex workP

Big Lottery Funding allowed the UKNSWP to build up a collection of materials on sex work. These comprise books, journal articles, research reports, project reports, leaflets and other materials such as reports from organizations, campaign documents and historical information. The main aim of the collection is to provide a place where material can be brought together securely and formally whilst allowing access to people who are researching and learning about the various aspects of the sex industry.

All the materials are housed in the specialist collections library within The Robertson Trust Library and Learning Resource Centre, Paisley Campus at the University of the West of Scotland. Borrowing from the library is straightforward and open to all:

- If the item you want is available electronically it will be emailed to you at no cost.
- If it is in the collection only in hard copy and it can be copied, it will be posted to you, you will simply need to cover the cost of postage and photocopying.
- With some items you'll be able to borrow the hard copy for a specified period as with any library, with you covering postage.

To do this you will need to contact the specialist librarian, Allison Watson (e-mail: allison.watson@uws.ac.uk).

Other sources of information include the Home Office RDS for certain studies (free of charge: www.homeoffice.gov.uk/rds/).

Notes

1 For further discussion on different research paradigms, see Denzin and Lincoln (1998).
2 O'Neill calls this process ethno-mimesis (2001, 2007b).

Suggested Reading

Hubbard, P. (1999) 'Researching female sex work: reflections on geographical exclusion, critical methodologies and 'useful' knowledge', *Area*, 31(3): 229–37.
O'Neill, M. (2001) *Prostitution and Feminism: Towards a Politics of Feeling*, Cambridge: Polity Press.
O'Neill, M., Campbell, R., James, A., Webster, M., Green, K., Patel, J., Akhtar, N. and Saleem, W. (2003) 'Red lights and safety zones', in D. Bell and M. Jayne (eds), *City of Quarters*, Aldershot: Ashgate.
Sanders, T. (2006) 'Sexing up the subject: methodological nuances in the female sex industry', *Sexualities*, 9(4): 471–90.
Shaver, F.M. (2005) 'Sex work research: methodological and ethical challenges', *Journal of Interpersonal Violence*, 20(3): 296–319.

Study Questions

Level one

• What relevance do feminist methodologies have to research into sex work?

Level two

• Can covert research methods ever be considered defensible when researching aspects of the sex industry?

Level three

• If you were designing a research study on clients of sex workers, what methods would you choose and why? Are there any practical and ethical considerations to take into account?

GLOSSARY

Arrest referral – usually relating to problem drug users, arrest referral schemes identify problem users as they pass through the criminal justice system and refer them to treatment agencies.

ASBO – a civil order made in court for which the police, local authorities and registered landlords can apply. Their aim is to protect neighbourhoods from anti-social behaviour that causes distress and harassment. An ASBO might prohibit a sex worker from entering a specific area. Breach of an order is a criminal offence.

Bondage – a sexual practice in which the partners derive additional pleasure through physical restraint or binding.

Breast relief – A sexual service which involves the stimulation of the penis by the breasts and/or cleavage.

Brothel – a house or establishment used by more than one woman, for the purposes of prostitution. Also known as a massage parlour.

Couch testing – 'testing' sexual performance to determine suitability for sex work.

Court diversion – similar to arrest referral schemes, court diversion schemes have been set up to divert specific groups, mainly sex workers, to services in place of receiving a fine or other penalty for prostitution-related offences. There is usually a minimum condition of engagement, such as two sessions with a support project.

Creative consultation – an approach to research and consultation that aims to incorporate the voices and views of communities directly into the process of policymaking and service delivery, through use of participatory arts and participatory action research.

Cruising – the activity of seeking and meeting sexual partners in public places.

Decriminalization – the removal of criminal penalties relating to adult prostitution.

Dodgy punters – dangerous clients. This usually relates to schemes for reporting dangerous/violent clients to projects so that information can be shared with other sex workers to improve their safety and to gather evidence for potential prosecution.

Emotional labour – jobs involving emotional labour are those which require face-to-face or voice-to-voice contact and require the worker to produce an emotional state in another person. Typical emotional labour jobs include restaurant workers and flight attendants. The concept was coined by sociologist Arlie Hochschild.

Escort – a sex worker who works for an agency or independently.

Exotic dance – sexualized dance in clubs – usually another term for stripping/striptease dance.

Fellatio – oral stimulation of the penis.

Gigolo – a professional male escort; a young man living at the expense of an older woman, particularly one to whom he gives sexual favours in return.

Grooming – exploitation of a young person or child by an older adult, usually a man, posing as a 'boyfriend', who coerces the young person into sexual activity and finally into prostitution.

Hand relief – masturbation.

Harm minimization – a philosophy of client-centred support that aims to reduce the harms to individuals caused by problems such as drug and alcohol dependency and to promote safer use rather than abstinence. Also used in relation to promoting safer sex.

Importuning – soliciting for immoral purposes.

Kerb-crawling – driving along slowly with the intention of enticing people into the car, for sexual purposes.

Lap dancer – a night club stripper who dances close to clients and sits briefly on their laps.

Legalization – making prostitution legal under certain conditions: for example, through use of toleration zones for street prostitution, or through regulation of premises. Legalization is often accompanied by conditions for sex workers, such as compulsory health checks.

Loitering – (for prostitutes) in a street or public place for the purposes of prostitution.

Maid – a receptionist in a brothel, massage parlour or sauna, who acts as the first point of contact for the client.

Needle exchange – a public health programme that allows injecting drug users to exchange used hypodermic needles for new ones in an effort to prevent the spread of infection.

Participatory Arts (PA) – Participatory Arts is sometimes referred to as Community Arts. It involves people working with an arts worker or an arts company, to create something new or original around a theme and when used in social research it is used to help participants to express their views creatively. The UK has a long history of using participatory arts as a means of giving a voice to marginalized communities (Webster, 1997, 5 2004).

Participatory action research (PAR) – a research methodology that typically enables the participation in the research process of those individuals or groups who are normally the subjects of traditional methods of research.

Pimp – a man who lives off the earnings of a prostitute, or who solicits for a prostitute or brothel and is paid for his services.

Punter – slang term for a male customer.

Receptionist *see* **maid**

Regulation – (in relation to sex work) a means of controlling legalized sex industry premises through licensing, where official agencies take control.

Rent boy – slang for young male prostitute who works on the street.

Sex market – the context in which buying and selling of sex takes place.

Sex tourism – travel undertaken to take advantage of the relatively lax laws on prostitution in some countries.

Sexually Transmitted Infections (STIs) – infections such as syphilis and chlamydia which are passed on during unprotected sex.

Soliciting – (for prostitutes) to make advances in a street or public place for the purposes of prostitution.

Tolerance zone – a location specifically designated for street prostitution, sometimes with services on site. Sex workers usually face arrest if they work outside the zone.

Trafficking – as distinct from people smuggling (where migrants are seen as willing participants), human trafficking is where the intention behind the facilitation is the exploitation of those migrants when they reach their destination (Home Office, 2004).

Travesti – term used to refer to male transvestites who work as sex workers, and appear as women, but do not have gender reassignment surgery.

Ugly Mugs *see* **Dodgy Punters**

'Whore' stigma – social stigma attached to sex work as a 'deviant' activity or occupation based on a woman's sexuality.

Window sex worker – sex workers (usually women) who sit on display behind windows. Found in certain cities, such as Amsterdam.

Zoning *see* **tolerance zone**

BIBLIOGRAPHY

Adkins, L. (1995) *Gendered Work: Sexuality, Family and Labour Market*, Buckingham: Open University Press.

Aggleton, P. (ed.) (1999) *Men Who Sell Sex: International Perspectives on Male Prostitution and HIV/AIDS*, London: Taylor and Francis.

Agustin, L.M. (2005) 'New research directions: the cultural studies of commercial sex', *Sexualities*, 8(5): 618–31.

Agustin, L.M. (2006) 'The conundrum of women's agency: migrations and the sex industry', in R. Campbell and M. O'Neill (eds), *Sex Work Now*, Cullompton: Willan.

Agustin, L.M. (2007a) *Sex at the Margins: Migration, Labour Markets and the Rescue Industry*, London: Zed Books.

Agustin, L.M. (2007b) 'Questioning solidarity: outreach with migrants who sell sex', *Sexualities*, 10(4): 519–34.

Allen, J.S. (2007) 'Means of desire's production: male sex labor in Cuba', *Identities*, 14(1): 183–202.

Anderson, B. (2006) *A Very Private Business: Migration and Domestic Work*, Centre on Migration, Policy and Society Working Paper No. 28, Oxford: University of Oxford.

Ayres, J. (2005) 'Developing services for migrant sex workers', presentation to UKNSWP conference 'Working with Diversity in Sex Work', Liverpool, 25 February.

Bamberger, M. and Podems, D.R. (2002) 'Feminist evaluation in the international development context', in D. Seigart and S. Brisola (eds), *Feminist Evaluation: Explorations and Experiences*, New Directions for Evaluation No. 96, San Francisco CA: Wiley.

Barnard, M., McKeganey, N. and Leyland, A. (1993) 'Risk behaviours among male clients of female prostitutes', *British Medical Journal*, 307(6900): 361–2.

Barrett, D. (1997) *Child Prostitution in Britain*, London: The Children's Society.

Barrett, D. and Ayre, P. (2000) 'Young people and prostitution: an end to the beginning?', *Children and Society*, 14(1): 48–59.

Barry, K. (1979) *Female Sexual Slavery*, New York: New York University Press.

Barry, K. (1995) *Prostitution and Sexuality*, New York: New York University Press.

Barry, K. (1996) *The Prostitution of Sexuality*, New York: New York University Press.

Barry, K. (1997) *The Idea of Prostitution*, Melbourne: Spinifex Press.

Bartley, P. (2000) *Prostitution, Prevention and Reform in England 1860–1914*, London: Routledge.

Barton, B. (2002) 'Dancing on the Mobius Strip: challenging the sex war paradigm', *Gender and Society*, 16(5): 585–602.

Barton, B. (2007) 'Managing the toll of stripping: boundary setting among exotic dancers', *Journal of Contemporary Ethnography*, 36(5): 571–96.

Bassermann, L. (1993) *The Oldest Profession: A History of Prostitution*, New York: Dorset Press.

Bauman, Z. (2001) *Community: Seeking Safety in an Insecure World*, Cambridge: Polity.

Becker, J. and Duffy, C. (2002) *Women Drug Users and Drugs Service Provision: Service Level Responses to Engagement and Retention*, DPAS Briefing Paper No. 17, London: Home Office.

Bell, S. (1994) *Reading, Writing and Rewriting the Prostitute Body*, Bloomington, IN: Indiana University Press.

Benhabib, S. (1990) 'Epistemologies of postmodernism: a rejoinder to Jean-François Leotard', in L.J. Nicholson (ed.), *Feminism/Postmodernism*, New York: Routledge.

Benson, C. and Matthews, R. (1995) *The National Vice Squad Survey*, Middlesex: Centre for Criminology, Middlesex University.

Benson, C. and Matthews, R. (2000) 'Police and prostitution vice squads in Britain', in R. Weitzer (ed.), *Sex for Sale*, London: Routledge.

Bernstein, E. (1999) 'What's wrong with prostitution? What's right with sex work? Comparing markets in female sexual labor', *Hastings Women's Law Journal*, 10(1): 91–119.

Bernstein, E. (2001) 'The meaning of the purchase: desire, demand and the commerce of sex', *Ethnography*, 2(3): 389–420.

Bernstein, E. (2007) 'Sex work for the middle classes', *Sexualities*, 10(4): 473–88.

Bimbi, D. (2007) 'Male prostitution: pathology, paradigms and progress in research', *Journal of Homosexuality*, 53(1/2): 7–35.

Bindman, J. (1997) *Redefining Prostitution as Sex Work on the International Agenda*, Available at: www.walnet.org/csis/papers/redefining.html (accessed 10 May 2008).

Bindman, J. (1998) 'An international perspective on slavery in the sex industry', in K. Kempadoo and J. Doezema (eds), *Global Sex Workers: Rights, Resistance and Redefinition*, New York and London: Routledge.

Bishop, R. and Robinson, L. (1997) *Nightmarket: Sexual Cultures and the Thai Economic Miracle*, New York and London: Routledge.

Boden, D. (2007) 'The alienation of sexuality in male erotic dancing', *Journal of Homosexuality*, 53(1/2): 129–52.

Bola, M. (1996) 'Questions of legitimacy?: The fit between researcher and researched', in S. Wilkinson and C. Kitzinger (eds), *Representing the Other: A Feminism and Psychology Reader*, London: Sage.

Bourne, J. (nd) *Attitudes Towards Prostitution in the Potteries*. Available at: www.staffs.ac.uk/ schools/humanities_and_soc_sciences/reports/fallen.htm

Boutellier, J. (1991) 'Prostitution, criminal law and morality in the Netherlands', *Crime, Law and Social Change*, 15(2): 201–11.

Boynton, P. (2002) 'Life on the streets: the experiences of community researchers in a study of prostitution', *Journal of Community and Applied Social Psychology*, 12(1): 1–12.

Boynton, P. and Cusick, L. (2006) 'Sex workers to pay the price', *British Medical Journal*, 332(28 January): 190–1.

Braiden, G. (2008) 'Glasgow turns to Sweden in attempt to tackle prostitution within', the Herald, 15 September. Available at http://www.theherald.co.uk/news/news/display.var. 2432449.0Glasgow_turns_to_Sweden_in_attempt_to_tackle_prostitution_within_city.php (accessed 17 September 2008)

Brazil's Labour and Employment Ministry website. Available at: www.mtecbo.gov.br/busca/ descricao. asp?codigo=5198 (accessed 27 May 2008).

Brents, B. and Hausbeck, K. (2005) 'Violence and legalized brothel prostitution in Nevada: examining safety, risk and prostitution policy', *Journal of Interpersonal Violence*, 20(3): 270–95.

Brents, B. and Hausbeck, K. (2007) 'Marketing sex: U.S. legal brothels and late capitalist consumption', *Sexualities*, 10(4): 425–39.

Brents, B. and Sanders, T. (forthcoming) 'The mainstreaming of the sex industry: economic inclusion and social ambivalence', *Journal of Law and Society*, Special Issue: Regulating Sex/Work: From Crime Control to Neo-liberalism.

Brewer, D., Muth, S. and Potterat, J. (2008) 'Demographic, biometric, and geographic comparison of clients of prostitutes and men in the US general population', *Electronic Journal of Human Sexuality*, 11(9). Available at: www.ejhs.org/volume11/brewer.htm

Brewis, J. and Linstead, S. (1998) 'Time after time: the temporal organization of red collar work', *Time and Society*, 7(2): 223–48.

Brewis, J. and Linstead, S. (2000a) '"The worst thing is the screwing" (1): consumption and the management of identity in sex work', *Gender, Work and Organization*, 7(2): 84–97.

Brewis, J. and Linstead, S. (2000b) '"The worst thing is the screwing" (2): context and career in sex work', *Gender, Work and Organization*, 7(2): 168–80.

Brewster, Z. (2003) 'Behavioural and interactional patterns of strip club patrons: tipping techniques and club attendance', *Deviant Behaviour*, 24(2): 221–43.

Bright, V. and Shannon, K. (2008) 'A participatory-action and interventional research approach to HIV prevention and treatment among women in survival sex work', *Research for Sex Work*, 10: 9–10.

Brooks-Gordon, B. (2005) 'Clients and commercial sex: reflections on *Paying the Price:* a consultation paper on prostitution', *Criminal Law Review,* 425–43.

Brooks-Gordon, B. (2006) *The Price of Sex: Prostitution, Policy and Society,* Cullompton: Willan.

Brown, A. (2004) 'Mythologies and panics: twentieth century constructions of child prostitution', *Children & Society,* 18(3): 344–54.

Brown, A. and Barrett, D. (2002) *'Knowledge of Evil': Child Prostitution and Child Sexual Abuse in Twentieth Century England,* Cullompton: Willan.

Browne, J. and Minichiello, V. (1995) 'The social meanings behind male sex work: implications for sexual interactions', *British Journal of Sociology,* 46(4): 598–622.

Bruinsma, G. and Meershoek, G. (1999) 'Organized crime and trafficking in women from Eastern Europe in the Netherlands', *Illegal Immigration and Commercial Sex,* London: Frank Cass.

Bryman, A. (1998) 'Quantitative and qualitative research strategies', in T. May and M. Williams (eds), *Knowing the Social World,* Buckingham: Open University Press.

Bullough, V. and Bullough, B. (1987) *Women and Prostitution: A Social History,* New York: Prometheus Books.

Busza, J. (2006) 'Having the rug pulled from under your feet: one project's experience of the US policy reversal on sex work', *Health Policy and Planning,* 21(4): 329–32.

Butcher, K. (2003) 'Confusion between prostitution and sex trafficking', *The Lancet,* 361(June 7): 1983.

Cabezas, A. (2004) 'Between love and money: sex, tourism and citizenship in Cuba and Dominican Republic', *Signs: Journal of Women in Culture and Society,* 29(6): 987–1015.

Campbell, C. (2000) 'Selling sex in the time of AIDS: the psycho-social context of condom use by sex workers on a Southern African mine', *Social Science & Medicine,* 50(4): 479–94.

Campbell, D. (2008) 'Working with male and trans sex workers: challenging times', paper presented at UK Network of Sex Work Projects Conference, Manchester, 6 June.

Campbell, R. (1998) 'Invisible men: making visible male clients of female prostitutes in Merseyside', in J. Elias, V. Bullough, V. Elias and G. Brewer (eds), *Prostitution: On Whores, Hustlers and Johns,* New York: Prometheus Books.

Campbell, R. (2001) *'Mushes' in Merseyside: Paying for Sex in Liverpool,* Liverpool: Hope University College.

Campbell, R. (2002) *Working on the Street: An Evaluation of the Linx Project,* Liverpool: Liverpool Hope/Nacro.

Campbell, R., Coleman, S. and Torkington, P. (1996) *Street Prostitution in Inner City Liverpool,* Liverpool: Liverpool City Council.

Campbell, R. and Kinnell, H. (2001) '"We shouldn't have to put up with this": street sex work and violence', *Criminal Justice Matters,* 42(Winter) 12.

Campbell, R. and O'Neill, M. (2004) *Sex Lies and Love? An Evaluation* (Report for Walsall Youth Offending Team), Coventry: NACRO and Staffordshire University.

Campbell, R. and Storr, M. (2001) 'Challenging the kerb crawler rehabilitation programme', *Feminist Review,* 67(Spring): 94–108.

Carael, M., Slaymaker, E., Lyerla, R. et al. (2006) 'Clients of sex workers in different regions of the world: hard to count', *Sexually Transmitted Infections,* 82: 26.

Castles, S. (2003) 'Towards a sociology of forced migration and social transformation', *Sociology,* 37(1): 13–34.

Chapkis, W. (1997) *Live Sex Acts: Women Performing Erotic Labour,* New York: Routledge.

Chevalier, A. (2007) 'The social role of an escort', paper presented at Sex Work: Regulating the Many Faces of Sexual Labour, University of Keele, 17 October.

Chun, S. (1999) 'An uncommon alliance: finding empowerment for exotic dancers through labour unions', *Hastings Women's Law Journal,* 10(1): 231–52.

Church, S., Henderson, M., Barnard, M. and Hart, G. (2001) 'Violence by clients towards female prostitutes in different work settings: questionnaire survey', *British Medical Journal,* 322: 524–5.

Clamen, J. and Lopes, A. (2003) 'Labour organising in the sex industry: the way forward?', *Research for Sex Work,* 6: 29–30.

Clark, J., Dyson, A., Meagher, N., Robson, E. and Wootten, M. (2001) *Young People as Researchers: Possibilities, Problems and Politics,* Leicester: Youth Work Press.

Clark, L. (2006) *Provision of Support for Imprisoned Adult Female Street-based Sex Workers*, Research Paper 2006/01, London: Griffins Society.

Collins, A. (2004) 'Sexuality and sexual services in the urban economy and socialscape: an overview', *Urban Studies*, 41(9): 1631–42.

Comella, L. (2008) 'It's sexy. It's big business. And it's not just for men', *Contexts*, 7(3): 61–3.

Connell, J. and Hart, G. (2003) 'An overview of male sex work in Edinburgh and Glasgow: the male sex work perspective', MRC Social and Public Health Sciences Unit, Occasional Paper, June. Available at: www.sphsu.mrc.ac.uk

Corbin, A. (1987) 'Commercial sexuality in nineteenth-century France: a system of images and regulations', in C. Gallagher and T. Laquer (eds), *The Making of the Modern Body: Sexuality and Society in the Nineteenth Century*, Berkeley, CA: University of California Press.

Corbin, A. (1990) *Women for Hire: Prostitution and Sexuality in France after 1850*, Cambridge, MA: Harvard University Press.

Coy, M. (2007a) 'Young women, local authority care and selling sex: findings from research', *British Journal of Social Work*, 38(7): 1408–24.

Coy, M. (2007b) 'This morning I'm a researcher, this afternoon I'm an outreach worker: ethical dilemmas in practitioner research', *International Journal of Social Research Methodology*, 9(5): 419–31.

Coy, M. (2008) 'The consumer, the consumed and the commodity: women and sex buyers talk about objectification in prostitution', in V. Munro and M. Della Giusta (eds), *Demanding Sex: Critical Reflections on the Regulation of Prostitution*, Hampshire: Ashgate.

Coy, M., Horvath, M. and Kelly, L. (2007) *'It's Just Like Going to the Supermarket': Men Buying Sex in East London*, London: Child & Woman Abuse Studies Unit, London Metropolitan University.

Cusick, L. and Berney, L. (2005) 'Prioritizing punitive responses over public health: commentary on the Home Office consultation document *Paying the Price*', *Critical Social Policy*, 25(4): 596–606.

Cusick, L. and Hickman, M. (2005) '"Trapping" in drug use and sex work', *Drugs: Education, Prevention and Policy*, 12(4): 369–79.

Cusick, L., Martin, A. and May, T. (2003) *Vulnerability and Involvement in Drug Use and Sex Work*, Home Office Research Study 268, London: Home Office.

Darch, T. (2004) 'Terrence Higgins Trust West Street Team: working with young men', in M. Melrose with D. Barrett (eds), *Anchors in Floating Lives: Interviews with Young People Sexually Abused Through Prostitution*, Lyme Regis: Russell House.

Davies, P. and Feldman, R. (1997) 'Prostitute men now', in G. Scambler and A. Scambler (eds), *Rethinking Prostitution: Purchasing Sex in the 1990's*, London: Routledge.

Davies, P. and Feldman, R. (1999) 'Selling sex in Cardiff and London', in P. Aggleton (ed.), *Men Who Sell Sex: International Perspectives on Male Prostitution and HIV/AIDS*, London: Taylor and Francis.

Davis, K. (1937) 'The sociology of prostitution', *American Journal of Sociology*, 2(5): 744–55.

Day, S. (2007) *On the Game: Women and Sex Work*, London: Pluto Press.

Day, S. and Ward, H. (2004) 'Approaching health through the prism of stigma', in S. Day and H. Ward (eds), *Sex Work, Mobility and Health in Europe*, London: Kegan Paul.

Delacoste, F. and Alexander, P. (1987) *Sex Work: Writings by Women in the Sex Industry*, London: Virago.

Denzin, N.K. and Lincoln, Y.S. (1998) *The Landscape of Qualitative Research: Theories and Issues*, Thousand Oaks, CA: Sage.

Department of Education and Skills (2003) *Every Child Matters*, London: HMSO. Available at: www.dfes. gov.uk

Department of Health (1999) *Working Together to Safeguard Children*, London: HMSO.

Department of Health (2000) *Safeguarding Children Involved in Prostitution: Supplementary Guidance to Safeguarding Children*, London: HMSO.

Department of Health/Home Office (1998) 'Guidance on Children Involved in Prostitution'. Available at: www.dohgov.uk/pdfs/qualitycp.pdf

Department of Health and Home Office (2000) *Safeguarding Children Involved in Prostitution*, London: HMSO.

Deshotels, T. and Forsyth, C.J. (2006) 'Strategic flirting and the emotional tab of exotic dancing', *Deviant Behavior*, 27(2): 223–41.

Diduck, A. and Wilson, W. (1997) 'Prostitutes and persons', *The Journal of Law and Society*, 24(4): 504–25.

Ditmore, M. (2008) 'Punishing sex workers won't curb HIV/AIDS, says Ban-Ki Moon', 24 June, RH Reality Check. Available at: www.rhrealitycheck.org/blog/2008/06/23/sex-workers-grateful-banki-moon (accessed 24 June 2008).

Ditmore, M. and Wijers, M. (2003) 'The negotiations on the UN Protocol on trafficking in persons', *Nemesis*, 4: 79–88.

Dixon, D. and Dixon, J. (1998) 'She-male prostitutes: who are they, what do they do and why do they do it?', in J. Elias, V. Bullough, V. Elias and G. Brewer (eds), *Prostitution: On Whores, Hustlers and Johns*, New York: Prometheus Books.

Doezema, J. (1998) 'Forced to choose: beyond the voluntary v forced prostitution dichotomy', in K. Kempadoo and J. Doezema (eds), *Global Sex Workers: Rights, Resistance and Redefinition*, New York and London: Routledge.

Dressel, P. and Petersen, D. (1982) 'Becoming a male stripper: recruitment, socialization, and ideological development', *Work and Occupations*, 9(4): 387–406.

Drinkwater, S., Greenwood, H. with M. Melrose (2004) 'Young people exploited through prostitution: a literature review', in M. Melrose, with D. Barrett (eds), *Anchors in Floating Lives: Interviews with Young People Sexually Abused through Prostitution*, Lyme Regis: Russell House.

Durbar Mahila Samanwaya Committe-website: www.durbar.org

Durkin, K. and Bryant, C. (1995) '"Log on to sex": some notes on the carnal computer and erotic cyberspace as an emerging research frontier', *Deviant Behaviour*, 16(2): 179–200.

Dworkin, A. (1981) *Pornography: Men Possessing Women?*, London: Women's Press.

Dworkin, A. (1996) 'Pornography', in S. Jackson and S. Scott (eds), *Feminism and Sexuality*, Edinburgh: Edinburgh University Press.

ECPAT International (2007) *Upholding the Right of Children to Live Free from Commercial Sexual Exploitation: Interventions and Recommendations*, Bangkok: ECPAT.

Edmunds, M., Hough, M., Turnbull, P. and May, T. (1999) *Doing Justice to Treatment: Referring Offenders to Drug Services*, London: Home Office/DPAS.

Edwards, S. (1991) 'Prostitution, whose problem?', unpublished paper, Wolverhampton Safer Cities Project.

Edwards, S. (1993) 'Policing: the under-representation of women's interests', in S. Jackson (ed.), *Women's Studies: A Reader,* Hemel Hempstead: Harvester Wheatsheaf.

Edwards, S. (1998) 'Abused and exploited – young girls in prostitution', in Barnardo's *Whose Daughter Next? Children Abused through Prostitution*, Ilford: Barnardo's.

Egan, D. (2003) 'I'll be your fantasy girl, if you'll be my money man: mapping desire, fantasy and power in two exotic dance clubs', *Journal for the Psychoanalysis of Culture and Society*, 8(1): 277–96.

Egan, D. (2005) 'Emotional consumption: mapping love and masochism in an exotic dance club', *Body & Society,* 11(4): 87–108.

Egan, D. and Frank, K. (2005) 'Attempts at a feminist and interdisciplinary conversation about strip clubs', *Deviant Behavior*, 26(2): 297–320.

Egan, D., Frank, K. and Johnson, M. (eds) (2006) *Flesh for Fantasy: Producing and Consuming Exotic Dance*, New York: Thunder's Mouth Press.

Ekberg, G. (2004) 'The Swedish law that prohibits the purchase of sexual services: best practices for prevention of prostitution and trafficking in human beings', *Violence Against Women*, 10(10): 1187–218.

Eisler, R. (1995) *Sacred Pleasure: Sex, Myth, and the Politics of the Body,* London: HarperCollins.

Elder, K. (2008) 'The PEPFAR "Anti-Prostitution Pledge": a case study from Nigeria', *Research for Sex Work*, 10: 15–18.

EMPOWER Foundation website: www.empowerfoundation.org

Ennew, J. (1986) The *Sexual Exploitation of Children*, Cambridge: Polity.

Epele, M. (2001) 'Excess, scarcity and desire among drug-using sex workers', *Body & Society*, 7(2–3): 161–79.

Erickson, D. and Tewkesbury, R. (2000) 'The "gentleman" in the club: a typology of strip club patrons', *Deviant Behaviour*, 21(3): 271–93.

Escoffier, E. (2007) 'Porn star/stripper/escort: economic and sexual dynamics in a sex work career', *Journal of Homosexuality*, 53(1): 173–200.

Europap (2003) *Practical Guidelines for Delivering Health Services to Sex Workers*, Ghent: European Network for HIV/STD Prevention in Prostitution (Europap).

Evans, C. and Lambert, H. (1997) 'Health seeking strategies and sexual health among female sex workers in urban India: implications for research and service provision', *Social Science and Medicine*, 44(12): 1791–803.

Farley, M. (2004) '"Bad for the body, bad for the heart": prostitution harms women even if legalized or decriminalized', *Violence Against Women*, 10(10): 1087–125.

Farley, M. (2005) 'Prostitution harms women even if indoors', *Violence Against Women*, 11(7): 950–64.

Faugier, J., Hayes, C. and Butterworth, C. (1992) *Drug-using Prostitutes, their Health Care Needs and their Clients*, Final Report to the Department of Health, London: Department of Health.

Faugier, J. and Sargeant, M. (1997) 'Boyfriends, "pimps" and clients', in G. Scambler and A. Scambler (eds), *Rethinking Prostitution: Purchasing Sex in the 1990's*, London: Routledge.

Finch, J. (1984) '"It's great to have someone to talk to": the ethics and politics of interviewing women' in C. Bell and H. Roberts (eds), *Social Researching: Politics, Problems, Practice*, London: Routledge.

Fine, M. (1998) 'Working the hyphens: reinventing self and other in qualitative research', in N.K. Denzin and Y.S. Lincoln (eds), *The Landscape of Qualitative Research: Theories and Issues*, Thousand Oaks, CA: Sage.

Finnegan, F. (1979) *Poverty and Prostitution: A Study of Victorian Prostitutes in York*, Cambridge: Cambridge University Press.

Fischer, C. (1996) 'Employee rights in sex work: the struggle for dancers' rights as employees', *Law and Inequality: A Journal of Theory and Practice*, 14(5): 521–54.

Foucault, M. (1979) *The History of Sexuality*, Vols 1 and 2, London: Allen Lane.

Frank, K. (1998) 'The production of identity and the negotiation of intimacy in a "gentleman's Club"', *Sexualities*, 1(2): 175–201.

Frank, K. (2002) *G-Strings and Sympathy*, Durham, NC: Duke University Press.

Frank, K. (2006) 'Observing the observers: reflections on my regulars', in D. Egan, K. Frank and M. Johnson (eds), *Flesh for Fantasy*, New York: Thunder's Mouth Press.

Frank, K. (2007) 'Thinking critically about strip club research', *Sexualities*, 10(4): 501–17.

Fraser, N. and Nicholson, L.J. (1990) 'Social criticism without philosophy: an encounter between feminism and postmodernism', in L.J. Nicholson (ed.), *Feminism/Postmodernism*, New York: Routledge.

Funari, V. (1997) 'Naked, naughty and nasty', in J. Nagel (ed.), *Whores and Other Feminists*, London: Routledge.

Gaffney, J. (2002) 'Guidelines for development of outreach work with men who sell sex', in K. Schiffer (ed.), *Manual: Tips, Tricks and Models of Good Practice for Service Providers Considering, Planning or Implementing Services for Male Sex Workers*, Amsterdam: European Network Male Prostitution.

Gaffney, J. (2007) 'A coordinated prostitution strategy and response to *Paying the Price* – but what about the men?', *Community Safety Journal*, 6(1): 27–33.

Gaffney, J. and Beverley, K. (2001) 'Contextualising the construction and social organisation of the commercial male sex industry in London at the beginning of the twenty-first century', *Feminist Review*, 67(Spring): 133–41.

Gagnon, J.H. and Simon, W. (1987) 'The sexual scripting of oral genital contacts', *Archives of Sexual Behavior*, 16(1): 1–25.

Galatowicz, L., Pitcher, J. and Woolley, A. (2005) *Report of the Community-Led Research Project Focusing on Drug and Alcohol Use of Women Sex Workers and Access to Services*, Coventry: Terrence Higgins Trust, for University of Central Lancashire and Department of Health.

Gall, G. (2006) *Sex Worker Union Organising: An International Study*, London: Palgrave Macmillan.
Gall, G. (2007) 'Sex worker unionisation: an exploratory study of emerging collective organisation', *Industrial Relations Journal*, 38(1): 70–88.
Gangoli, G. (2007) 'Immorality, hurt or choice: how Indian feminists engage with prostitution', *International Feminist Journal of Politics*, 9(1): 1–19.
Gangoli, G. and Westmarland, N. (eds) (2006) *International Approaches to Prostitution: Law and Policy in Europe and Asia*, Bristol: The Policy Press.
Garland, D. (2001) *The Culture of Control: Crime and Social Order in Contemporary Society*, Oxford: Oxford University Press.
Garland, J., Spalek, B. and Chakraborti, N. (2006) 'Hearing lost voices: issues in researching "hidden" minority ethnic communities', *British Journal of Criminology*, 46(4): 423–37.
Gibson, B. (1995) *Male Order: Life Stories from Boys who Sell Sex*, London: Cassell.
Gil, P. (2006) *Body Count: Fixing the Blame for the Global AIDS Catastrophe*, New York: Thunder's Mouth Press.
Gillespie, T. (2000) 'Virtual violence?: Pornography and violence against women on the internet', in J. Radford, M. Friedlberg and L. Harne (eds), *Women, Violence and Strategies for Action*, Buckingham: Open University Press.
Goodchild, S. and Thompson, J. (2007) '5,000 child sex slaves in UK', *Independent on Sunday*, 25 February. Available at: www.independent.co.uk/news/uk/crime/5000-child-sex-slaves-in-uk-437800.html (accessed 25 May 2009).
Goodey, J. (2003) 'Migration, crime and victimhood: responses to sex trafficking in the EU', *Punishment and Society*, 5(4): 415–31.
Goodyear, M.D. (2008) 'Incarceration of female sex workers in China and STI/HIV programmes that are not rights-based are doomed to fail', *Sexually Transmitted Infections*, 84(1): 1–2.
Gould, A. (1999) *Punishing the Punter: The Politics of Prostitution in Sweden*, Loughborough: Department of Social Science, Loughborough University.
Green, J. (1992) *'It's No Game': Responding to the Needs of Young Women at Risk or Involved in Prostitution*, Leicester: National Youth Agency.
Green, J., Mulroy, S. and O'Neill, M. (1997) 'Young people and prostitution from a youth services perspective', in D. Barrett (ed.), *Children and Prostitution: Current Dilemmas, Practical Responses*, London: The Children's Society.
Grentz, S. (2005) 'Intersections of sex and power in research on prostitution: a female researcher interviewing male heterosexual clients', *Signs: Journal of Women in Culture and Society*, 30(4): 2091–113.
Groom, T. and Nandwini, R. (2006) 'Characteristics of men who pay for sex: a UK sexual health clinic survey', *Sexually Transmitted Infections*, 82(5): 364–7.
Hall, T.M. (2007) 'Rent boys, barflies and kept men: men involved in sex with men for compensation in Prague', *Sexualities*, 10(4): 457–72.
Hallgrimsdottir, H., Phillips, R. and Beniot, C. (2006) 'Fallen women and rescued girls: social stigma and media narratives of the sex industry in Victoria, BC from 1980 to 2005', *The Canadian Review of Sociology and Anthropology*, 43(3): 265–82.
Hancock, L. (2006) 'Community safety and social exclusion', in P. Squires (ed.), *Community Safety: Critical Perspectives on Policy and Practice*, Bristol: The Policy Press.
Hancock, L. and Matthews, R. (2001) 'Crime, community safety and toleration', in R. Matthews and J. Pitts (eds), *Crime, Disorder and Community Safety*, London: Routledge.
Hanmer, J. and Maynard, M. (1987) *Women, Violence and Social Control*, Basingstoke: Macmillan.
Hanmer J., Radford, J. and Stanko, E. (1989) *Women, Policing and Male Violence*, London: Routledge.
Hanmer, J. and Saunders, S. (1984) *Well Founded Fear: A Community Study of Violence to Women*, London: Hutchinson.
Harcourt, C. and Donovan, B. (2005a) 'Sex work and the law', *Sexual Health*, 2: 121–8.
Harcourt, C. and Donovan, B. (2005b) 'The many faces of sex work', *Sexually Transmitted, Infections*, 81(3): 201–6.

Harcourt, C., van Beek, I., Heslop, J., McMahon, M. and Donovan, B. (2001) 'The health and welfare needs of female and transgender street sex workers in New South Wales', *Australian and New Zealand Journal of Public Health*, 25(1): 84–9.

Harding, R. and Hamilton, P. (2008) 'Working girls: abuse and choice in street-level sex work? A study of homeless women in Nottingham', *British Journal of Social Work*. Available at: http://bjsw.oxfordjournals.org/cgi/content/abstract/bcm157 (accessed 1 June 2009).

Harding, S. (ed.) (1987) *Feminism and Methodology*, Milton Keynes: Open University Press.

Harding, S. (1990) 'Feminism, science and the anti-Enlightenment critiques', in L.J. Nicholson (ed.), *Feminism/Postmodernism*, New York: Routledge.

Hart, G. and Barnard, M. (2003) '"Jump on top, get the job done": strategies employed by female prostitutes to reduce the risk of client violence', in E.A. Stanko (ed.), *The Meanings of Violence*, London: Routledge.

Hartsock, N. (1983) 'The feminist standpoint: developing the ground for a specifically feminist historical materialism', in S. Harding and M.B. Hintikka (eds), *Discovering Reality*, Amsterdam: D. Reidel.

Hausbeck, K. and Brents, B. (2000) 'Inside Nevada's brothel industry', in R. Weitzer (ed.), *Sex for Sale*, London: Routledge.

Hausbeck, K. and Brents, B. (2002) 'McDonaldization of the sex industries? The business of sex', in G. Ritzer (ed.), *McDonaldization: The Reader*, Thousand Oaks, CA: Pine Forge Press.

Hawkes, G. (1996) *A Sociology of Sex and Sexuality*, Buckingham: Open University Press.

Henriques, F. (1962) *Prostitution and Society*, London: MacGibbon and Kee.

Hester, M. and Westmarland, N. (2004) *Tackling Street Prostitution: Towards an Holistic Approach*, Home Office Research Study 279, Development and Statistics Directorate, London: Home Office.

Hinchberger, B. (2005) *Brazilian Sex Workers Don't Mourn, They Organize*, 19 October 2005. Available at: www.brazilmax.com/news.cfm/tborigem/fe_society/id/23 (accessed 25 May 2008).

Hoigard, C. and Finstad, L. (1992) *Backstreets: Prostitution, Money and Love*, Cambridge: Polity.

Holzman, H. and Pines, S. (1982) 'Buying sex: the phenomenology of being a john', *Deviant Behaviour*, 4(1): 89–116.

Home Office (1957) *Report of the Committee on Homosexual Offences and Prostitution* cmnd. 247, London: HMSO.

Home Office (2004) *Paying the Price: A Consultation on Prostitution*, London: Home Office.

Home Office (2006) *A Coordinated Prostitution Strategy*, London: Home Office.

Howe, C., Zaraysky, S. and Lorentzen, L. (2008) 'Transgender sex workers and sexual transmigration between Guadalajara and San Francisco', *Latin American Perspectives*, 35(1): 31–50.

Howell, P. (2001) 'Sex and the city of bachelors: sporting guidebooks and urban knowledge in nineteeth century Britain and America', *Cultural Geographies*, 8(1): 20–50.

Hubbard, P. (1998) 'Community action and the displacement of street prostitution: evidence from British Cities', *Geoforum*, 29(3): 269–86.

Hubbard, P. (1999a) *Sex and the City: Geographies of Prostitution in the Urban West*, Aldershot: Ashgate.

Hubbard, P. (1999b) 'Researching female sex work: reflections on geographical exclusion, critical methodologies and "useful" knowledge', *Area*, 31(3): 229–37.

Hubbard, P. (2002) 'Maintaining family values? Cleansing the streets of sex advertising', *Area*, 34(4): 353–60.

Hubbard, P. (2007) 'Out of touch and out of time? The contemporary policing of sex work', in R. Campbell and M. O'Neill (eds), *Sex Work Now*, Cullompton: Willan.

Hubbard, P., Campbell, R., Pitcher, J., O'Neill, M. and Scoular, J. (2006) 'An urban renaissance for all?', in R. Atkinson and G. Helms (eds), *Securing an Urban Renaissance: Crime, Community and British Urban Policy*, Bristol: The Policy Press.

Hubbard, P., Matthews, R. and Scoular, J. (2007) *Regulating the Spaces of Sex Work: Assessing the Impact of Prostitution Law: Full Research Report*. ESRC End of Award Report, RES-000-22-1001. Swindon: ESRC.

Hubbard, P., Matthews, R. and Scoular, J. (2008a) 'Regulating sex work in the EU: prostitute women and the new spaces of exclusion', *Gender, Place and Culture*, 15(2): 137–52.

Hubbard, P., Matthews, R., Scoular, J. and Agustin, L.M. (2008b) 'Away from prying eyes? The urban geographies of "adult entertainment"', *Progress in Human Geography*, 32(3): 363–81.

Hubbard, P. and Sanders, T. (2003) 'Making space for sex work: female street prostitution and the production of urban space', *International Journal of Urban and Regional Research*, 27(1): 73–87.

Hughes, D. (2001) 'Prostitution online'. Available at: www.uri.edu/artsci/wms/Hughes/demads.htm,

Hughes, D. (2004) 'The use of new communication technologies for sexual exploitation of women and children', in R. Whisnant and C. Stark (eds), *Not for Sale: Feminists Resisting Prostitution and Pornography*, Toronto: Spinifex Press.

Hunt, N. and Stevens, A. (2004) 'Whose harm? Harm reduction and the shift to coercion in UK drug policy', *Social Policy & Society*, 3(4): 333–42.

Hunter, G. and May, T. (2004) *Solutions and Strategies: Drugs Problems and Street Sex Markets, Guidance for Partnerships and Providers*, London: Home Office.

Hwang, S. and Bedford, O. (2004) 'Juveniles' motivations for remaining in prostitution', *Psychology of Women Quarterly*, 28(2): 136–46.

Janus, M.D., Scanton, B. and Price, V. (1984) 'Youth prostitution', in A.W. Burgess (ed.), *Child Pornography and Sex Rings*, Lexington, MA: Lexington Books.

Jarvinen, M. (1993) *Of Vice and Women: Shades of Prostitution*, Oslo: Scandinavian University Press.

Jeal, N. and Salisbury, C. (2004) 'Self-reported experiences of health services among female street-based prostitutes: a cross-sectional survey', *British Journal of General Practice*, 54(504): 515–19.

Jeal, N. and Salisbury, C. (2007) 'Health needs and service use of parlour-based prostitutes compared with street-based prostitutes: a cross-sectional survey', *British Journal of Obstetrics and Gynaecology*, 114(March): 875–81.

Jeffreys, S. (1997) *The Idea of Prostitution*, Melbourne: Spinifex Press.

Jeffreys, S. (2003) 'Sex tourism: do women do it too?', *Leisure Studies*, 22(3): 223–38.

Jeffreys, S. (2008) *The Industrial Vagina: The Political Economy of the Global Sex Trade*, London: Routledge.

Jenness, V. (1990) 'From sex as sin to sex as work: COYOTE and the reorganization of prostitution as a social problem', *Social Problems*, 27(3): 403–20.

Jesson, J. (1993) 'Understanding adolescent female prostitution: a literature review', *British Journal of Social Work*, 23(5): 517–30.

Johnson, P. (2007) 'Ordinary folk and cottaging: law, morality and public sex', *Journal of Law and Society*, 34(4): 520–43.

Jones, P. and Pratten, J. (1999) 'Buying and selling sex: a preliminary examination of the service encounter', *Management Research News*, 22(12): 38–42.

Jones, P., Shears, P. and Hillier, D. (2003) 'Retailing and the regulatory state: a case study of lap dancing clubs in the UK', *International Journal of Retail and Distribution Management*, 31(4/5): 214–19.

Jordan, J. (2005) *The Sex Industry in New Zealand*, Wellington: Ministry of Justice.

Kantola, J. and Squires, J. (2004) 'Discourses surrounding prostitution policies in the UK', *European Journal of Women's Studies*, 11(1): 77–101.

Kelly, L. and Regan, L. (2000) *Stopping Traffic: Exploring the Extent of, and Responses to, Trafficking in Women for Sexual Exploitation in the UK*, Police Research Series Paper 125, London: Home Office Research, Development and Statistics Directorate. Available at: www.homeoffice.gov.uk/rds/prgpdfs/fprs125.pdf

Kelly, L., Wingfield, R., Burton, S. and Regan, L. (1995) *Splintered Lives: Sexual Exploitation of Children in the Context of Children's Rights and Child Protection*, Ilford: Barnardo's and the Child Abuse and Women's Studies Unit, University of North London.

Kempadoo, K. (1998) 'The Exotic Dancers Alliance: an interview with Dawn Prassar and Johanna Breyer', in K. Kempadoo and J. Doezema (eds), *Global Sex Workers: Rights, Resistance and Redefinition*, New York: Routledge.

Kempadoo, K. (ed.) (1999a) *Sun, Sex and Gold: Tourism and Sex Work in the Caribbean*, London: Rowman and Littlefield.

Kempadoo, K. (1999b) 'Continuities and change: five centuries of prostitution in the Caribbean', in K. Kempadoo (ed.), *Sun, Sex and Gold: Tourism and Sex Work in the Caribbean*, London: Rowman and Littlefield.

Kempadoo, K. and Doezema, J. (eds) (1998) *Global Sex Workers: Rights, Resistance, and Redefinition*, London: Routledge.

Kesler, K. (2002) 'Is a feminist stance in support of prostitution possible? An exploration of current trends', *Sexualities*, 5(2): 219–35.

Kilvington, J., Day, S. and Ward, H. (2001) 'Prostitution policy in Europe: a time for change?', *Feminist Review*, 67(Spring): 78–93.

Kinnell, H. (2006a) 'Murder made easy: the final solution to prostitution?', in R. Campbell and M. O'Neill (eds), *Sex Work Now*, Cullompton: Willan.

Kinnell, H. (2006b) 'Clients of female sex workers: men or monsters?', in R. Campbell and M. O'Neill (eds), *Sex Work Now*, Cullompton: Willan.

Kinnell, H. (2008) *Violence and Sex Work in Britain*, Cullompton: Willan.

Kinnell, H. and Griffiths, R.K. (1989) 'Male clients of female prostitutes in Birmingham, England: a bridge for transmission of HIV?', poster presentation, fifth International Conference on AIDS, Montreal, Canada June 1989.

Kishtainy, K. (1982) *The Prostitute in Progressive Literature*, London: Allison and Busby.

Kitzinger, C. and Wilkinson, S. (1996) 'Theorizing representing the other', in S. Wilkinson and C. Kitzinger (eds), *Representing the Other: A Feminism and Psychology Reader*, London: Sage.

Klauser, F.R. (2007) 'Difficulties in revitalizing public space by CCTV: street prostitution surveillance in the Swiss city of Olten', *European Urban and Regional Studies*, 14(4): 337–48.

Korn, J. (1998) 'My sexual encounters with sex workers: the effects on a consumer', in J. Elias, V. Bullough, V. Elias and G. Brewer (eds), *Prostitution: On Whores, Hustlers and Johns*, New York: Prometheus Books.

Kulick, D. (1998) *Travesti: Sex, Gender and Culture among Brazilian Transgendered Prostitutes*, Chicago, IL: University of Chicago Press.

Kulick, D. (2003) 'Sex in the new Europe: the criminalization of clients and Swedish fear of penetration', *Anthropological Theory*, 3(2): 199–218.

Kulick, D. (2005) 'Four hundred thousand Swedish perverts', *GLQ: A Journal of Lesbian and Gay Studies*, 11(2): 205–35.

Kurtz, S.P., Surratt, H.L., Inciardi, J.A. and Kiley, M. (2004) 'Sex work and "date" violence', *Violence Against Women*, 10(4): 357–85.

Laite, J.A. (2008) 'The association of moral and social hygiene: abolitionism and prostitution law in Britain (1915–1959)', *Women's History Review*, 17(2): 207–23.

Law, L. (2000) *Sex Work in Southeast Asia: The Place of Desire in a Time of AIDS*, London: Routledge.

Leander, K. (2005) 'Reflections on Sweden's measures against men's violence against women', *Social Policy & Society*, 5(1): 115–25.

Lee, M. and O'Brien, R. (1995) *The Game's Up: Redefining Child Prostitution*, London: The Children's Society.

Leichtentritt, R. and Davidson-Arad, B. (2004) 'Adolescent and young adult male-to-female transsexuals: pathways to prostitution', *British Journal of Social Work*, 34(4): 349–74.

Letherby, G. (2003) *Feminist Research in Theory and Practice*, Buckingham: Open University Press.

Lever, J. and Dolnick, D. (2000) 'Clients and call girls: seeking sex and intimacy', in R. Weitzer (ed.), *Sex for Sale*, London: Routledge.

Levi-Minzi, M. and Shields, M. (2007) 'Serial sexual murderers and prostitutes as their victims: difficulty profiling perpetrators and victim vulnerability as illustrated by the Green River Case', *Brief Treatement and Crisis Intervention*, 7(1): 77–89.

Lewis, J., Maticka-Tyndale, E., Shaver, F. and Schramm, H. (2005) 'Managing risk and safety on the job: the experiences of Canadian sex workers', *Journal of Psychology & Human Sexuality*, 17(1/2): 147–67.

Lewis, T. (2008) 'Tax sex workers', *Jamaica Observer*, 19 June. Available at: www.jamaicaobserver.com/news/html/20080619T000000-0500_136918_OBS_TAX_SEX_WORKERS.asp (accessed 24 June 2008).

Lim, L.L. (1998) *The Sex Sector: The Economic and Social Bases of Prostitution in Southeast Asia*, Geneva: International Labour Office.

Lloyd, R. (1977) *Playland: A Study of Boy Prostitution*, London: Blond and Briggs.

Lombroso, C. and Ferrero, G. (2004) *Criminal Woman, the Prostitute, and the Normal Woman*, translated with a new introduction by N. Hahn Rafter and M. Gibson, Durham, NC: Duke University Press.

Lopes, A. (2001) 'Sex workers of the world unite', *Feminist Review*, 67(Spring): 151–3.

Lopes, A. (2006) 'Sex workers and the labour movement in the UK', in R. Campbell and M. O'Neill (eds), *Sex Work Now*, Cullompton: Willan.

Lowman, J. (1987) 'Taking young prostitutes seriously', *Canadian Review of Sociology and Anthropology*, 24(1): 99–116.

Lowman, J. (1992) 'Street prostitution control: some Canadian reflections on the Finsbury Park experience', *British Journal of Criminology*, 32(1): 1–17.

Lowman, J. (2000) 'Violence and outlaw status of street prostitution in Canada', *Violence Against Women*, 6(9): 987–1011.

Lowman, J. and Atchison, C. (2006) 'Men who buy sex: a survey in the Greater Vancouver Regional District', *Canadian Journal of Sociology and Anthropology*, 43(3): 281–96.

Lucas, A. (2005) 'The work of sex work: elite prostitutes' vocational orientations and experiences', *Deviant Behavior*, 26(5): 513–46.

Lupton, D. (ed.) (1999) *Risk and Sociocultural Theory: New Directions and Perspectives*, Cambridge: Cambridge University Press.

MacKinnon, C. (1987) *Feminism Unmodified: Discourses on Life and Law*, Cambridge, MA: Harvard University Press.

MacKinnon, C. (1989) 'Pornography: not a moral issue', in R. Klein and D. Steinberg (eds), *Radical Voices: A Decade of Feminist Resistance from Women's Studies International Forum*, Oxford: Pergamon.

Maher, L. (2000) *Sexed Work: Gender, Race and Resistance in a Brooklyn Drug Market*, Oxford: Oxford University Press.

Mai, N. (2007) 'Errance, migration and male sex work: on the socio-cultural sustainability of a third space', in S. Ossman (ed.), *Places We Share: Migration, Subjectivity, and Global Mobility*, Lanham, MD: Lexington Books.

Malina, D. and Schmidt, R.A. (1997) 'It's a business doing pleasure with you: Sh! A women's sex shop case', *Marketing Intelligence and Planning*, 15(7): 352.

Mansson, S.A. (2006) 'Men's demand for prostitutes', *Sexologies*, 15(2): 87–92.

Mansson, S.A. and Hedin, U. (1999) 'Breaking the Matthew effect on women leaving prostitution', *International Journal of Social Welfare*, 8: 67–77.

Marie Claire (2007) 'From red light to runway', 26 July. Available at: www.marieclaire.co.uk/news/168050/from-red-light-to-runway.html (accessed 27 May 2008).

Marlowe, J. (2006) 'Thinking outside the box: men in the sex industry', in J. Spector (ed.), *Prostitution and Pornography: Philosophical Debate about the Sex Industry*, Stanford, CA: Stanford University Press.

Mathieu, L. (2003) 'The emergence and uncertain outcomes of prostitutes' social movements', *The European Journal of Women's Studies*, 10(1): 29–50.

Matthews, R. (1986) 'Beyond Wolfendon? Prostitution, policies and the law', in R. Matthews and J. Young (eds), *Confronting Crime*, London: Sage.

Matthews, R. (1993) *Kerb Crawling, Prostitution and Multi-Agency Policing*, Police Research Group, Crime Prevention Unit Services Paper No. 43, London: Home Office.

Matthews, R. (2003) 'Beyond Wolfenden: prostitution, politics and the law', in R. Matthews and M. O'Neill (eds), *Prostitution*, Aldershot: Ashgate.

Matthews, R. (2005) 'Policing prostitution: 10 years on', *British Journal of Criminology*, 45(1): 1–20.

Matthews, R. and O'Neill, M. (eds) (2003) *Prostitution*, Aldershot: Ashgate.

May, T. (1997) *Social Research: Issues, Methods and Process*, Buckingham: Open University Press.

May, T., Edmunds, M. and Hough, M. (1999) *Street Business: The Links between Sex and Drug Markets*, Crime Detection and Prevention Series Paper 118, London: Home Office.

May, T., Harocopos, A. and Hough, M. (2000) *For Love or Money: Pimps and the Management of Sex Work*, London: Home Office Policing and Reducing Crime Unit.

May, T., Harocopos, A. and Turnbull, P. (2001) *Selling Sex in the City: An Evaluation of a Targeted Arrest Referral Scheme for Sex Workers in Kings Cross*, London: Home Office.

May, T. and Hunter, G. (2006) 'Sex work and problem drug use in the UK: the links, problems and possible solutions', in R. Campbell and M. O'Neill (eds), *Sex Work Now*, Cullompton: Willan.

Maynard, M. (1998) 'Feminists' knowledge and the knowledge of feminisms: epistemology, theory, methodology and method', in T. May and M. Williams (eds), *Knowing the Social World*, Buckingham: Open University Press.

Mayorga, L. and Velásquez, P. (1999) 'Bleak pasts, bleak futures: life paths of thirteen young prostitutes in Cartagena, Columbia', in K. Kempadoo (ed.), *Sun, Sex, and Gold: Tourism and Sex Work in the Caribbean*, London and New York: Rowman and Littlefield.

Mazo-Karras, R. (1989) 'The regulation of brothels in later Medieval England', *Signs*, 14(3): 399–433.

McClintock, A. (1992) 'Sex workers and sex work', *Social Text*, 37(1): 1–10.

McDowell, L. (1997) *Capital Culture: Gender at Work in the City*, Oxford: Blackwell.

McIntosh, M. (1978) 'Who needs prostitutes? The ideology of male sexual needs', in C. Smart and B. Smart (eds), *Women, Sexuality and Control*, London: Routledge and Kegan Paul.

McKeganey, N. (1994) 'Why do men buy sex and what are their assessments of the HIV-related risks when they do?', *Aids Care,* (6)3: 289–301.

McKeganey, N. and Barnard, M. (1996) *Sex Work on the Streets*, Buckingham: Open University Press.

McLeod, E. (1982) *Working Women: Prostitution Now*, London: Croom Helm.

McMullen, R.J. (1987) 'Youth prostitution: a balance of power', *Journal of Adolescence*, 10(1): 35–43.

McNair, B. (2002) *Striptease Culture: Sex, Media and the Democratization of Desire*, London: Routledge.

McNaughton, C. and Sanders, T. (2007) 'Housing and transitional phases out of "disordered" lives: a case of leaving homelessness and street sex work', *Housing Studies*, 22(6): 885–900.

Meil Hobson, B. (1990) *Uneasy Virtue: The Politics of Prostitution and the American Reform Tradition*, Chicago, IL: The University of Chicago Press.

Melrose, M. (2002) 'Labour pains: some considerations on the difficulties of researching juvenile prostitution', *International Journal of Social Research Methodology*, 5(4): 333–51.

Melrose, M. (2004) 'Fractured transitions: disadvantaged young people, drug taking and risks', *Probation Journal*, 51(4): 327–41.

Melrose, M. (2007a) 'Trying to make a silk purse from a sow's ear? A comment on the government's prostitution strategy', *Community Safety Journal*, 5(2): 4–13.

Melrose, M. (2007b) 'The government's new prostitution strategy: a cheap fix for drug-using sex workers?', *Community Safety Journal*, 6(1): 18–26.

Melrose, M. and Barrett, D. (eds) (2004) *Anchors in Floating Lives: Interventions with Young People Sexually Abused through Prostitution*, London: Russell House.

Melrose, M., Barrett, D. and Brodie, I. (1999) *One-Way Street: Retrospectives on Childhood Prostitution*, London: The Children's Society.

Minichiello, V., Marino, R., Browne, J., Jamieson, M., Peterson, K., Reuter, B. and Robinson, K. (2002) 'Male sex workers in three Australian cities: socio-demographic and sex work characteristics', *Journal of Homosexuality*, 42(1): 29–51.

Montemurro, B. (2001) 'Strippers and screamers: the emergence of social control in a noninstitutionalized setting', *Journal of Contemporary Ethnography*, 30(3): 275–304.

Monto, M. (2000) 'Why men seek out prostitutes', in R. Weitzer (ed.), *Sex for Sale*, London: Routledge.

Monto, M. (2001) 'Prostitution and fellatio', *Journal of Sex Research*, 38(1): 140–5.

Monto, M. and Garcia, S. (2001) 'Recidivism among the customers of female street prostitutes: do intervention programs help?', *Western Criminology Review*, 3(2).

Monto, M. and Hotaling, N. (2001) 'Predictors of rape myth acceptance among male clients of female street prostitutes', *Violence Against Women*, 7(3): 275–93.

Morrison, T. and Whitehead, B. (2005) 'Strategies of stigma resistance among Canadian gay-identified sex workers', *Journal of Psychology & Human Sexuality*, 17(1/2): 169–79.

Muir, J. (2008) 'Are you taking notes on us?' Reflections on case study research in urban environments', in P.J. Maginn, S. Thompson and M. Tonts (eds), *Qualitative Urban Analysis: An International Perspective*, Oxford: Elsevier.

Muntarbhorn, V. (1996) *Sexual Exploitation of Children*, New York and Geneva: UN Centre for Human Rights.

Murphy, A.G. (2003) 'The dialectical gaze: exploring the subject–object tension in the performances of women who strip', *Journal of Contemporary Ethnography*, 32(3): 305–35.

Murray, L., Moreno, L., Rosario, S., E. J., Sweat, M. and Kerrigan, D. (2007) 'The role of relationship intimacy in consistent condom use among female sex workers and their regular paying partners in the Dominican Republic', *AIDS Behaviour*, 11: 463–70.

Nagel, J. (1997) *Whores and Other Feminists*, London: Routledge.

Nath, M.B. (2000) 'Women's health and HIV: experience from a sex workers' project in Calcutta', *Gender and Development*, 8(1): 100–8.

Nencel, L. (2001) *Ethnography and Prostitution in Peru*, London: Pluto Press.

Newman, J. (2003) 'New Labour, governance and the politics of diversity', in J. Barry, M. Dent and M. O'Neill (eds), *Gender and the Public Sector: Professionals and Managerial Change*, London: Routledge.

NSPCC (2007) Briefing for Policy Makers. Available at: www.nspcc.org/uk/inform/ policyandpublicaffairs/Europe/Briefings/councilofeurope_wdf.51232.pdf (accessed 17 February 2008).

Oakley, A. (1981) 'Interviewing women: a contradiction in terms?', in H. Roberts (ed.), *Doing Feminist Research*, London: Routledge.

Oakley, A. (2000) *Experiments in Knowing: Gender and Method in the Social Sciences*, Cambridge: Polity.

Oakley, A. (2002) *Gender on Planet Earth*, Oxford: Polity.

O'Connell Davidson, J. (1995) 'The anatomy of "free choice" prostitution', *Gender Work and Organisation*, 2(1): 1–10.

O'Connell Davidson, J. (1998) *Prostitution, Power and Freedom*, Cambridge: Polity.

O'Connell Davidson, J. (2002) 'The rights and wrongs of prostitution', *Hypatia*, 17(2): 84–98.

O'Connell Davidson, J. (2003) '"Sleeping with the enemy"? Some problems with feminist abolitionist calls to penalise those who buy commercial sex', *Social Policy and Society*, 2(1): 55–64.

O'Connell Davidson, J. (2005) *Children in the Global Sex Trade*, Cambridge: Polity.

O'Connell Davidson, J. (2006) 'Will the real sex slave please stand up?', *Feminist Review*, 83(1): 4–23.

O'Connell Davidson, J. and Layder, D. (1994) *Methods, Sex and Madness*, London: Routledge.

O'Connell Davidson, J. and Sanchez Taylor, J. (1999) 'Fantasy islands: exploring the demand for sex tourism', in K. Kempadoo (ed.), *Sun, Sex and Gold: Tourism and Sex Work in the Caribbean*, London: Rowman and Littlefield.

Oldenburg, V.T. (1990) 'Lifestyle as resistance: the case of the courtesans of Lucknow, India', *Feminist Studies*, 16(2): 259–87.

Olesen, V. (1998) 'Feminisms and models of qualitative research', in N.K. Denzin and Y.S. Lincoln (eds), *The Landscape of Qualitative Research: Theories and Issues*, Thousand Oaks, CA: Sage.

O'Neill, M. (1996) 'Prostitution, feminism and critical praxis: profession prostitute?', *The Austrian Journal of Sociology*, special edition on 'Work and Society', edited by Johanna Hofbauer and Jorg Flecker, Winter.

O'Neill, M. (1997) 'Prostitute Women Now', in G. Scambler and A. Scambler (eds), *Rethinking Prostitution: Purchasing Sex in Britain in the 1990s*, London: Routledge.

O'Neill, M. (2001) *Prostitution and Feminism*, Cambridge: Polity.

O'Neill, M. (2007a) 'Community safety, rights and recognition: towards a coordinated prostitution strategy?', *Community Safety Journal*, 6(1): 45–52.

O'Neill, M. (2007b) 'Feminist knowledge and socio-cultural research: ethno-mimesis, feminist praxis and the visual turn', in T. Edwards (ed.), *Cultural Theory*, London: Sage.

O'Neill, M. (2009) 'Community Safety, Rights, Redistribution and Recognition: Towards a Coordinated Prostitution Strategy?', in J. Phoenix (ed.), *Regulating Sex for Sale: Prostitution Policy Reform in the UK*, Bristol: The Policy Press.

O'Neill, M. and Barbaret, R. (2000) 'Victimisation and the social organisation of prostitution in England and Spain', in R. Weitzer (ed.), *Sex for Sale: Prostitution, Pornography and the Sex Industry*, London: Routledge.

O'Neill, M. and Campbell, R. (2004) *Working Together To Create Change*. Walsall prostitution consultation research. A participatory action research project. January 2004. Staffordshire University and Liverpool Hope University College.

O'Neill, M. and Campbell, R. (2006) 'Street sex work and local communities: creating discursive space for *genuine* consultation and inclusion', in R. Campbell and M. O'Neill (eds), *Sex Work Now*, Cullompton: Willan.

O'Neill, M., Campbell, R., Hubbard, P., Pitcher, J. and Scoular, J. (2008) 'Living with the other: street sex work, contingent communities and degrees of tolerance', *Crime, Media and Culture*, 4(1): 73–93.

O'Neill, M., Campbell, R., James, A., Webster, M., Green, K., Patel, J., Akhtar, N. and Saleem, W. (2004) 'Red lights and safety zones', in D. Bell and M. Jayne (eds), *City of Quarters: Urban Villages in the Contemporary City*, Aldershot: Ashgate.

O'Neill, M., Goode, N. and Hopkins, K. (1995) 'Juvenile prostitution: the experience of young women in residential care', *Childright*, December. 113.

O'Neill, M., Johnson, S., McDonald, M., Webster, M., Wellik, M. and McGregor, S. (1994) 'Prostitution, feminism and the law: feminist ways of seeing, knowing and working with women working as prostitutes', *Rights of Women Bulletin*, Spring.

O'Neill, M. and Webster, M. (2005) 'Creativity, community and change: creative approaches to community consultation', in J. Thompson and C. Turner (eds), *Rise up and Become..: A Toolkit to Put Learners at the Heart of RISE*, Leicester: NIACE.

Outshoorn, J. (2004) 'Pragmatism in the polder: changing prostitution policy in the Netherlands', *Journal of Contemporary European Studies*, 12(2): 165–76.

Outshoorn, J. (2005) 'The political debates on prostitution and trafficking of women', *Social Politics*, 12(1): 141–55.

Padilla, M. (2007) *Caribbean Pleasure Industry: Tourism, Sexuality and AIDS in the Dominican Republic*, Chicago, IL: University of Chicago Press.

Palmer, T. (2002) *No Son of Mine! Children Abused through Prostitution*, Basildon: Barnardo's.

Pasko, L. (2002) 'Naked power: the practice of stripping as a confidence game', *Sexualities*, 5(1): 49–66.

Pateman, C. (1988) *The Sexual Contract*, Oxford: Blackwell.

Patton, M.Q. (1997) *Utilization-Focused Evaluation: The New Century Text*, Thousand Oaks, CA: Sage.

Pearce, J. (1997) *Prostitution and Drugs in Sheffield: Exploring the Links*, London: Middlesex University.

Pearce, J. (2006) 'Finding the "I" in sexual exploitation: young people's voices within policy and practice', in R. Campbell and M. O'Neill (eds), *Sex Work Now*, Cullompton: Willan.

Pearce, J. with M. Williams and Galvin, C. (2002) *'Its Someone Taking a Part of You': A Study of Young Women and Sexual Exploitation*, London: National Children's Bureau for Joseph Rowntree Foundation. Available at: www.jrf.org.uk/knowledge/findings/socialpolicy/513.asp

Penfold, C., Hunter, G., Campbell, R. and Barham, L. (2004) 'Tackling client violence in female street prostitution: inter-agency working between outreach agencies and the police', *Policing & Society*, 14(4): 365–79.

Peng, Y.W. (2007) 'Buying sex: domination and difference in the discourses of Taiwanese Piao-ke', *Men and Masculinities*, 9(3): 315–36.

Perkins, R. (1999) '"How much are you, love?" The customer in the Australian sex industry', *Social Alternatives*, 18(3): 38–47.

Perkins, R. and Lovejoy, F. (2007) *Call Girls: Private Sex Workers in Australia*, Crawley, Western Australia: University of Western Australia Press.

Petzer, S. (1998) Personal correspondence, 23 January 1998.

Pheterson, G. (ed.) (1989) *A Vindication of the Rights of Whores*, Seattle, WA: Seal.

Pheterson, G. (1993) 'The whore stigma', *Social Text*, 37(1): 37–64.

Pheterson, G. (1996) *The Prostitution Prism*, Amsterdam: Amsterdam University Press.

Philpot, T. (1990) 'Male prostitution: the boys' own story', *Community Care*, 820(1): 19–22.

Phoenix, J. (1999) *Making Sense of Prostitution*, London: Macmillan.

Phoenix, J. (2000) 'Prostitute identities: men, money and violence', *British Journal of Criminology*, 40(1): 37–55.

Phoenix, J. (2007/8) 'Sex, money and the regulation of women's "choices": a political economy of prostitution', *Criminal Justice Matters*, 70(Winter): 25–6.

Phoenix, J. (2009) 'Frameworks of understanding', in J. Phoenix (ed.), *Regulating Sex for Sale: Prostitution, Policy Reform in the UK*, Bristol: The Policy Press.

Phoenix, J. and Oerton, S. (2005) *Illicit and Illegal: Sex, Regulation and Social Control*, Cullompton: Willan.

Piscitelli, A. (2007) 'Shifting boundaries: sex and money in the North-East of Brazil', *Sexualities*, 10(4): 489–500.

Pitcher, J. (2006a) 'Support services for women working in the sex industry', in R. Campbell and M. O'Neill (eds), *Sex Work Now*, Cullompton: Willan.

Pitcher, J. (2006b) 'Evaluating community safety programmes and community engagement: the role of qualitative methods and collaborative approaches to policy research', *Urban Policy and Research*, 24(1): 67–82.

Pitcher, J. and Aris, R. (2003) *Women and Street Sex Work: Issues Arising from an Evaluation of an Arrest Referral Scheme*, London: Nacro.

Pitcher, J., Campbell, R., Hubbard, P., O'Neill, M. and Scoular, J. (2006) *Living and Working in Areas of Street Sex Work: From Conflict to Coexistence*, Bristol: The Policy Press.

Pitcher, J., Campbell, R., Hubbard, P., O'Neill, M. and Scoular, J. (2008) 'Diverse community responses to controversial urban issues: the contribution of qualitative research to policy development', in P.J. Maginn, S. Thompson and M. Tonts (eds), *Qualitative Urban Analysis: An International Perspective*, Oxford: Elsevier.

Pitts, M.K., Smith, A., Grierson, J., O'Brien, M. and Misson, S. (2004) 'Who pays for sex and why? An analysis of social and motivational factors associated with male clients of sex workers', *Archives of Sexual Behaviour*, 33(4): 353–8.

Plant, M. (1997) 'Alcohol, drugs and social milieu', in G. Scambler and A. Scambler (eds), *Rethinking Prostitution: Purchasing Sex in the 1990s*, London: Routledge.

Plummer, K. (1995) *Telling Sexual Stories: Power, Change and Social Worlds*, London: Routledge.

Plumridge, E., Chetwynd, S.J., Reed, A. and Gifford, S. (1997) 'Discourses of emotionality in commercial sex: the missing client voice', *Feminism and Psychology*, 7(2): 165–81.

Poel, S. (1995) 'Solidarity as boomerang: the fiasco of the prostitutes' rights movement in the Netherlands', *Crime, Law and Change*, 23(1): 41–65.

Public Now (2007) 'Brazil's Congress rejected legalized prostitution'. Available at: www.now public.com/politics/brazils-congress-rejected-legalized-prostitution (accessed 25 May 2008).

Punch, M. (1998) 'Politics and ethics in qualitative research', in N.K. Denzin and Y.S. Lincoln (eds), *The Landscape of Qualitative Research: Theories and Issues*, Thousand Oaks, CA: Sage.

Pyett, P. (1998) 'Doing it together: sex workers and researchers', *Research for Sex Work*. Available at: http://hcc.med.vu.nl/artikelen/pyett.htm

Pyett, P. and Warr, D. (1997) 'Vulnerability on the streets: female sex workers and HIV risk', *AIDS Care*, 9(5): 539–47.

Quassoli, F. (2004) 'Making the neighbourhood safer: social alarm, police practices and immigrant exclusion in Italy', *Journal of Ethnic and Migration Studies*, 30(6): 1163–81.

Quayle, E., Holland, G., Linehan, C. and Taylor, M. (2000) 'The Internet and offending behaviour: a case study', *The Journal of Sexual Aggression*, 6(1/2): 78–96.

Quayle, E. and Taylor, M. (2002) 'Child pornography and the Internet: perpetuating a cycle of abuse', *Deviant Behaviour*, 23(3): 365–95.

Raphael, J. and Shapiro, D. (2004) 'Violence in indoor and outdoor prostitution venues', *Violence Against Women*, 10(2): 126–39.

Ramazanoglu, C. and Holland, J. (2002) *Feminist Methodology: Challenges and Choices*, London: Sage.

Raymond, J.G. (1999) 'Prostitution as violence against women', *Women's International Forum*, 21(1): 1–9.

Reinharz, S. (1992) *Feminist Methods in Social Research*, New York: Oxford University Press.

Ren, X. (1999) 'Prostitution and economic modernization in China', *Violence Against Women*, 5(12): 1411–36.

Richters, J. (2007) 'Through a hole in the wall: setting and interaction in sex-on-premises venues', *Sexualities*, 10(3): 275–97.

Rickard, W. (2001) '"Been there, seen it, done it , I've got the T-shirt": British sex workers reflect on jobs', *Feminist Review*, 67(Spring): 111–32.

Rickard, W. and Growney, T. (2001) 'Occupational health and safety amongst sex workers: a pilot peer education resource', *Health Education Research*, 16(3): 321–33.

Roberts, N. (1992) *Whores in History: Prostitution in Western Society*, London: Harper Collins.

Roberts, R., Bergstronm, S. and La Rooy, D. (2007) 'Commentary: UK students and sex work: current knowledge and research issues', *Journal of Community and Applied Social Psychology*, 17(1): 141–6.

Ronai, C. (1992) 'The reflective self through narrative', in C. Ellis and M. Flaherty (eds), *Investigating Subjectivity: Research on Lived Experience*, Newbury Park, CA: Sage.

Ronai, C. and Ellis, C. (1989) 'Turn-ons for money: interactional strategies of the table dancers', *Journal of Contemporary Ethnography*, 18(3): 271–98.

Rosen, E. and Venkatesh, S. (2008) 'A "perversion" of choice: sex work offers just enough in Chicago's urban ghetto', *Journal of Contemporary Ethnography*, 37(4): 417–41.

Ruggiero, V. (1997) 'Trafficking in human beings: slaves in contemporary Europe', *International Journal of the Sociology of Law*, 25(2): 231–44.

Ryan, C. and Hall, M. (2001) *Sex Tourism: Marginal People and Liminalities*, London: Routledge.

Sagar, T. (2005) 'Street watch: concept and practice', *British Journal of Criminology*, 45(1): 98–112.

Sagar, T. (2007) 'Tackling on-street sex work: anti-social behaviour orders, sex workers and inclusive inter-agency initiatives', *Criminology and Criminal Justice*, 7(2): 153–68.

Sanchez Taylor, J. (2001) 'Dollars are a girl's best friend? Female tourists' sexual behaviour in the Caribbean', *Sociology*, 35(3): 749–64.

Sanchez Taylor, J. (2006) 'Female sex tourism: a contradiction in terms?', *Feminist Review*, 83(1): 42–59.

Sanders, T. (2004) 'The risks of street prostitution: punters, police and protesters', *Urban Studies*, 41(8): 1703–17.

Sanders, T. (2005a) *Sex Work: A Risky Business*, Cullompton: Willan.

Sanders, T. (2005b) 'It's just acting: sex workers' strategies for capitalising on sexuality', *Gender, Work and Organization*, 12(4): 319–42.

Sanders, T. (2005c) 'Researching the online sex work community', in C. Hine (ed.), *Virtual Methods in Social Research on the Internet*, Oxford: Berg.

Sanders, T. (2006a) 'Behind the personal ads: the indoor sex markets in Britain', in R. Campbell and M. O'Neill (eds), *Sex Work Now*, Cullompton: Willan.

Sanders, T. (2006b) 'Sexing up the subject: methodological nuances in researching the female sex industry', *Sexualities*, 9(4): 449–68.

Sanders, T. (2007a) 'Becoming an ex-sex worker: making transitions out of a deviant career', *Feminist Criminology*, 2(1): 1–22.

Sanders, T. (2007b) 'The politics of sexual citizenship: commercial sex and disability', *Disability & Society*, 22(5): 439–55.

Sanders, T. (2008a) *Paying for Pleasure: Men who Buy Sex*, Cullompton: Willan.

Sanders, T. (2008b) 'Male sexual scripts: intimacy, sexuality and pleasure in the purchase of commercial sex', *Sociology*, 42(1): 400–17.

Sanders, T. (2008c) 'Selling sex in the shadow economy', *International Journal of Social Economics*, 35(10): 704–28.

Sanders, T. (2009) 'Kerbcrawler rehabilitation programmes: curing the "deviant" male and reinforcing the "respectable" moral order', *Critical Social Policy*, 29(1).

Sanders, T. and Campbell, R. (2007) 'Designing out violence, building in respect: violence, safety and sex work policy', *British Journal of Sociology*, 58(1): 1–18.

Sanders, T. and Campbell, R. (2008) 'Why hate men who pay for sex? Investigating the shift to tackling demand and the calls to criminalise paying for sex', in V. Munro (ed.), *Demanding Sex? Critical Reflections on the Supply/Demand Dynamic in Prostitution*, Aldershot: Ashgate.

Sassen, S. (2002) 'Women's burden: counter-geographies of globalization and the feminization of survival', website: *Nordic Journal of International Law*, 71: 255–74.

Scambler, G. (2007) 'Sex work stigma: opportunist migrants in London', *Sociology*, 41(6): 1079–96.

Scarlet Alliance website: www.scarletalliance.org.au (accessed 10 May 2008).

Schloenhardt, A. (1999) 'Organised crime and the business of migrant trafficking', *Crime, Law and Social Change*, 32(2): 203–33.

Schwant, T.A. (1998) 'Approaches to human inquiry', in N.K. Denzin and Y.S. Lincoln (eds), *The Landscape of Qualitative Research: Theories and Issues*, Thousand Oaks, CA: Sage.

Scott, J. (1998) 'Changing attitudes to sexual morality: a cross-national comparison', *Sociology*, 32(4): 815–45.

Scott, J. (2007) 'Understanding prostitution in a rural context', paper presented at Sex Work: Regulating the Many Faces of Sexual Labour conference, university of Keele, 17 October.

Scott, J., Hunter, J., Hunter, V. and Ragusa, A. (2006) 'Sex outside the city: sex work in rural and regional NSW', *Rural Society*, 16(2): 151–68.

Scott, J., Minichiello, V., Marino, R., Harvey, G., Jamieson, M. and Browne, J. (2005) 'Understanding the new context of the male sex work industry', *Journal of Interpersonal Violence*, 20(3): 320–42.

Scottish Executive (2005) *Being Outside: Constructing a Response to Street Prostitution. Report of the Expert Group on Prostitution in Scotland*, Edinburgh: Scottish Executive.

Scoular, J. (2004a) 'The "subject" of prostitution: interpreting the discursive, symbolic and material position of sex/work in feminist theory', *Feminist Theory*, 5(3): 343–55.

Scoular, J. (2004b) 'Criminalising "punters": evaluating the swedish position on prostitution', *Journal of Social Welfare and Family Law*, 26(2): 195–210.

Scoular, J., Gilchrist, G. and Cameron, J. (2004) *Streetlife: Women's Perspectives on Prostitution in Glasgow*, Glasgow: University of Strathclyde.

Scoular, J. and O'Neill, M. (2007) 'Regulating prostitution: social inclusion, responsibilization and the politics of prostitution reform', *British Journal of Criminology*, 47(5): 764–78.

Scoular, J., Pitcher, J., Campbell, R., Hubbard, P. and O'Neill, M. (2007) 'What's anti-social about sex work? The changing representation of prostitution's incivility', *Community Safety Journal*, 6(1): 11–17.

Segal, L. and McIntosh, M. (eds) (1992) *Sex Exposed: Sexuality and the Pornography Debate*, London: Virago.

Self, H. (2003) *Prostitution, Women and Misuse of the Law: The Fallen Daughters of Eve*, London: Frank Cass.

Self, H. (2004) *History Repeating Itself: The Regulation of Prostitution and Trafficking* (accessed 22 February 2008).

Sereny, G. (1984) *The Invisible Children: Child Prostitution in America, Germany and Britain*, London: Deutsch.

Shannon, K., Rusch, M., Shoveller, J., Alexson, D., Gibson, K. and Tyndall, M.W. (2008) 'Mapping violence and policing as an environmental–structural barrier to health service and syringe availability among substance-using women in street-level sex work', *International Journal of Drug Policy*, 19(1): 140–7.

Sharp, K. and Earle, S. (2003) 'Cyberpunters and cyberwhores: prostitution on the Internet', in Y. Jewkes (ed.), *Dot Cons: Crime, Deviance and Identity on the Internet*, Cullompton: Willan.

Shaver, F. (2005) 'Sex work research: methodological and ethical challenges', *Journal of Interpersonal Violence*, 20(3): 296–319.

Shaw, I. and Butler, I. (1998) 'Understanding young people and prostitution: a foundation for practice?', *British Journal of Social Work*, 28(2): 177–96.

Shelter (2004) *Off the Streets: Tackling Homelessness among Female Sex Workers*, London: Shelter.

Silbert and Pines (1981) 'Sexual abuse as an antecedent to prostitution', *Child Abuse and Neglect*, 5(3): 407–11.

Simmons, C., Lehmann, P. and Collier-Tenison, S. (2008) 'Linking male use of the sex industry to controlling behaviours in violent relationships: an exploratory analysis', *Violence Against Women*, 14(4): 406–417.

Skodbo, S., Brown, G., Deacon, S., Cooper, A., Hall, A., Millar, T., Smith, J. and Whitham, K. (2007) *The Drug Interventions Programme (DIP): Addressing Drug Use and Offending through 'Tough Choices'*, Home Office Research Report 2, London: Home Office.

Slamah, K. (1999) 'Transgenders and sex work in Malaysia', in K. Kempadoo and J. Doezema (eds), *Global Sex Workers*, London: Routledge.

Sloan, L. and Wahab, S. (2000) 'Feminist voices on sex work: implications for social work', *Affilia*, 15(4): 457–79.

Sloss, C. and Harper, G. (2004) 'When street sex workers are mothers', *Archives of Sexual Behaviour*, 33(4): 329–41.

Smith, C. (2002) 'Shiny chests and heaving G-strings: a night out with the Chippendales', *Sexualities*, 5(11): 67–89.

Sobey, M. (1994) *Young People Involved in Prostitution: A Study of Literature and A Research Project Examining Incidence and Agency Responses in Nottinghamshire*, Derby: University of Derby.

Social Research Association (2003) *Ethical Guidelines*, London: SRA (also available from www.the-sra.org.uk).

Sondhi, J., O'Shea, J. and Williams, T. (2002) *Arrest Referral: Emerging Findings from the National Monitoring and Evaluation Programme*, DPAS Paper 18, London: Home Office.

Soothill, K. and Sanders, T. (2005) 'The geographical mobility, preferences and pleasures of prolific punters: a demonstration study of the activities of prostitutes' clients', *Sociological Research Online*, 10(1).

Spivey, S.E. (2005) 'Distancing and solidarity as resistance to sexual objectification in a nude dancing bar', *Deviant Behavior*, 26(4): 417–37.

Stallybrass, P. and White, A. (1986) *The Politics and Poetics of Transgression*, London: Methuen.

Stanley, L. (1996) 'The mother of invention: necessity, writing and representation', in S. Wilkinson and C. Kitzinger (eds), *Representing the Other: A Feminism and Psychology Reader*, London: Sage.

Storr, M. (2003) *Latex and Lingerie: The Sexual Dynamics of Ann Summers Parties*, Oxford: Berg.

Sullivan, E. and Simon, W. (1998) 'The client: a social, psychological and behavioural look at the unseen patron of prostitution', in J.E. Elias, V.L. Bullough, V. Elias and G. Brewer (eds), *Prostitution: On Whores, Hustlers and Johns*, Amherst, NY: Prometheus.

Surratt, H.L., Inciardi, J.A., Kurtz, S.P. and Kiley, M.C. (2004) 'Sex work and drug use in a subculture of violence', *Crime and Delinquency*, 50(1): 43–59.

Svanstrom, Y. (2004) 'Criminalising the John – a Swedish gender model?', in J. Outshoorn (ed.), *The Politics of Prostitution*, Cambridge: Cambridge University Press.

Swann, S. (1998) *Whose Daughter Next? Children Abused Through Prostitution*, Ilford: Barnardo's.

TAMPEP (2005) *Position Paper on Trafficking in Women*, TAMPEP International Foundation. Available at: www.tampep.com.

Tandon, T. (2008a) *Sex Work Law Reform – Eyes on GOM*. March. Lawyer's Collective. Available at: www.lawyerscollective.org/content/sex-work-law-reform-eyes-gom (accessed 15 May 2008).

Tandon, T. (2008b) *Lawyer's Collective Interview with Dr. Smarajit Jana*, March 2008. Lawyer's Collective. Available at: www.lawyerscollective.org/content/interview-1 (accessed 15 May 2008).

Taylor, D. (2006) 'Sex workers are a soft target in the asylum figures battle', *Guardian*, 22 June.

Thompson, W. and Harred, J. (1992) 'Topless dancers: managing stigma in a deviant occupation', *Deviant Behaviour*, 13(2): 291–311.

Thompson, W., Harred, J.L. and Burks, B.E. (2003) 'Managing the stigma of topless dancing: a decade later', *Deviant Behavior*, 24(5): 551–70.

Thukral, J. and Ditmore, M. (2003) *Revolving Door: An Analysis of Street-based Prostitution in New York City*, New York: Urban Justice Center/Sex Workers Project.

Trautner, M.L. (2005) 'Doing gender, doing class: the performance of sexuality in exotic dance clubs', *Gender and Society*, 19(6): 771–88.

Truman, C. (2002) 'Doing feminist evaluation with men: achieving objectivity in a sexual health needs assessment', in D. Seigart and S. Brisola (eds), *Feminist Evaluation: Explorations and Experiences*, New Directions for Evaluation No. 96, San Francisco, CA: Wiley.

Truong, T. (1990) *Sex, Money and Morality: Prostitution and Tourism in Southeast Asia*, London: Zed Books.

UKHT (2006) UKHT Factsheet. Available at: www.ukhtc.org/includes/press-pack.pdf (accessed 17 February 2008).

UKNSWP (UK Network of Sex Work Projects) (2004) *Response to* Paying the Price. Available at: www.uknswp.org/UKNSWP_Paying_the_Price_response.pdf

UKNSWP (UK Network of Sex Work Projects) (2008) *Working with Migrant Sex Workers*. Good practice guidance 03. Manchester: UKNSWP. Available at: www.uknswp.org

UNDP and You and Aids (2003) 'Self-regulatory boards: Kolkata's sex workers show the way', in S.Y. Rana, R. Debabrata, G.P. Kumar, C. Castillejo and M. Mishra, *From Challenges to Opportunities: Responses to Trafficking and HIV/AIDS in South Asia*, New Delhi: UND. Available at: www.youandaids.org/UNDP_REACH_publications/From%20Challenges%20to%20 Opportunities/Chapter4%20replace%20photo.pdf (accessed 14 May 2008).

UNHCHR (UN Office of the High Commissioner for Human Rights) (1999) *Concluding Observations of the Committee on the Elimination of Discrimination Against Women: China*. A/54/38, paragraphs 288–89. 3 February 1999. Available at: www.unhchr.ch/tbs/doc. nsf/(Symbol)/1483ffb5a2a626a980256732003e82c8?Opendocument (accessed 8 May 2008).

UNHCHR (UN Office of the High Commissioner for Human Rights) (2000) *Concluding Observations of the Committee on the Elimination of Discrimination Against Women: Germany*. A/55/38, paragraphs 325 and 326. 2 February 2000. Available at: www.unhchr.ch/tbs/doc.nsf/(Symbol)/64d8644 ed9ea3f788025688c0054c3f4?Opendocument (accessed 8 May 2008).

UNHCHR (UN Office of the High Commissioner for Human Rights) (2001) *Concluding Observations of the Committee on the Elimination of Discrimination Against Women: Sweden*. A/56/38, paragraph 355. 31 July 2001. Available at: www.unhchr.ch/tbs/doc.nsf/(Symbol)/80bb4b9d 34212c1fc1256acc004f72e2?Opendocument (accessed 8 May 2008).

Van Brunschot, E.G. (2003) 'Community policing and "John Schools"', *Canadian Review of Sociology and Anthropology*, 40(2): 215–32.

Van Doorninck, M. and Campbell, R. (2006) '"Zoning" street sex work: the way forward?', in R. Campbell and M. O'Neill (eds), *Sex Work Now*, Cullompton: Willan.

Vanwesenbeeck, I. (2005) 'Burnout among female indoor sex workers', *Archives of Sexual Behavior*, 34(6): 627–639.

Veena, N. (2007) 'Revisiting the prostitution debate in the technology age: women who use the Internet for sex work in Bangkok', *Gender, Technology and Development*, 11(1): 97–107.

Visano, L.A. (1991) 'The impact of age on paid sexual encounters', *Journal of Homosexuality*, 20(2): 207–25.

Vitaliano, P.D. et al. (1981) 'Perceptions of juvenile experiences: females involved In prostitution versus property offences', *Criminal Justice and Behaviour*, 8(3): 325–42.

Voeten, H., Egesah, O., Varkevisser, C. and Habbema, J. (2007) 'Female sex workers and unsafe sex in urban and rural Nyanza, Kenya: regular partners may contribute more to HIV transmission than clients', *Tropical Medicine and International Health*, 12(2): 174–82.

Voices Heard Group (2007) *Hidden for Survival*, GAP project, Newcastle: Tyneside Cyrenians Ltd.

Voices Heard Group, Seebohm, L. and Smiles, S. (2008) *Hidden for Survival: Peer Research into the lives of sex workers within Newcastle, Gateshead, Sunderland, South Tyneside and North Tyneside*, Research Study TC-02, Newcastle: Tyneside Cyrenians and Counted4. Available at: www.tynesidecyrenians.co.uk/viewpage.aspx?pageid=24

Wahab, S. (2003) 'Creating knowledge collaboratively with female sex workers: Insights from a qualitative, feminist and participatory study', *Qualitative Inquiry*, 9: 625–42.

Wahab, S. (2004) 'Tricks of the trade: what social workers can learn about female sex workers through dialogue', *Qualitative Social Work*, 3(2): 139–60.

Walker, C. et al. (1994) 'Evaluation of urban crime funding in West Yorkshire: extract from Final Report to the West Yorkshire Police Authority 1994', appendix to *Centre for Criminal Justice Studies Sixth Annual Report*, Leeds: Centre for Criminal Justice Studies, University of Leeds. Available at: www.leedsac.uk.law/ccjs/an-reps/an-rep93. htm (accessed 1 June 2009).

Walkowitz, J. (1977) 'The making of an outcast group: prostitutes and working women in nineteenth-century Plymouth and Southampton', in M. Vicinus (ed.), *A Widening Sphere: Changing Roles of Victorian Women*, London: Methuen.

Walkowitz, J. (1980) *Prostitution and Victorian Society*, Cambridge: Cambridge University Press.

Walkowitz, J. (1992) *City of Dreadful Delight: Narratives of Sexual Danger in Late-Victorian London*, London: Virago Press.

Walsh, J. (1996) 'The world's first prostitutes: union', *Marie Claire*, January 1996 48–51. Available at: www.walnet.org/csis/news/world_96/mclaire-9601.html (accessed 28 May 2008).

Ward, H. and Aral, O. (2006) 'Globalisation, the sex industry, and health', *Sexually Transmitted Infections*, 82: 345–7.

Ward, H. and Day, S. (1997) 'Health care and regulation: new perspectives', in G. Scambler and A. Scambler (eds), *Rethinking Prostitution: Purchasing Sex in the 1990s*, London: Routledge.

Ward, H., Day, S., Green, K. and Weber, J. (2004) 'Declining prevalence of STI in the London sex industry, 1985–2002', *Sexually Transmitted Infections*, 80(3): 374–6.

Ward, H., Day, S., Mezzone, J., Dunlop, L., Dionegan, C. and Farrar, S. (1993) 'Prostitution and risk of HIV: female prostitues in London', *British Medical Journal*, 307: 356–8.

Ward, H., Green, A. and Day, S. (2000) *Sex Work and Crack Cocaine: Summary Report*, London: Imperial College, Department of Epidemiology and Public Health.

Ward, H., Mercer, C.H., Wellings, K., Fenton, K., Erens, B., Copas, A. and Johnson, A.M. (2005) 'Who pays for sex? An analysis of the increasing prevalence of female commercial sex contacts among men in Britain', *Journal of Sexually Transmitted Infections*, 81(6): 467–71.

Warr, D. and Pyett, P. (1999) 'Difficult relations: sex work, love and intimacy', *Sociology of Health and Illness*, 21(3): 290–309.

Webster, M. (ed.) (1997) *Community Arts Workers: Finding Voices, Making Choices, Creativity for Social Change*. Nottingham: Educational Heretics Press.

Webster, M. (ed.) (2005) *Finding Voices, Making Choices: Creativity for Social Change*. Nottingham: Educational Heretics Press.

Weinberg, M.S., Shaver, F.M. and Williams, C.J. (1999) 'Gendered sex work in the San Francisco Tenderloin', *Archives of Sexual Behavior*, 28(3): 503–21.

Weitzer, R. (1991) 'Prostitutes' rights in the US: the failure of a movement', *The Sociological Quarterly*, 32(1): 23–41.

Weitzer, R. (2000) 'Why we need more research on sex work', in R. Weitzer (ed.), *Sex for Sale*, London: Routledge.

Weitzer, R. (2005) 'New directions in research on prostitution', *Crime, Law and Social Change*, 43: 211–35.

Weitzer, R. (2006) 'Moral crusade against prostitution', *Society*, 43 (March–April): 33–8.

Weitzer, R. (2007) 'The social construction of sex trafficking: ideology and institutionalization of a moral crusade', *Politics & Society*, 35(3): 447–75.

West, D.J. and de Villiers, B.D. (1992) *Male Prostitution*, London: Duckworth.

West, J. (2000) 'Prostitution: collectives and the politics of regulation', *Gender, Work and Organisation*, 7(2): 106–18.

West, J. and Austrin, T. (2002) 'From work as sex to sex as work: networks, "others" and occupations in the analysis of work', *Gender, Work and Organization*, 9(5): 482–503.

Whittaker, D. and Hart, G. (1996) 'Research note: managing risks: the social organisation of indoor sex work', *Sociology of Health and Illness*, 18(3): 399–413.

Whowell, M. (2008) *Escorts, Porn Stars, Strippers and Rent Boys: Exploring Forms and Practices of Male Sex Work*, Manchester: UK Network of Sex Work Projects.

Whowell, M. and Gaffrey, J. (2009) 'Male sex work in the UK: forms, practice and policy implications' in Phoenix, J. (ed.) *Regulating Sex for Sale: Prostitution Policy Reforms in the UK*.

Wilkinson, R. (1955) *Women of the Streets*, London: Secker and Warburg.

Wilkinson, S. and Kitzinger, C. (eds) (1996) *Representing the Other: A Feminism and Psychology Reader*, London: Sage.

Williamson, C. and Folaron, G. (2003) 'Understanding the experience of street-level prostitutes', *Qualitative Social Work*, 2(3): 271–87.

Wilson, J. and Kelling, G. (1982) 'Broken windows', *The Atlantic Monthly*, 29 March: 29–38.

Wojcicki, J. and Malala, J. (2001) 'Condom use, power and HIV/AIDS risk: sex-workers bargain for survival in Hillbrow/Joubert Park/Berea, Johannsburg', *Social Science and Medicine*, 53(1): 99–121.

Wolfenden (1957) *Report of the Committee on Homosexual Offences and Prostitution*, London: HMSO.

Wood, E. (2000) 'Working in the fantasy factory: the attention hypothesis and the enacting of masculine power in strip clubs', *Journal of Contemporary Ethnography*, 29(1): 5–31.

INDEX

Wilson, J. and Kelling, G., 132
window sex workers, 36, 189
Wolfendon Report, 112, 114–15, 132
Wolverhampton City Council, 90
working conditions, 96–7
World Charter for Prostitutes' Rights, 94, 96–7
World Congress on commercial sexual
    exploitation of children (CSEC),
    Stockholm, 55

World Health Organisation, 54

young people *see* children and
    young people

zero tolerance, 137, 147
zoning, 4, 137, 189

Supporting researchers for more than forty years

Research methods have always been at the core of SAGE's publishing. Sara Miller McCune founded SAGE in 1965 and soon after, she published SAGE's first methods book, *Public Policy Evaluation*. A few years later, she launched the Quantitative Applications in the Social Sciences series – affectionately known as the 'little green books'.

Always at the forefront of developing and supporting new approaches in methods, SAGE published early groundbreaking texts and journals in the fields of qualitative methods and evaluation.

Today, more than forty years and two million little green books later, SAGE continues to push the boundaries with a growing list of more than 1,200 research methods books, journals, and reference works across the social, behavioural, and health sciences.

From qualitative, quantitative and mixed methods to evaluation, SAGE is the essential resource for academics and practitioners looking for the latest in methods by leading scholars.

www.sagepublications.com